T0213691

Lecture Notes in Computer Science　　10380

Commenced Publication in 1973
Founding and Former Series Editors:
Gerhard Goos, Juris Hartmanis, and Jan van Leeuwen

Editorial Board

David Hutchison
  Lancaster University, Lancaster, UK
Takeo Kanade
  Carnegie Mellon University, Pittsburgh, PA, USA
Josef Kittler
  University of Surrey, Guildford, UK
Jon M. Kleinberg
  Cornell University, Ithaca, NY, USA
Friedemann Mattern
  ETH Zurich, Zurich, Switzerland
John C. Mitchell
  Stanford University, Stanford, CA, USA
Moni Naor
  Weizmann Institute of Science, Rehovot, Israel
C. Pandu Rangan
  Indian Institute of Technology, Madras, India
Bernhard Steffen
  TU Dortmund University, Dortmund, Germany
Demetri Terzopoulos
  University of California, Los Angeles, CA, USA
Doug Tygar
  University of California, Berkeley, CA, USA
Gerhard Weikum
  Max Planck Institute for Informatics, Saarbrücken, Germany

More information about this series at http://www.springer.com/series/7408

Khalil Drira · Hongbing Wang
Qi Yu · Yan Wang
Yuhong Yan · François Charoy
Jan Mendling · Mohamed Mohamed
Zhongjie Wang · Sami Bhiri (Eds.)

Service-Oriented Computing – ICSOC 2016 Workshops

ASOCA, ISyCC, BSCI, and Satellite Events
Banff, AB, Canada, October 10–13, 2016
Revised Selected Papers

 Springer

Editors

Khalil Drira
Université de Toulouse
Toulouse
France

Hongbing Wang
Southeast University
Jiangsu
China

Qi Yu
Rochester Institute of Technology
Rochester, NY
USA

Yan Wang
Macquarie University
Sydney, NSW
Australia

Yuhong Yan
Concordia University
Montreal, QC
Canada

François Charoy
CNRS
Université de Lorraine
Nancy
France

Jan Mendling
Vienna University of Economics
and Business
Vienna
Austria

Mohamed Mohamed
IBM Research
San Jose, CA
USA

Zhongjie Wang
Harbin Institute of Technology
Harbin
China

Sami Bhiri
University of Monastir
Monastir
Tunisia

ISSN 0302-9743   ISSN 1611-3349   (electronic)
Lecture Notes in Computer Science
ISBN 978-3-319-68135-1   ISBN 978-3-319-68136-8   (eBook)
https://doi.org/10.1007/978-3-319-68136-8

Library of Congress Control Number: 2017957543

LNCS Sublibrary: SL2 – Programming and Software Engineering

© Springer International Publishing AG 2017
This work is subject to copyright. All rights are reserved by the Publisher, whether the whole or part of the material is concerned, specifically the rights of translation, reprinting, reuse of illustrations, recitation, broadcasting, reproduction on microfilms or in any other physical way, and transmission or information storage and retrieval, electronic adaptation, computer software, or by similar or dissimilar methodology now known or hereafter developed.
The use of general descriptive names, registered names, trademarks, service marks, etc. in this publication does not imply, even in the absence of a specific statement, that such names are exempt from the relevant protective laws and regulations and therefore free for general use.
The publisher, the authors and the editors are safe to assume that the advice and information in this book are believed to be true and accurate at the date of publication. Neither the publisher nor the authors or the editors give a warranty, express or implied, with respect to the material contained herein or for any errors or omissions that may have been made. The publisher remains neutral with regard to jurisdictional claims in published maps and institutional affiliations.

Printed on acid-free paper

This Springer imprint is published by Springer Nature
The registered company is Springer International Publishing AG
The registered company address is: Gewerbestrasse 11, 6330 Cham, Switzerland

Preface

This volume presents the proceedings of the scientific satellite events that were held in conjunction with the 2016 International Conference on Service-Oriented Computing, which took place in Alberta, Canada, October 10–13, 2016.

The satellite events provide venues for specialist groups to meet, to generate focused discussions on specific sub-areas within service-oriented computing, and to engage in community-building activities. These events helped significantly enrich the main conference by both expanding the scope of research topics and attracting participants from a wider community.

The selected scientific satellite events were organized around three main tracks, including a workshop track, a PhD symposium track, and a demonstration track.

The ICSOC 2016 workshop track consisted of three workshops on a wide range of topics that fall into the general area of service computing:

- ASOCA 2016: the First Workshop on Adaptive Service-Oriented and Cloud Applications
- ISyCC 2016: the First Workshop on IoT Systems Provisioning and Management in Cloud Computing
- BSCI 2016: the Second International Workshop on Big Data Services and Computational Intelligence

The workshops were held on October 10, 2016. Each workshop had its own chairs and Program Committee who were responsible for the selection of papers. The overall organization for the workshop program, including the selection of the workshop proposals, was carried out by Khalil Drira, Hongbing Wang, and Qi Yu.

The ICSOC PhD Symposium is an international forum for PhD students to present, share, and discuss their research in a constructive and critical atmosphere. It also provides students with fruitful feedback and advice on their research approach and thesis. The PhD Symposium Track was chaired by Yan Wang, Yuhong Yan, and François Charoy.

The ICSOC Demonstration Track offers an exciting and highly interactive way to show research prototypes/work in service-oriented computing (SOC) and related areas. The Demonstration Track was chaired by Jan Mendling, Mohamed Mohamed, and Zhongjie Wang.

We would like to thank the workshop, PhD symposium, and demonstration authors, as well as keynote speakers and workshop Organizing Committees, who together contributed to this important aspect of the conference.

We hope that these proceedings will serve as a valuable reference for researchers and practitioners working in the SOC domain and its emerging applications.

June 2017

Khalil Drira
Hongbing Wang
Qi Yu
Yan Wang
Yuhong Yan
François Charoy
Jan Mendling
Mohamed Mohamed
Zhongjie Wang
Sami Bhiri

ICSOC 2016 Organization

General Chairs

Barbara Pernici — Politecnico di Milano, Italy
Munindar P. Singh — North Carolina State University, USA

Program Chairs

Michael Sheng — University of Adelaide, Australia
Eleni Stroulia — University of Alberta, Canada
Samir Tata — Institute Mines-Telecom, France

Steering Committee

Boualem Benatallah — University of New South Wales, Australia
Fabio Casati — University of Trento, Italy
Bernd J. Krämer — Fern Universität in Hagen, Germany
Winfried Lamersdorf — University of Hamburg, Germany
Heiko Ludwig — IBM, USA
Mike Papazoglou — Tilburg University, The Netherlands
Jian Yang — Macquarie University, Australia
Liang Zhang — Fudan University, China

Publication Chair

Sami Bhiri — University of Monastir, Tunisia

Workshop Chairs

Khalil Drira — University of Toulouse, France
Hongbing Wang — Southeast University, China
Qi Yu — Rochester Institute of Technology, USA

Panel Chairs

Boualem Benatallah — University of New South Wales, Australia
Heiko Ludwig — IBM, USA
Jianwen Su — UC Santa Barbara, USA

Finance Chair

Bernd Krämer — Fern Universität in Hagen, Germany

Demonstration Track Chairs

Jan Mendling   Vienna University of Economics and Business, Austria
Mohamed Mohamed   IBM Almaden, USA
Zhongjie Wang   Harbin Institute of Technology, China

PhD Symposium Chairs

Yan Wang   Macquarie University, Australia
Yuhong Yan   Concordia University, Canada
François Charoy   University of Lorraine, France

Publicity Chairs

Naouel Moha   University of Québec in Montréal, Canada
Mohamed Sellami   ISEP, France
Lucinéia Heloisa   Universidade Federal do Rio Grande do Sul, Brazil
  Thom
Lina Yao   University of New South Wales, Australia

Local Organization Chair

Ying Zou   Queen's University, Canada

Web Chairs

Nguyen Khoi Tran   University of Adelaide, Australia
Wei Emma Zhang   University of Adelaide, Australia

Workshop on Adaptive Service-Oriented and Cloud Applications

Slim Kallel   ReDCAD Laboratory, University of Sfax, Tunisia
Ismael Bouassida   ReDCAD Laboratory, University of Sfax, Tunisia
  Rodriguez
Mohamed Jmaiel   Digital Research Center of Sfax, Tunisia

Workshop on Big Data Services and Computational Intelligence

Zhangbing Zhou   China University of Geosciences (Beijing), China
Patrick C.K. Hung   University of Ontario Institute of Technology, Canada
Yucong Duan   Hainan University, Haikou, China
Richard Lomotey   The Pennsylvania State University, Beaver, USA

Workshop for IoT Systems Provisioning and Management in Cloud Computing

Sami Yangui   Concordia University, QC, Canada
Mohamed Mohamed   IBM Research, CA, USA
Diala Naboulsi   Concordia University, QC, Canada

Contents

Adaptive Service-Oriented and Cloud Applications

ASOCA: Workshop on Adaptive Service-Oriented and Cloud Applications

Slim Kallel[1], Ismael Bouassida Rodriguez[1], and Mohamed Jmaiel[1,2]

[1] ReDCAD Laboratory, University of Sfax, Sfax, Tunisia
{slim.kallel,ismaelbouassida.rodriguez,
mohamed.jmaiel}@redcad.tn
[2] Digital Research Center of Sfax, Sfax, Tunisia

1 Introduction

The ASOCA 2016 workshop address the adaptation and reconfiguration issues of the Service-oriented and cloud applications and architectures.

An adaptive and reconfigurable service oriented applications can repair itself if any execution problems occur, in order to successfully complete its own execution, while respecting functional and Non-Functional agreements. In the design of an adaptive and reconfigurable software system, several aspects have to be considered. For instance, the system should be able to predict or to detect degradations and failures as soon as possible and to enact suitable recovery actions.

2 Topics

The main topics of the ASOCA 2016 workshop are devoted to the design and the implementation of adaptive and reconfigurable service oriented and cloud applications and architectures. Specifically, the relevant topics include, but are not limited to:

- Distributed and centralized solutions for the diagnosis and repair of service-oriented and cloud applications.
- Design for the diagnosability and repairability
- Monitoring simple and composite architectures, components and services
- Semantic (or analytic) architectural and behavioral models for monitoring of software systems
- Dynamic reconfiguration of service-oriented and cloud applications.
- Planning and decision making Technologies for ensuring autonomic properties Predictive management of adaptability.
- Management of autonomic properties Experiences in practical adaptive and reconfigurable service-oriented and cloud applications.
- Tools and prototypes for managing adaptability.

3 Accepted Papers

The program committee selected 5 papers from 8 received papers based on the originality, quality, and relevance to the topics of the workshop. Each submission is reviewed at least by three reviewers. The list of accepted papers is as follows:

- Antoine Auger, Ernesto Exposito and Emmanuel Lochin, *A generic framework for quality-based autonomic adaptation within sensor-based systems.*
- Yataghene Lydia, *Using Formal model for Evaluation of Business Processes Elasticity in the Cloud.*
- Antonio Bucchiarone, Martina De Sanctis and Annapaola Marconi, *Decentralized Dynamic Adaptation for Service-based Collective Adaptive Systems.*
- Hela Malouche, Youssef Ben Halima and Henda Hajjami Ben Ghezala, *A brokerage architecture: cloud service selection.*
- Amir Taherkordi, Peter Herrmann, Jan Olaf Blech, and lvaro Fernndez, *Service Virtualization for Self-Adaptation in Mobile Cyber-Physical Systems.*

Acknowledgement. We are grateful to all program committee members and the external reviewers for their effort to read and discuss the papers in their area of expertise. We would also like to thank the authors for their submissions and for ensuring the success of this track.

Decentralized Dynamic Adaptation
for Service-Based Collective Adaptive Systems

Antonio Bucchiarone$^{(\boxtimes)}$, Martina De Sanctis, and Annapaola Marconi

Fondazione Bruno Kessler, Via Sommarive, 18, Trento, Italy
{bucchiarone,msanctis,marconi}@fbk.eu

Abstract. Modern service-based systems are progressively becoming more heterogeneous. They form a socio-technical system, composed of distributed entities, software and human participants, interacting with and within the environment. These systems operate under constant perturbations that are due to unexpected changes in the environment and to the unpredictable behavior of the participants. We argue that for a service-based system to be resilient, adaptation must be collective. Multiple participants must adapt their behavior in concert to respond to critical runtime impediments. In this work, we present a framework for the modeling and execution of large-scale service-based Collective Adaptive Systems, where adaptation needs are solved in a decentralized and collective manner.

1 Introduction

The term *Collective Adaptive Systems* (CASs) has been introduced in the literature to denote large-scale systems that may present substantial socio-technical embedding [22]. They typify systems with complex design, engineering and management, whose level of complexity comes specifically from gathering and combining in the same operating environment heterogeneous and autonomous components, systems and users, with their specific concerns. To be robust against the high degree of dynamism of their operating environments, and to sustain the continuous variations induced by their socio-technical nature, these systems need to *self-adapt*. Self-adaptation is an important feature of complex software systems, but it is often seen as a mean to automate management activities in order to meet desired requirements, such as minimize resources and costs (e.g. [12]). In a CAS instead, self-adaptation is a feature of the collectiveness. Individual entities may "opportunistically" enter the system and self-adapt in order to leverage other entities' resources, functionalities and capabilities to perform their task more efficiently or effectively. But, the collaborative nature of the system, makes this self-adaptation much trickier [18]. Changes in the behaviour of one entity may break the consistency of the whole collaboration, or have negative repercussions on other participants. Adaptation must, therefore, be *collective*. Entities must be able to self-adapt simultaneously, while preserving the collaboration and benefits

© Springer International Publishing AG 2017
K. Drira et al. (Eds.): ICSOC 2016 Workshops, LNCS 10380, pp. 5–20, 2017.
https://doi.org/10.1007/978-3-319-68136-8_1

of the system (or sub-system) they are within. Self-adaptation of an individual entity is therefore not only finalized to the achievement of its own goals but also to the fulfillment of emerging goals of the dynamically formed sub-systems.

This paper addresses the challenge of *collective adaptation in service-based systems* through an *adaptive by-design* approach that exploits the key features of service-oriented design to support the modeling, development, and execution of CASs operating in dynamic environments. Key properties of our approach are the emphasis on collaboration towards fulfillment of individual diverse goals and the heterogeneous nature of the system with respect to roles, behaviours and goals of its participants. These properties distinguish our approach from other types of collective adaptation approaches, like for instance swarms, where all elements of a community have a uniform behavior and global shared goal [13], and multi-agent systems and agent-based organizations [9], where there may be several distinct roles and behaviors, but the differentiation is still limited and often pre-designed. The approach presented here is an extension of the model proposed in [5], and further formalized in [6]. While existing approaches normally deal with CASs through isolated adaptation, we propose a framework to build CASs that fully addresses the challenge of collective behavior of systems by fulfilling the following requirements:

R1. Support for a highly dynamic environment and an open and dynamic nature of the system where entities communication and adaptation handling are context-aware.
R2. Support for large-scale distributed configuration of the system, with different decision management strategies (from hierarchical to peer–to–peer).
R3. A collective adaptation approach allowing entities to collectively adapt at runtime and in a decentralized fashion, guaranteeing the reliability of the system.

The approach is evaluated in two different application domains, namely a Urban Mobility System that handles the multi-modal and collaborative mobility in a Smart City, and a Surveillance System, devoted to the detection of intruders in private companies. The application and evaluation of the approach allow us to demonstrate its *scalability* and *reliability* when applied to real-world scenarios, and to prove its capability of successfully deal with different type of problems.

The reminder of the paper is structured as follows. Section 2 describes the class of systems we intend to approach. In Sect. 3, a comparison with other related works is presented. Section 4 illustrates in details the proposed approach for modeling and executing CASs to address the requirements depicted in this Section (**R1–R3**). In Sect. 5, an evaluation of the approach is given. Section 6 closes the paper providing some conclusions and future works.

2 Motivating Examples

To better understand the class of systems we intend to approach, in this Section we give two motivating examples of systems characterized by the aforementioned requirements.

The Urban Mobility System. It refers to the specification of a multi-modal and collaborative Urban Mobility System (UMS). Its goal consists in the collaborative exploitation of the city transport facilities, while providing real-time, and customized mobility services supporting the whole travel duration. The UMS exploits a variety of *heterogeneous* services, often provided by *autonomous* entities: from city mobility resources (e.g., public transportation, bike sharing), with their transport service functionalities (e.g., registration, booking), to general-purpose ones (e.g., diverse payment services). The UMS purpose is twofold: (i) integrate the available services supporting the multi-modal journey planning, organization (booking and payment services), and execution (real-time availability of services) of a trip; (ii) help citizens to deal with context changes that may affect a journey, by exploiting the adaptation abilities of the involved entities, in a collective manner. Moreover, the UMS operates in a continuously changing and complex environment. Each service may enter or leave the system at any time (e.g., a new bike-sharing service), and it may change or extend its offered functionalities, making the system *open* and *dynamic*. Moreover, the system's context changes can affect the operation of the system (e.g., traffic jams, services unavailability) (**R1**). Different entities and actors, playing different roles, participate in the UMS: citizens are actively involved; each transport service is handled by an entity manager mediating between the passengers and third party services; drivers dynamically interact both with the system and with the passengers of their routes. Eventually, the UMS entity provides integration between all the involved parts. The system results in an adaptive *hierarchy* of entities that dynamically evolves in response to the evolution of the environment and the context (**R2**). Moreover, in order to support a sustainable mobility within the city, the system's intent is that of inducing users to prefer collective mobility solutions (e.g., flexibuses, car sharing), both during the normal execution of the system and in case of adaptation needs (e.g., intense traffic on the route). To this aim, each entity is able to interact with other entities, to *notify*, *solve* or *manage* problems, as well as to adapt its own process to apply collective and adaptive solutions (e.g., the FlexiBus changes its path) (**R3**).

The Surveillance System. It refers to a Surveillance System (SurSys) for the premises of a private company [2]. Its objective is the detection of intruders entering the factory buildings. The system involves *heterogeneous* entities: (i) *smart devices*, such as (a) *Unmanned Aerial Vehicles* (UAVs) following specific protocols as defined in the service agreement of the company; (b) *movable cameras* placed on the top of the buildings; (c) *fixed sensors* in strategic places monitoring movements in the environment. Next there are (ii) *physical persons*, such as *guards* controlling the surveillance process and *maintainers* that are in charge of maintaining the used equipment (e.g., drones, cameras). Eventually, (iii) *manager entities* for the whole management of the system, such as *ground stations* handling multiple drones and receiving telemetry data, and a *central station*. As regards the behavior of the SurSys, besides its application logic, from an adaptation point of view each entity provides its adaptation logic to be played in case adaptation needs arise (e.g., the detection of obstacles by a drone). The number and the type (e.g., new type of drone) of the entities in the system can vary according to the size of the area, the number of buildings and other characteristics of the client company. Moreover, services can change their functionalities, or offer new ones (e.g., a drone starting to take photos), requiring for an open and dynamic system (**R1**). Differently from the UMS, the SurSys follows a peer–to–peer decision management strategy that better fits its characteristics. Indeed, in this system there is neither a central supervisor nor different abstraction levels between the involved entities. In contrast, according to the current context and to the specific goal to reach, entities can dynamically organize themselves in sub-systems which collaborate in a peer–to–peer manner to accomplish their work (**R2**). Moreover, the entities must avoid to bring the system to a halt, being able to react to dynamic context changes. To this aim, entities must collaborate to better deal with unexpected problems, by adapting their own processes applying collective solutions (e.g., the Maintainer can manually drive a drone with problems, while the Ground Station sends a new drone) (**R3**).

3   Related Work

In this Section we focus on reviewing recent works dealing with runtime collective adaptation in those systems that address some of the three requirements defined in Sect. 1. In the field of mission-critical software systems, these are often expected to safely adapt to changes in their execution environment, where run-time adaptation mechanisms reduce the complexity of the system. For example, in [15], an adaptive run-time model used to establish a flexible information processing within a group of heterogeneous robots is presented. In [23], a reusable framework for developing adaptive multi-agent systems for heterogeneous teams, using an organization based approach, is given. Furthermore, existing works for distributed self-adaptive systems are typically based on multi-agents and MAPE (Monitor, Analyze, Plan and Execute) loop paradigms [17, 19]. More specifically, the system is decomposed in self-handling software units, which collaborate and coordinate in a distributed way.

The creation of *coalitions* is a commonly used approach and it has been widely studied in game theory and economics. In [21], the authors tackle the problem of coalitions making in multi-agents systems in a neighborhood agent network (a network in which agents directly communicate only with their neighbors). Each agent can participate to several coalitions at the same time, by indicating for each of them the degree of involvement. A coalition is initiated by an agent (the initiator) issuing a task. Then, the initiator contacts its neighbors trying to find a subset of them able to satisfy the proposed task. If there is not such a subset, then it randomly selects a neighbor as mediator, in order to contact the mediator's neighbors.

There exist a lot of solutions regarding coalitions of coordinating entities, where each entity plays a specific role, known as *choreography*. In [7], a formal framework incorporating the notion of self-adaptation in the context of choreographies is presented. Here we find the concept of global types, each of which represents the communication choreography that can be updated at runtime, in response to changing conditions in the global state. These approaches deal with runtime adaptation but without a collective approach.

A group of interacting entities can also be seen as an *ensemble*. For instance, SCEL [8] is a formal language that provides abstractions for autonomic systems in terms of behaviors, knowledge, aggregation and policies. We found interesting how the abstraction for aggregation is modeled. In SCEL it is possible to define ensembles as a set of entities. The runtime selection of entities participating to some ensemble is based on the satisfaction of specific predicates.

In [10], the authors give a formal foundation for the ensemble modeling. An ensemble is defined in terms of roles and role connectors. Moreover, the runtime behaviour of an ensemble is given by means of an automaton. The idea of role is close to ours, but in our approach instead of defining predefined and fixed connections among roles, we leave roles to freely interact.

Decision making in large distributed systems has been widely explored in different research areas (e.g., multi-agent systems). Centralized approaches become impractical for systems with a large number of entities. However, these difficulties can be overcome by allowing entities to cooperate or self-organize in solving distributed decision problems. The main issue in this decentralized approach is identifying which entities need to communicate, what information should be sent, and how frequently [14].

To sum up, we can notice that none of the reviewed studies are well-suited to fully address all the three requirements characterizing the type of systems that are the focus of this paper. In contrast, our approach gives us the possibility to handle both collective and selfish behavior between autonomous and heterogeneous entities. Furthermore, the management of coalition is decentralized and this eliminates the single point of failure and the potential bottleneck in the system. In the following Section, we describe our approach in details and show how it allows the system to meet all requirements **R1–R3**.

4   General Framework and Approach

In this Section we present our service-based approach for modeling (Sect. 4.1) and executing (Sect. 4.2) CASs addressing the three requirements identified in Sect. 1.

4.1   Modeling of Service-Based Collective Adaptive Systems

The Domain Object (DO) model has been defined with the purpose of modeling and executing adaptive service-based systems. It has been proposed in [5] and further formalized and evaluated in [6]. We want to highlight that the focus of this paper is on the collective adaptation approach of service-based CASs, rather than on the model we use to design these systems. Thus, for lack of space, here we give only some hints on the DO model, while we report and describe the extensions made to it, in order to deal with collective adaptation. Briefly, each system entity is modeled as a DO in terms of its own behaviour (i.e., *core process*), as well as the functionalities (i.e., *fragments*) it provides. Each DO has a partial view on the operational environment, representing its *domain knowledge*, which may also span at runtime. Moreover, the model is suitable for the application of advanced techniques for dynamic and incremental service composition [4], to effectively deal with changes occurring at different levels in the system operating in dynamic environment. The resulting adaptive system is a *dynamic network* of DOs connected through a set of dependencies established through their runtime interactions by means of their offered/required functionalities. For more details on the modeling approach, please refer to [5,6].

To allow system entities to collectively adapt, dealing with adaptation needs that can be raised both by the environment and by the entities themselves, the model has been extended with specific constructs. A key concept are *ensembles*, that are modeled over the dynamic network of DOs, as groups of DOs and that, although autonomous in their execution, share common goals and might need to collectively handle run-time adaptation problems. For instance, in the UMS scenario, an ensemble is that made by the *flexibus driver*, the *route manager* handling the specific route, and all the *passengers* subscribed to the route (see Fig. 1). Each of them is modeled as a DO and behaves autonomously, but if something occurs (e.g., the route is blocked), they should collectively adapt to fulfill collective goals (e.g., being on time

```
1 <tns:ensemble name="RouteA" xmlns:tns="http://das.fbk.eu/Ensemble"
2     xmlns:xsi="http://www.w3.org/2001/XMLSchema-instance"
3     xsi:schemaLocation="http://das.fbk.eu/Ensemble_Ensemble.xsd">
4     <tns:domainObjectType>RouteManager</tns:domainObjectType>
5     <tns:domainObjectType>FlexibusDriver</tns:domainObjectType>
6     <tns:domainObjectType>RoutePassenger</tns:domainObjectType>
7 </tns:ensemble>
```

Fig. 1. Example of the route ensemble model.

at the destination point). Moreover, ensembles can also involve entities at different levels. An ensemble can be made by the *flexibus company* and the *car pooling company*, to allow different companies to support each other, in case of adaptation needs spanning over the scope of a single transportation mean.

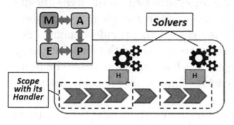

Fig. 2. Extended domain object process.

Lastly, when an *intra-ensemble* adaptation can not be solved, *inter-ensembles* adaptation can be performed. To enable collective adaptation, each DO's core process implements a set of *collective adaptation solvers* (from here on, simply *solvers*), as well as a set of *collective adaptation handlers* (from here on, simply *handlers*) (see Fig. 2). Solvers model the ability of a DO to handle one or more *issues*. Each solver relates to the particular issue that it can handle. Handlers are used to capture issues, during the nominal execution of a DO, and to trigger the appropriate solver. Each handler refers to a finite *scope* in the process of a DO, and it can be of two different types: (i) *onExternalIssue* handlers are used to catch issues coming from other DOs in the system (both in the same or in a different ensembles); (ii) *onInternalIssue* handlers are devoted to monitor properties expressed on the own knowledge of the DO, and catch the issues arising when this properties are violated. For instance, in Fig. 3 we report the XML listing modeling the handlers related to the scope in the flexibus driver process. The flexibus driver can catch the **intense traffic** external issue, coming from the external environment, as well as the **bus broken** internal issue, thanks to its knowledge. A collective adaptation process is triggered by a run-time occurrence of an extraordinary circumstance corresponding to an issue. The resolution of the issue is the outcome of the triggered adaptation process in which all the affected DOs adapt collaboratively and with a possible minimal impact on their execution. In the next Section we describe in details the collective, yet decentralized, handling of a collective adaptation.

```
1 <tns:scope name="FD_scope1">
2      <tns:invoke name="FD_RouteStartedNotice"></tns:invoke>
3      <!--Here the activities in the scope of the following handlers-->
4      <tns:eventHandlers>
5          <tns:eventHandler name="IntenseTraffic">
6              <tns:onExternalIssue onEventName="IntenseTraffic"/>
7              <tns:callSolver solverType="Route-IntenseTraffic"/>
8          </tns:eventHandler>
9          <tns:eventHandler name="BusBroken">
10             <tns:onInternalIssue onInternalKnowledge="DP-BusStatus.broken"/>
11             <tns:callSolver solverType="Route-BusDamaged"/>
12         </tns:eventHandler>
13     </tns:eventHandlers>
14 </tns:scope>
```

Fig. 3. Collective adaptive handlers example.

4.2   Execution of Service-Based Collective Adaptive Systems

During the normal execution of the system, through the interactions between DOs, ensembles are formed. Ensembles can be created spontaneously and change over time: different entities may join or leave an existing ensemble dynamically and autonomously. Their termination is also spontaneous: participants have reached their goals, or the ensemble itself has ceased to provide benefits. For instance, in the UMS scenario, users subscribe to a specific flexibus route, by exploiting functionalities of the route manager, which has previously set the route and assigned a driver to it. In this way, the ensemble made by the route manager, the flexibus driver and the passengers is set up. While the execution goes on, the ensemble can evolve. New passengers can subscribe to the route, while others can leave it. However, to deal with unpredictable changes, local adaptation is not enough, since the scope of these changes goes beyond the single entity. Typical changes occurring in dynamic environments are characterized by the fact of affecting different entities: (i) the entity directly related to the change (e.g., a route interrupted directly affects the flexibus driver); (ii) the entities belonging to the same ensemble (e.g., both the passengers on board and the ones waiting at the bus stops); (iii) the entities involved as a consequence of the adaptation executed to solve the problem (e.g., the UMS provides a new plan for the waiting passengers); these entities can also belong to different ensembles. This demonstrates the need for collective adaptation approaches able to deal with dynamic changes, and whose scope can be, in the worst case, the entire system. Thus, such an approach must provide one or more decision management strategies, to allow different entities to communicate and cooperate in a collective manner.

The collective adaptation process is handled in a decentralized manner by the DOs involved, directly or indirectly, in an adaptation need. Each DO implements a *Monitor - Analyze - Plan - Execute* (MAPE) loop [11] that allows for the dynamic interaction with the other DOs. In Fig. 4, the *state machine* (SM) representing the operation of a MAPE loop is shown. We use a color code to distinguish the four phases of the MAPE loop. In the following, we highlight the most interesting states of the SM. In the Monitoring phase, each DO monitors the environment through active handlers. Issues can come both from the DO itself (`Issue Triggered`) or from a different DO, asking support for solving an issue (`Issue Received`). This starts the Analyze phase, where the issue solver is called (`Local Solver Called`). In the Planning phase, if the solver has found a solution (`Solution Found`), the *collective planning* phase starts. All the DOs involved in the issue resolution process will collectively collaborate to solve it. Here, we explore the more interesting `solution with targets` edge, representing the case in which the solution provided by the solver foresees the involvement of other DOs, which are firstly found (`Targets Found`), and then triggered (`Issues Targeted`) to be involved in the resolution process. Once the current DO receives feedback from the triggered DOs (`Solution Received`), it selects the best solution (`Solution Chosen`) (e.g., by applying the approach in [3,16]). At this point, we should distinguish two cases. If the issue was triggered internally (`root node` edge), the DO asks the involved targets to commit their local best solution

(Ask Partners To Commit), it waits for their commit to be done (All Partners Commit Done), and eventually it commits its local solution (Commit Local Solution). Otherwise, if the issue was coming from outside (not root node edge), the DO reports the feedback to the issue's sender (Solution Forwarded), and it waits for a future commit (Commit Requested). The DO can receive a positive or a negative reply for its proposed solution. In both cases, it executes a solution commit (Commit Local Solution), which will be empty in the negative case.

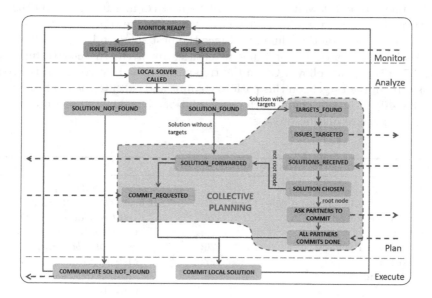

Fig. 4. MAPE state machine.

In the Algorithm 1, we report the pseudo-code of our *Collective Adaptation Algorithm* that is supported by the MAPE loops, handlers and solvers used in the DOs modeling. We focus on the main procedures, by giving the point of view of a single DO whose monitor captures an issue. The issue resolution process generates a resolution tree, modeling all possible solutions for a given issue, over which the best solution is selected. The function startCA (lines 1–7) takes the detected issue and calls the main function resolveIssue. After the issue resolution process, if a collective solution has not been found, the entity will self adapt (line 5). The resolveIssue function (lines 8–36) is called locally by the DO detecting the issue. If needed, the function is recursively invoked to trigger the issue resolution across multiple DOs in a distributed way. Indeed, the DO initially calls its solver for the specific issue, if any (line 10). The called solver provides a solution, which may comprise, in turn, one or more sub-issues (line 11) that are triggered as a consequence of the first one. In order to solve each sub-issue, the DO must establish one or more communications with other connected DOs (line 12). For each communication, the set of potential solvers is identified through all reachable DOs (e.g., targets) (line **16**). Once all targets have been identified, to understand if and how they can handle the sub-issue, the `resolveIssue` function is called remotely on each target by a remote procedure call (rpc) (lines **17–20**). When the DO receives all the potential solutions for the invoked targets, the Analytic Hierarchy Process (AHP) algorithm [3,16] is executed to identify the best solution (line **22**). If a best solution has been found, we can observe two different behaviors: (i) if the DO running the algorithm is not the root (i.e., the one starting the resolution process), it stores the solution locally (line **26**) and it waits for a commit request coming from the DO that is its father in the issue resolution tree. Otherwise, (ii) the root DO executes the commit of the best solution (line **28**). Since the best solution is implicitly made of sub-solutions related to the different entities involved, the `commit` function (lines **37–42**) acts as follows. Given the tree-path of the best solution, the root DO asks to all the targets on this path to commit and execute their sub-solution (lines **38–40**). Lastly, it commits the best solution (line **41**) and executes it, by ending the issue resolution process.

Algorithm 1. Collective Adaptation Algorithm.

1: **function** STARTCA($issue$)
2:    **if** RESOLVEISSUE($issue, this$) **then**
3:       Issue solved via CA.
4:    **else**
5:       $this.selfAdapt$
6:    **end if**
7: **end function**

8: **function** RESOLVEISSUE($issue, entity$)
9:    $solutionFound = False$
10:    $solution = $ CALLSOLVER($issue$)
11:    **for all** $issue \in solution.issues$ **do**
12:       $Coms = $ DERIVECOMS($issue$)
13:       **for all** $comm \in Coms$ **do**
14:          $S = \emptyset$
15:          $bestSol = null$
16:          $T = $ FINDTARGETS($comm$)
17:          **for all** $target \in T$ **do**
18:             $S = S\cup$
19: rpc(RESOLVEISSUE($comm.issue, target$))
20:          **end for**
21:       **end for**

22:          $bestSol = \text{AHP}(S)$
23:          **if** $bestSol! = null$ **then**
24:             $solutionFound = True$
25:             **if** $entity\ != $ root **then**
26:                STORE($bestSol$)
27:             **else**
28:                COMMIT($bestSol, T$)
29:             **end if**
30:          **else**
31:             $this.selfAdapt$
32:             **return**
33:          **end if**
34:       **end for**
35:    **return** $solutionFound$
36: **end function**

37: **function** COMMIT($bestSol, T$)
38:    **for all** $target \in T$ **do**
39:       EXECUTE($target.bestSol$)
40:    **end for**
41:    EXECUTE($bestSol$)
42: **end function**

In Fig. 5, we give an example of the communication between two single entities. We show the possible flow of information when an issue (e.g., `RouteABlocked`) is raised internally by an entity (e.g., `FlexiBus Driver`). This is just a simplification with the aim of showing the communication and synchronization between entities. However, in normal scenarios, our framework is able to deal with multiple entities that collaborate. The labels with ordered numbers represent the order in which the computational states of the respective MAPE SMs are executed.

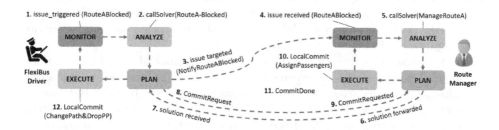

Fig. 5. Overview of the communication between two entities.

5   Evaluation

We realized a Java implementation of the first version of our framework[1], and we evaluated it by executing experiments in the two different scenarios described in Sect. 2. In our experiments we concern with measuring and understanding how the framework performs in providing solutions in terms of collective adaptation. In the following we present the experiment design and the discussion of its results.

Experiment Design. The main goal of our evaluation is to analyze the framework with respect to its *feasibility* and *scalability*. This goal can be refined into the following research questions:

– **RQ1:** Can the framework be used at run-time to manage the adaptation of service-based Collective Adaptive Systems?
– **RQ2:** Is the framework scalable for managing real-sized applications?

In our experiments we perform a stratified random sampling [20]: the population of all possible sequences of raised issues is divided into a set of *treatments* with a uniform distribution between the groups in terms of the number of raised issues. Random sampling is then applied within the groups. Each *treatment* models a sequence of raised issues. More specifically, in each treatment t we can have a set of different raised issues with one of the following cardinality: $< 1, 250, 500, 750, 1000 >$. Moreover, both the order of the raised issues

---

[1] **Replication Package.** To allow the easy replication and verification of our experiments, we provide a complete and portable replication package, which is publicly available at the link https://github.com/das-fbk/CAS-ICSOC2016.

within the sequence and the entities raising them is randomly chosen. As an example, considering the UMS scenario, the value < 250 > represents the treatment in which the total number of different raised issues (e.g., `RouteBlocked`, `PassengerDelay`, etc.) sums up to 250 issues in total. After the treatments generation, the experiment has been run.

Discussion of the Results. The specification of the UMS scenario we used to evaluate our approach contains 8 ensembles models and 23 domain object models, while the SurSys scenario contains 5 ensembles models and 24 domain object models. We have evaluated our techniques using a dual-core CPU running at 2.7 GHz, with 8Gb memory. We created 500 treatments for each scenario resulting in a total of 1000 runs of the experiment.

Table 1 shows the average execution time per number of raised issues, after a sequential execution of 500 treatments, for both the scenarios. We can observe that after a full loaded execution, our framework can solve a burst of 1000 issues in under 42 and 30 seconds (s), in the UMS and SurSys scenarios, respectively[2].

In order to better understand how the framework performs when the complexity of the collective adaptation problems increase, we did as follows. We consider the number of roles involved in the issue resolution as the complexity index for each problem. Then, we take into account the subset of treatments of 500 issues, to evaluate the performance on a set of equivalent problems. In Tables 2 and 3 we report the obtained results. For the UMS scenario (see Table 2), we can see that the considered set of problems involves a number of roles in a range between 4 and 9, while for the SurSys scenario (see Table 3) the range is between 7 and 11.

This shows that the problems complexity is almost uniformly distributed. We can notice that the average execution time moderately increases with respect to the increasing of the problem complexity, but not in a linear way. In the UMS scenario we can observe a particular increase of the execution time for the problems with complexity 9. However, by analyzing the data, we can say that in a set of 2500 issues resolutions, only one problem involves 9 roles reducing the performance.

Concerning the scalability of the framework in real-size problems, we decided to measure the distribution of the total number of issue resolutions both over the ensembles and roles number, in the different scenarios. As shown in Fig. 6, the number of ensembles is between 1 and 4. In the UMS scenario, for the majority of the problems, the issue resolutions happens in the scope of 2 ensembles. While, for the SurSys scenario, the majority of the problems is solved involving

Table 1. Execution time per number of raised issues (SurSys in grey).

Issues	1		250		500		750		1000	
Time in ms	51.7	51.6	10168.5	7423.6	20434.3	14792.8	30925.7	22197.1	41349.8	29607.1

---

[2] It is important to consider that having burst of 1000 issues all together is very rare.

Table 2. Execution time per number of involved roles for the UMS.

Num. of roles	4	5	6	7	8	9
Time in ms	19941.65	20191.67	20449.2	20677.1	21111.67	22381.6

Table 3. Execution time per number of involved roles for the SurSys.

Num. of roles	7	8	9	10	11
Time in ms	13919.42	14521.99	14842.67	14774.4	15153.72

3 ensembles. Observing the distribution of the issue resolutions over the roles, as reported in Fig. 7, we can notice that the trend is almost equivalent to the distribution measured over the ensembles. In the UMS scenario, in most cases the issue resolution involves 5 or 6 roles. As regard the SurSys scenario, this number increases around 9 and 10. These results clearly demonstrate the scalability of our framework when dealing with real-sized applications.

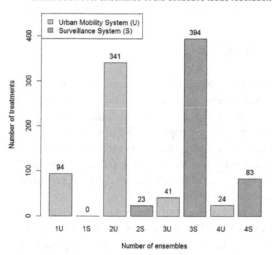

Fig. 6. Distribution of issue resolutions over ensembles.

In conclusion, to demonstrate the generality of our approach, we considered two large-scale and distributed systems that typically use two different decision management strategies. The UMS is hierarchical by nature, while the SurSys follows a peer-to-peer communication strategy. The experiments showed that our framework performed well while dealing with both the scenarios. Moreover, by looking at the resulting graphics it is possible to clearly distinguish between the different decision management strategies used by the two different scenarios. For instance, as emerges from Fig. 6, in the UMS scenario the system is often able to solve the problem within the ensemble in which it arises (e.g., intra-ensembles resolution). To the contrary, in the SurSys scenario, the system always solve the problem in the scope of more than one ensemble (e.g., inter-ensembles resolution). Furthermore, Fig. 7 reflects the strategy used by the systems, by showing that systems with a hierarchical strategy, as the UMS, involves a less number of roles, with respect to those with a peer-to-peer strategy, as the SurSys.

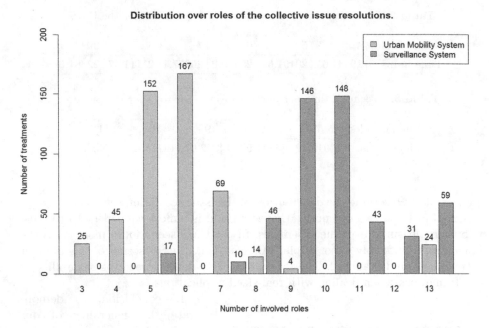

Fig. 7. Distribution of issue resolutions over the number of roles.

6   Conclusion and Future Work

This paper addresses the challenge of collective adaptation in service-based systems through an adaptive by-design approach that exploits the key features of service-oriented design to support the modeling, development, and execution of CASs operating in dynamic environments. Key properties of our approach are **R1**) the capability of handling with an open and dynamic system environment; **R2**) the support for different decision management strategies, from peer-to-peer to hierarchical models; **R3**) the emphasis on a collaborative, yet distributed, management of adaptation problems among entities.

Following this principle, we have presented a framework that supports the design, development, and operation of CASs that are resilient to a wide range of changes. We have defined an algorithm to solve adaptation issues within an ensemble, which discovers the entities able to solve an issue and to apply adaptation with minimal impact, guaranteeing the system reliability.

As future work we are planning to use our framework in real environments. Our idea is to integrate the *Surveillance System* with a suitable extension of the FLYAQ platform [1] that permits to graphically define civilian missions for a team of autonomous multi-copters via a domain specific language. A future step for the *Urban Mobility System* would be that of integrating it with an extension of the `Open Trip Planner`,[3] to provide also collective mobility solutions (e.g. car pooling, flexi-buses).

References

1. Bozhinoski, D., Di Ruscio, D., Malavolta, I., Pelliccione, P., Tivoli, M.: FLYAQ: enabling non-expert users to specify and generate missions of autonomous multicopters. In: 30th IEEE/ACM ASE (2015)
2. Bozhinoski, D., Malavolta, I., Bucchiarone, A., Marconi, A.: Sustainable safety in mobile multi-robot systems via collective adaptation. In: IEEE SASO, pp. 172–173 (2015)
3. Bucchiarone, A., Dulay, N., Lavygina, A., Marconi, A., Raik, H., Russo, A.: An approach for collective adaptation in socio-technical systems. In: IEEE SASO Workshops, pp. 43–48 (2015)
4. Bucchiarone, A., Marconi, A., Mezzina, C.A., Pistore, M., Raik, H.: On-the-fly adaptation of dynamic service-based systems: incrementality, reduction and reuse. In: Basu, S., Pautasso, C., Zhang, L., Fu, X. (eds.) ICSOC 2013. LNCS, vol. 8274, pp. 146–161. Springer, Heidelberg (2013). doi:10.1007/978-3-642-45005-1_11
5. Bucchiarone, A., De Sanctis, M., Marconi, A., Pistore, M., Traverso, P.: Design for adaptation of distributed service-based systems. In: Barros, A., Grigori, D., Narendra, N.C., Dam, H.K. (eds.) ICSOC 2015. LNCS, vol. 9435, pp. 383–393. Springer, Heidelberg (2015). doi:10.1007/978-3-662-48616-0_27
6. Bucchiarone, A., Sanctis, M.D., Marconi, A., Pistore, M., Traverso, P.: Incremental composition for adaptive by-design service based systems. In: Proceedings of the IEEE ICWS, pp. 236–243 (2016)
7. Coppo, M., Dezani-Ciancaglini, M., Venneri, B.: Self-adaptive monitors for multiparty sessions. In: PDP 2014, pp. 688–696. IEEE (2014)
8. De Nicola, R., Loreti, M., Pugliese, R., Tiezzi, F.: A formal approach to autonomic systems programming: the SCEL language. TAAS 9(2), 7 (2014)
9. Far, B.H., Wanyama, T., Soueina, S.O.: A negotiation model for large scale multiagent systems. In: IRI, pp. 589–594 (2006)
10. Hennicker, R., Klarl, A.: Foundations for ensemble modeling - the helena approach - handling massively distributed systems with elaborate ensemble architectures. In: Specification, Algebra, and Software - Essays Dedicated to Kokichi Futatsugi, pp. 359–381 (2014)
11. IBM: An architectural blueprint for autonomic computing. Technical report, IBM (2006)
12. Lalanda, P., McCann, J.A., Diaconescu, A.: Autonomic Computing - Principles, Design and Implementation. Undergraduate Topics in Computer Science. Springer, London (2013). doi:10.1007/978-1-4471-5007-7
13. Levi, P., Kernbach, S.: Symbiotic-Robot Organisms: Reliability, Adaptability, Evolution, vol. 7. Springer, Heidelberg (2010). doi:10.1007/978-3-642-11692-6
14. Mathews, G., Durrant-Whyte, H., Prokopenko, M.: Decentralized decision making for multiagent systems. In: Prokopenko, M. (ed.) Advances in Applied Self-organizing Systems. Advanced Information and Knowledge Processing, pp. 77–104. Springer, London (2008). doi:10.1007/978-1-84628-982-8_5
15. Niemczyk, S., Geihs, K.: Adaptive run-time models for groups of autonomous robots. In: IEEE/ACM SEAMS 2015, pp. 127–133 (2015)

---

[3] http://www.opentripplanner.org/.

16. Saaty, T.L.: What is the analytic hierarchy process? In: Mitra, G., Greenberg, H.J., Lootsma, F.A., Rijkaert, M.J., Zimmermann, H.J. (eds.) Mathematical Models for Decision Support. NATO ASI Series. Springer, Heidelberg (1988). doi:10.1007/978-3-642-83555-1_5

17. Vromant, P., Weyns, D., Malek, S., Andersson, J.: On interacting control loops in self-adaptive systems. In: IEEE/ACM SEAMS 2011, pp. 202–207 (2011)

18. Weyns, D., Andersson, J.: On the challenges of self-adaptation in systems of systems. In: SESoS@ECOOP 2013. pp. 47–51 (2013)

19. Weyns, D., Malek, S., Andersson, J.: FORMS: unifying reference model for formal specification of distributed self-adaptive systems. TAAS **7**(1), 8 (2012)

20. Wohlin, C., Runeson, P., Höst, M., Ohlsson, M., Regnell, B., Wesslén, A.: Experimentation in Software Engineering. Computer Science. Springer, Heidelberg (2012). doi:10.1007/978-3-642-29044-2

21. Ye, D., Zhang, M., Sutanto, D.: Self-adaptation-based dynamic coalition formation in a distributed agent network: a mechanism and a brief survey. IEEE Trans. Parallel Distrib. Syst. **24**(5), 1042–1051 (2013)

22. Zambonelli, F., Bicocchi, N., Cabri, G., Leonardi, L., Puviani, M.: On self-adaptation, self-expression, and self-awareness in autonomic service component ensembles. In: SASOW, pp. 108–113 (2011)

23. Zhong, C., DeLoach, S.A.: Runtime models for automatic reorganization of multi-robot systems. In: IEEE/ACM SEAMS 2011, pp. 20–29 (2011)

A Generic Framework for Quality-Based Autonomic Adaptation Within Sensor-Based Systems

Antoine Auger[1]([⊠]), Ernesto Exposito[2], and Emmanuel Lochin[1]

[1] Institut Supérieur de l'Aéronautique et de l'Espace (ISAE-SUPAERO),
Université de Toulouse, 31055 Toulouse Cedex 4, France
{antoine.auger,emmanuel.lochin}@isae.fr
[2] Laboratoire Informatique de l'Université de
Pau et des Pays de l'Adour (LIUPPA), Anglet, France
ernesto.exposito@univ-pau.fr

Abstract. With the growth of the Internet of Things (IoT), sensor-based systems deal with heterogeneous sources, which produce heterogeneous observations of disparate quality. Since network QoS is rarely sufficient to expertise Quality of Observation (QoO), managing such diversity at the application level is a very complex task and requires high levels of experience from application developers. Given this statement, this paper proposes a generic framework for QoO-based autonomic adaptation within sensor-based systems. An abstract architecture is first introduced, intended to bridge the gap between sensors capabilities and application needs thanks to the Autonomic Computing paradigm. Then, the framework is instantiated and practical considerations when implementing an autonomous sensor-based system are given. We illustrate this instantiation with concrete examples of sensor middlewares and IoT platforms.

Keywords: Internet of things · Sensors · Observations · Information quality · Adaptation · Autonomic computing · Service-oriented architectures

1 Introduction

With the accelerated development of Internet of Things (IoT), more and more information sources are available to applications, generally through intermediate sensor-based systems such as sensor middlewares [9,15] or IoT platforms [25]. Whether physical or virtual, sensors represent a huge opportunity for collecting and processing information to provide enhanced services and improve the quality of life within cities.

Only few sensor-based systems have been designed to adapt their behavior according to application needs. Instead, these systems usually define their own metrics before delegating the management of observation quality to end

© Springer International Publishing AG 2017
K. Drira et al. (Eds.): ICSOC 2016 Workshops, LNCS 10380, pp. 21–32, 2017.
https://doi.org/10.1007/978-3-319-68136-8_2

applications. However, this adaptation strategy has several drawbacks since it assumes that application developers have the knowledge to understand those metrics and their meaning. Furthermore, some metrics could be missing or poorly implemented.

On one hand, sensor-based systems deal with various sensors, which constitute as many heterogeneous sources that produce observations of disparate quality. These systems receive and process observations to enrich them with additional information or make them more meaningful for end applications. On the other hand, applications may have specific observation needs, in particular concerning the Quality of Observation (QoO). These needs, which differ from one application to another, may be dynamic and therefore vary over time. For instance, two applications may ask for the same kind of observations (temperature, wind, etc.) but may not require the same granularity (e.g., frequency, coverage).

In order to bridge the gap between heterogeneous observations and application-specific QoO needs, we envision dynamic adaptation with only few interventions from developers/experts. By following the Autonomic Computing [12] approach, we propose sensor-based systems to play the role of autonomic mediators that adapt their behavior to fit application needs thanks to the definition of Service Level Agreements (SLAs). In this paper, a generic framework for QoO-based autonomic adaptation will be presented. This framework, suitable to a large number of sensor-based systems, consists in two parts: (i) an abstract architecture composed of different layers for observation consumption and (ii) a description of five autonomic maturity levels from a sensor perspective.

The remainder of this paper is organized as follows. Section 2 introduces the required background. Section 3 presents our contribution which consists in a generic framework. Section 4 focuses on framework instantiation, giving concrete implementation examples from sensor middlewares and IoT platforms. Finally, we present existing and relevant work in Sect. 5 before concluding and giving some research perspectives in Sect. 6.

2   Required Background

This Section aims to give the reader the required background about sensor observations, QoO and the Autonomic Computing paradigm. These notions are the three foundations of the framework that will be described later in Sect. 3.

2.1   Terminology for Sensor Observations

Sensor-based systems provide observations to applications. Each observation may be considered as the representation of a physical-observed phenomenon (the temperature of a place, a person that enters a room, etc.) or a virtual-occurred event (a new tweet from someone, an incoming e-mail, the availability of a new software update, etc.).

Previous studies have proposed taxonomies to denote the different types of observations that applications can consume. Indeed, the same phenomenon or event can be reported in different ways, including more or less details about the unit of the measure, sensor type, location, etc. As a matter of fact, these taxonomies use ladder representations to denote the different observation types. For instance, in 2013, the National Institute of Standards and Technology (NIST) conducted a sensor ontology literature review [7] that introduced "raw data", "primitive" and "object" perception levels. More recently, Sheth has proposed the "data, information, knowledge, and wisdom (DIKW) ladder" for the IoT [23]. Such taxonomies aim to estimate the level of complexity required to process and "understand" them by observation consumers (applications or users).

In this paper, we only envision applications as observation consumers. Reusing existing terminologies, we define three levels for observation consumption that we define as follows, from the most basic to the most complex:

Sensor Raw Data. The first observation level corresponds to unprocessed observations coming from sensors. At this level, these observations are encoded in the key/value form and do not contain additional information. We denote them as sensor Raw Data (e.g., {sensor_id: 34, value: 20}).

Sensor Information. The second observation level corresponds to sensor Information. Sensor Information is sensor Raw Data that has been processed or enriched with additional Context information [17] (e.g., {sensor_id: 34, value: 20, unit: Celsius, location: (43.564509, 1.468910), accuracy: 0.8}).

Sensor Knowledge. The third observation level is reached with the use of semantics. By implementing a semantic annotation process, sensor-based systems are able to model domain-specific observations and thus to deal with machine-understandable information. We denote by sensor Knowledge any semantic-based observation representation (e.g., {sensor_type: temperature, value: comfort, location: room3, accuracy: good}).

These three observation types mainly refer to observation representation (broadly speaking their content and their format). In the next Section, we introduce attributes to characterize them more precisely and assess their intrinsic quality.

2.2 Quality of Observation

Since the goal of our framework is to provide application-specific high-quality observations, we present some popular quality dimensions and examples of metrics, which may later serve as a basis for SLAs' definition:

Data Quality (DQ). In this work, we use DQ notion to refer to the intrinsic quality of sensor Raw Data. Broadly speaking, it can be seen as the distance between the sensed value (the observation) and the corresponding event (the occurred event). Quite complex to assess, DQ is mainly impacted by the sensor device quality and performances of the underlying network.

Quality of Information (QoI). In [2], Bisdikian et al. define QoI as "*the collective effect of information characteristics (or attributes) that determine the* *degree by which the information is (or perceived to be) fit-to-use for a purpose"*. Some examples of QoI attributes are latency, reputation and spatio-temporal Context. In a sensor context, these metrics may be particularly useful for an application to assess more accurately how fit-for-use sensor Information is.

Quality of Context (QoC). According to Dey, Context can be defined as *"any information that can be used to characterize the situation of an entity. An entity is a person, place, or object that is considered relevant to the interaction between a user and an application, including the user and applications themselves"* [6]. QoC denotes Quality of Information applied to Context [3].

Quality of Knowledge (QoK). Some sensor-based systems, such as Semantic Sensor Webs [24], use ontologies to model sensor observations and describe the capabilities of their sensors. This semantic representation allows query inference and high-level reasoning on sensor Knowledge. QoK assesses the quality of the ontology-based modelisation. Some metrics (such as completeness, coverage and ease to use) have been proposed for Knowledge management systems [20] and may be applied to sensor Knowledge.

Quality of Service (QoS). QoS has been defined in the E.800 recommendation [10] by the ITU-T. Although this definition encompasses above quality dimensions, it is not the case in practice. Indeed, the term "Quality of Service" generally refers to packet transportation from source to destination within the network. As a matter of fact, the set of QoS metrics is often restricted to bandwidth, delay, jitter and loss probability. We will denote this quality dimension as "network QoS" in the rest of this paper.

Above quality dimensions may be used to characterize the general quality of sensor observations. Depending on sensors, applications and use cases, it may be relevant to use many of them to improve this characterization process. For instance, using both network QoS and QoI, one can better understand if some outdated observations are the result of poor network performances or due to a sensor sampling rate too low. In this paper, independently of their consumption level, we use the generic term "Quality of Observation" (QoO) to denote observation quality that sensor-based systems provide to upper applications.

2.3   Autonomic Computing Paradigm

Autonomic Computing has been defined by IBM as the ability of systems to *"manage themselves given high-level objectives from administrators"* [12]. Since it makes a clear distinction between goals and means, the Autonomic Computing paradigm is commonly considered as a convenient way to build interoperable, evolving and easy-to-use systems.

Autonomic systems are a set of Autonomic Elements. Each Autonomic Element is composed of one or many Managed Elements controlled by a single Autonomic Manager. This entity continuously monitors the internal state of its different Managed Elements; then analyses this information; and finally takes appropriate decisions based on both its knowledge base and high-level objectives.

At last, these decisions are converted into actions and transmitted to appropriate Managed Elements for execution. These different steps form the MAPE-K adaptation control loop (Monitor, Analyse, Plan, Execute, Knowledge base), also denoted as "MAPE-K loop" in the rest of this paper.

Autonomic systems relieve end-users to manually implement logic to comply with their needs. Instead, users express their goals, leaving to one or many Autonomic Managers the task of managing the different Autonomic Elements. This process implements the required self-properties. In [12], IBM has identified four *self-** fundamental adaptation properties for autonomic systems, namely self-configuration, self-optimization, self-healing and self-protection.

3   Generic Framework Proposal

In this Section, we present our generic framework for quality-based adaptation. This framework describes an abstract architecture and describes five autonomic maturity levels for sensor-based systems.

3.1   Abstract Architecture

Figure 1 depicts a high-level representation of a sensor-based system providing QoO-based adaptation. Inspired by the representation of standard IT protocol stacks, it shows the different flows that exist between components: while solid arrows represent observation consumption flows, dashed arrows indicate adaptation-related flows (control, management, etc.).

As previously stated, we only consider three different types of observations that applications can consume. We denote as "Raw Data layer", "Information layer" and "Semantic layer" the layers at which applications can consume Raw Data, Information or Knowledge observations, respectively. In fact, one may see each layer as an abstract service provider offering collection and digitization, characterization and semantic annotation to upper layers, respectively. In the following, we give more details about these three layers:

Raw Data layer. The Raw Data layer deals with observations that are produced by sensors. Raw observations can either refer to phenomena (for physical sensors) or events (for virtual sensors). This layer offers collection and digitization of these observations to upper layers. Regarding physical sensors, the digitization process consists in the translation of observations from the physical world into the digital world (e.g., using sensor adapters/wrappers).

Information layer. The Information layer offers Raw Data characterization. The fact of annotating sensor Raw Data with Context information adds value to it since end applications can then use this Context information to assess QoO. For instance, sensor provenance, spatio-temporal information and sensor confidence level are some concrete Context attributes that can be added to sensor Raw Data.

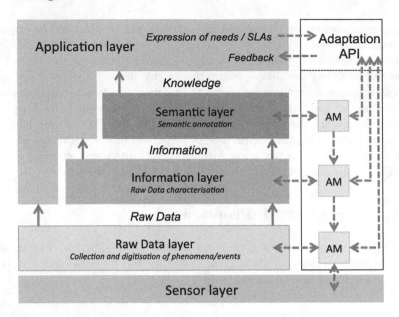

Fig. 1. Abstract architecture for application-specific QoO adaptation. AM: **A**utonomic **M**anager, SLAs: **S**ervice **L**evel **A**greements.

Semantic layer. The Semantic layer offers semantic-based annotation of sensor Information. The use of semantic-based representations (in general using ontologies) allows applications to consume machine-understandable Knowledge. Since ontologies are conceptual representations of a specific domain, we denote as Knowledge any semantic-based observation representation. Remember that this kind of observations allows high-level inference and reasoning.

According to the proposed architecture, applications can customize the behavior of the sensor-based system by expressing needs through the adaptation API. For instance, a classic application for environmental monitoring may be less sensitive to delay than another one for military battlefield management. Therefore, these two applications can ask for the same kind of observations (temperature, wind, etc.) by specifying different QoO levels (with the definition of SLAs). Then, these SLAs are routed to the appropriate Autonomic Manager(s). Each Autonomic Manager (AM) should take into account these application needs and add them to its Knowledge base. When the QoO needs are not or no longer fulfilled, the Autonomic Manager will enforce the required corrective actions to be implemented by the corresponding layer. In addition to possibly consuming observations at three different levels, applications can also subscribe to feedback (statuses of the different layers, statistics of the MAPE-K loops, QoO metrics, etc.) sent by the autonomic sensor-based system.

This framework considers each observation layer as a Managed Element, managed by its own Autonomic Manager for scalability reasons. To adapt QoO according to application needs, we assume that each observation layer implements the required adaptation mechanisms. Some examples of these mechanisms are observation Filtering, Formatting, Fusion, Caching or Machine Learning. Please note that the study of these mechanisms is out of the scope of the framework.

3.2   Autonomic Maturity Levels for Sensor-Based Systems

With the presence of Autonomic Managers and adaptation-related flows, our abstract architecture falls within the Autonomic Computing paradigm. Inspired by the work of IBM on Autonomic Computing [11], we adapt and describe five maturity levels to quantify *how autonomous an existing sensor-based system is*:

Basic (level 1). At this level, no customization is available for applications. The entire behavior of the system is hard-coded by developers during the design phase. The monitoring of the system is done manually by developers who also replace or update different elements and components accordingly.

Managed (level 2). At this autonomic level, adaptation is based on predefined rules written by developers or domain experts (e.g., meteorologists). These rules are simple (*if value < 0 then drop(wind_speed_observation)* for instance) and are generally written by a skilled person.

Predictive (level 3). Predictive behavior is reached with the implementation of reasoning processes in some components of the sensor-based system. These processes can consist in Fusion, Machine Learning, etc. but they must not take into account any macroscopic goal. At this maturity level, components are generally selfish entities.

Adaptive (level 4). Adaptive behavior is characterized by the definition of SLAs. SLAs mostly correspond to the definition of application profiles with specific QoO needs. At this maturity level, components take into account SLAs to self-adapt their local behavior. By implementing such mechanisms, a sensor-based system can be seen as a system driven by a macroscopic goal.

Autonomic (level 5). The last maturity level is the autonomic one. A sensor-based system may be considered as autonomic when its behavior is driven by the expression of business rules coming from end applications. Such system automatically derives appropriate SLAs from these rules and routes them to its different Autonomic Elements. Then, these autonomic entities accordingly adapt their behavior and collectively fulfill application needs.

To fully take advantage of the Autonomic Computing paradigm, we recommend to instantiate our framework to build adaptive or autonomic sensor-based systems (level 4 or 5) with definition of SLAs. These SLAs should include both observation needs (e.g., {type: `temperature`, level: `information`}) and the QoO level required by the application (e.g., {timeliness: `60`, trust: `0.8`}).

Since it is composed of generic components (conceptual layers), this framework can be adapted to a large number of platform-specific implementations. For example, one could imagine a sensor-based system where sensors semantically annotate their observations. In this case, the Sensor, Raw Data, Information and Semantic layers would be only one. Regarding adaptation, our framework is also generic about the chosen autonomic maturity level, the SLAs definition and the available adaptation mechanisms.

4   Framework Instantiation

In this Section, we focus on practical considerations when implementing an autonomous sensor-based system. QoO metrics, mediation and SLAs are required by our framework in order to provide application-specific QoO adaptation. We illustrate each of these features by giving concrete examples of existing sensor-based systems. These examples aim to instantiate our framework and validate the abstract architecture previously introduced.

4.1   QoO Metrics Definition

In Sect. 2, we have seen that numerous quality dimensions may be considered to derive metrics and define new SLAs.

Some sensor-based systems define their own custom QoO metrics. For instance, the MASTAQ middleware [9] proposes "standard deviation" and "confidence level" as QoO metrics while MiddleWhere [19] defines "resolution", "confidence" and "freshness" metrics to assess the quality of location information. Other sensor-based systems use frameworks to define QoO metrics. For instance, INCOME [15] is a QoC-based middleware for Context distribution. It allows Context consumers to express SLAs according to their QoC needs. The distribution of Context information is then performed according to these needs. In order to model heterogeneous QoC metrics, INCOME uses the QoCIM framework [14].

Although it allows finer metric tuning, defining custom metrics may decrease the system interoperability. Indeed, a simple name is rarely sufficient to understand how a metric is computed or how it should be used. As a result, sensor-based systems that define their own metrics must provide adequate documentation, which details and clarifies the metrics used to avoid any ambiguities.

4.2   Mediation

Mediation feature has gained attention with Service-Oriented Architectures. A Service-Oriented Architecture (SOA) is an architectural framework for building software systems based on distributed services which may be offered by different service providers. SOA software architectures are based, among other things, on the key concepts of service, service provider and service consumer [13]. A service is a well-defined and self-contained function or functionality offered by a service producer. Service consumers are the entities that make use of the services provided. Sometimes, the use of a service must respect a SLA, which specifies the purpose, functionalities, constraints and usage of the service.

Sensor-based systems often play the role of mediators, bridging the gap between sensors and applications. Even if all sensor-based systems are not built following SOA framework, the underlying sensors may be considered as "observation providers" while upper applications can be seen as "observation consumers". In some cases, it may occur that several sensors have similar capabilities. Although they offer the same kind of observation, they may not offer the same QoO level. To optimise resources, some sensor-based systems only select a subset of service providers that are sufficient to fill customer needs. This mechanism is called sensor composition/selection and it has gained popularity with Semantic Web Services. For instance, in [18], Perera et al. propose CASSARAM, a Context-aware tool to select an optimal subset of sensors according to specific QoO attributes (availability, accuracy, etc.).

Implementation choices have an effect on mediation feature. While a SOA-based system can rely on a service bus playing the role of mediator, other architectures (such as microservice-based architectures) should implement their own mediation mechanism.

4.3   Application Needs and Sensor Capabilities

In order to provide adaptation, our abstract architecture relies on the expression of application needs. This requirement supposes that (i) applications must be able to express their needs regarding observations and (ii) sensors must be able to express their capabilities and describe the characteristics of the service that they provide.

To cope with these challenges, several sensor-based systems have used semantics, and in particular ontologies, to model sensor observations and describe the capabilities of their sensors. Ontology-based representation involves the definition of concepts and their relationships. Using semantics for observation modeling corresponds to transform sensor Raw Data or sensor Information into machine-understandable Knowledge. Within semantic-based systems, sensors can also express their capabilities in a semantic way (what is their type, their sampling rate, their units, etc.).

Numerous sensors and observations ontologies have been developed, creating a need for standardisation. Between 2009 and 2011, the Semantic Sensor Network Incubator Group[1] of the W3C initiated a standardisation process. After reviewing 17 sensors and observations ontologies, they identified the most relevant concepts and developed the Semantic Sensor Network (SSN) ontology [5]. SSN ontology has been reused within CASSARAM middleware [18] for instance. In CASSARAM, sensors are semantically described using an extended SSN ontology while observations are semantically annotated with Context. Finally, OpenIoT project [25] also extends SSN ontology to generalize the notion of sensor, supporting both physical devices and virtual sensors.

---

[1] http://www.w3.org/2005/Incubator/ssn/.

Ontologies are efficient to build extensible, reusable and interoperable systems. The W3C SSN ontology is currently one of the most popular standard within sensor-based systems to both represent observations and describe sensor capabilities.

5 Related Work

QoS within Wireless Sensor Networks has been largely investigated [4]. Studies generally present network QoS as a way to improve general information quality within WSNs. By contrast, this assumption does not longer holds for other sensor-based systems such as IoT platforms. Indeed, within these observation-centric systems, network QoS is rarely sufficient to ensure observation quality. Therefore, other quality dimensions (like QoI) need to be considered. Until now, QoO has often been addressed thanks to Context-awareness feature [1,3]. Therefore, Context information and QoC have received much attention, especially in the areas of sensor middlewares [22] and IoT [17]. However, Context information is rarely used by sensor-based systems to perform autonomic adaptation but is rather added to sensor observations as meta-data for later analysis by applications.

Few research efforts have been made to manage QoO with Autonomic Computing. For instance, AcoMS [8] is a sensor middleware for Context distribution. It enables autonomic adaptation by providing several self-* features such as configuration, reconfiguration and healing. The solution of Pathan et al. [16] allows sensor plug-and-play, as well as self-reconfiguration processes according to application scenarios and Context. Finally, SPACES [21] focuses on web-service adaptation by implementing an autonomic MAPE-K loop to dynamically change web services behavior according to Context information. Overall, the above solutions have highlighted the benefits to provide autonomic adaptation. However, they do not consider intrinsic QoO but only rely on the execution Context to define SLAs and provide adaptation. Finally, they do not take into account application-specific needs.

To the best of our knowledge, we are the first to propose a generic framework to achieve application-specific QoO adaptation within sensor-based systems.

6 Conclusion and Perspectives

In this paper, we introduce and describe a generic framework for autonomic adaptation within sensor-based systems relying on Quality of Observation (QoO). This framework aims to bridge the gap between sensors and applications thanks to the Autonomic Computing paradigm. In this paper, a layered architecture able to provide various levels of observation consumption according to application-specific QoO needs has been introduced. This abstract architecture relies on the definition of Service Level Agreements (SLAs) and can be instantiated according to different autonomic maturity levels.

By considering QoO, sensor-based systems go beyond commonly-used network QoS, which has shown its limitations within information-centric systems such as sensor middlewares and IoT platforms. We hope that our generic framework will help researchers and developers to build autonomous sensor-based systems that focus on their primary function, i.e., deliver high-quality observations to applications. Further experimentations are needed to estimate the relevancy of certain QOO metrics depending on use cases. Moreover, further investigation into MAPE-K autonomic control loop is strongly recommended, in particular concerning the Knowledge base (decision rules and execution plans).

As future work, we are currently developing a Cloud-based integration platform for QoI Assessment as a Service. Designed according to the framework presented in this paper, this platform will be applied to a Smart City use case. Such contribution will help the different Smart City stakeholders to assess, better understand and improve QoI in a collaborative way.

Acknowledgements. This research was supported in part by the French Ministry of Defense through financial support of the Direction Générale de l'Armement (DGA).

References

1. Bettini, C., Brdiczka, O., Henricksen, K., Indulska, J., Nicklas, D., Ranganathan, A., Riboni, D.: A survey of context modelling and reasoning techniques. Pervasive Mob. Comput. **6**(2), 161–180 (2010)
2. Bisdikian, C., Branch, J., Leung, K., Young, R.: A letter soup for the quality of information in sensor networks. In: IEEE International Conference on Pervasive Computing and Communications, PerCom 2009, pp. 1–6, March 2009
3. Buchholz, T., Küpper, A., Schiffers, M.: Quality of context information: What it is and why we need it. In: Proceedings of the 10th HP-OVUA Workshop, vol. 2003 (2003)
4. Chen, D., Varshney, P.K.: QoS support in wireless sensor networks: a survey. In: International Conference on Wireless Networks, vol. 13244, pp. 227–233 (2004)
5. Compton, M., Barnaghi, P., Bermudez, L., García-Castro, R., Corcho, O., Cox, S., Graybeal, J., Hauswirth, M., Henson, C., Herzog, A.: The SSN ontology of the W3C semantic sensor network incubator group. Web Semant. Sci. Serv. Agents World Wide Web **17**, 25–32 (2012)
6. Dey, A.K.: Understanding and using context. Pers. Ubiquit. Comput. **5**(1), 4–7 (2001)
7. Eastman, R., Schlenoff, C., Balakirsky, S., Hong, T.: A Sensor Ontology Literature Review. Technical report NIST IR 7908, National Institute of Standards and Technology. http://nvlpubs.nist.gov/nistpubs/ir/2013/NIST.IR.7908.pdf
8. Hu, P., Indulska, J., Robinson, R.: An autonomic context management system for pervasive computing. In: Sixth Annual IEEE International Conference on Pervasive Computing and Communications, PerCom 2008, pp. 213–223, March 2008
9. Hwang, I., Han, Q., Misra, A.: MASTAQ: a middleware architecture for sensor applications with statistical quality constraints. In: Third IEEE International Conference on Pervasive Computing and Communications Workshops, PerCom 2005 Workshops, pp. 390–395. IEEE (2005)

10. ITU-T: E.800: Definitions of terms related to quality of service. International Telecommunication Union-Telecommunication Standardisation Sector (ITU-T), September 2008
11. Jacob, B., Lanyon-Hogg, R., Nadgir, D.K., Yassin, A.F.: A practical guide to the IBM autonomic computing toolkit. IBM, International Technical Support Organization (2004)
12. Kephart, J.O., Chess, D.M.: The vision of autonomic computing. Computer **36**(1), 41–50 (2003)
13. Krafzig, D., Banke, K., Slama, D.: Enterprise SOA: service-oriented architecture best practices. Prentice Hall Professional (2005)
14. Marie, P., Desprats, T., Chabridon, S., Sibilla, M.: The QoCIM framework: concepts and tools for quality of context management. In: Brézillon, P., Gonzalez, A.J. (eds.) Context in Computing, pp. 155–172. Springer, New York (2014). doi:10.1007/978-1-4939-1887-4_11
15. Marie, P., Lim, L., Manzoor, A., Chabridon, S., Conan, D., Desprats, T.: QoC-aware context data distribution in the internet of things. In: Proceedings of the 1st ACM Workshop on Middleware for Context-Aware Applications in the IoT, M4IOT 2014, pp. 13–18. ACM, New York (2014)
16. Pathan, M., Taylor, K., Compton, M.: Semantics-based plug-and-play configuration of sensor network services. In: SSN, Citeseer (2010)
17. Perera, C., Zaslavsky, A., Christen, P., Georgakopoulos, D.: Context aware computing for the internet of things: a survey. IEEE Commun. Surv. Tutorials **16**(1), 414–454 (2014)
18. Perera, C., Zaslavsky, A., Liu, C., Compton, M., Christen, P., Georgakopoulos, D.: Sensor search techniques for sensing as a service architecture for the internet of things. IEEE Sens. J. **14**(2), 406–420 (2014)
19. Ranganathan, A., Al-Muhtadi, J., Chetan, S., Campbell, R., Mickunas, M.D.: MiddleWhere: a middleware for location awareness in ubiquitous computing applications. In: Jacobsen, H.-A. (ed.) Middleware 2004. LNCS, vol. 3231, pp. 397–416. Springer, Heidelberg (2004). doi:10.1007/978-3-540-30229-2_21
20. Rao, L., Osei-Bryson, K.M.: Towards defining dimensions of knowledge systems quality. Expert Syst. Appl. **33**(2), 368–378 (2007)
21. Romero, D., Rouvoy, R., Seinturier, L., Chabridon, S., Conan, D., Pessemier, N.: Enabling context-aware web services: a middleware approach for ubiquitous environments. Enabling context-aware web services: methods, architectures, and technologies, pp. 113–135 (2010)
22. Sheikh, K., Wegdam, M., van Sinderen, M.: Middleware support for quality of context in pervasive context-aware systems. In: Fifth Annual IEEE International Conference on Pervasive Computing and Communications Workshops, PerCom Workshops 2007, pp. 461–466, March 2007
23. Sheth, A.: Internet of things to smart IoT through semantic, cognitive, and perceptual computing. IEEE Intell. Syst. **31**(2), 108–112 (2016)
24. Sheth, A., Henson, C., Sahoo, S.: Semantic sensor web. IEEE Internet Comput. **12**(4), 78–83 (2008)
25. Soldatos, J., Kefalakis, N., Hauswirth, M., Serrano, M., Calbimonte, J.P., Riahi, M., Aberer, K., Jayaraman, P.P., Zaslavsky, A.: OpenIoT: Open Source Internet-of-Things in the Cloud (2015)

Using Formal Model for Evaluation of Business Processes Elasticity in the Cloud

Lydia Yataghene[1]([✉]), Malika Ioualalen[1], Mourad Amziani[2], and Samir Tata[3]

[1] University of Science and Technology Houari Boumediene, Algiers, Algeria
{lyataghene,mioualalen}@usthb.dz
[2] Beamap, SopraSteria Group, Courbevoie, France
mamziani@beamap.fr
[3] Institut Mines-Telecom, TELECOM SudParis, Evry, France
samir.tata@telecom-sudparis.eu

Abstract. As it has been the case with other technologies, the availability of Service-based Business Processes (SBPs) in the Cloud allows imagining new usage scenarios. Typically, these scenarios include the execution of thousands of processes during a very short period of time requiring temporarily a very important amount of resources. Novel and innovative approaches for modeling of business processes should be developed to allow supporting these scenarios and others in a safer and cost-effective way. For instance, it is necessary to define strategies to scale resource consumed by business processes up and down to ensure their adaptation to the workload changes. In this paper, we focus on how to model and evaluate SBPs elasticity strategies. We propose an analytical model based on queuing model with variable number of servers to represent SBPs adaptation to demands' variation. We consider a queuing model as Markov chain to evaluate elasticity strategies in the steady state, and to calculate the indices of performance. Our analytical model allows Cloud providers to evaluate and decide about the elasticity strategy to consider before implementing it in real environments.

Keywords: Cloud environments · Elasticity · Queuing model · Markov chain

1 Introduction

Cloud Computing is a model for enabling ubiquitous, convenient, on demand network access to a shared pool of configurable computing resources. These resources should be rapidly provisioned and released with minimal effort and service provider interaction [7]. Services in this paradigm are basically delivered under three layers, which are: Infrastructure as a Service (IaaS), Platform as a Service (PaaS) and Software as a Service (SaaS).

Cloud services can be provided with the elasticity property which allows these services to adapt their resources usage according to demands evolution while maintaining the desired QoS. The elasticity of a Cloud service is the ability

© Springer International Publishing AG 2017
K. Drira et al. (Eds.): ICSOC 2016 Workshops, LNCS 10380, pp. 33–44, 2017.
https://doi.org/10.1007/978-3-319-68136-8_3

to large scale dynamically, without requiring a reset and without causing side effects (loss of QoS). The provisioning of resources may be made using horizontal or vertical elasticity. Vertical elasticity increases or decreases the resources of a specific Cloud service while horizontal elasticity adds and removes instances of Cloud services.

Cloud environments are being increasingly used for deploying and executing business processes and particularly Service-based Business Processes (SBPs) that are made of components that provide business services. As it has been the case with other technologies, the availability of SBPs in the Cloud allows imagining new usage scenarios. Typically, these scenarios include the execution of thousands of processes during a very short period of time requiring temporarily a very important amount of resources. Novel and innovative approaches for modeling of business processes should be developed to allow supporting these scenarios and others in a safer and cost-effective way. For instance, it is necessary to define strategies to scale resource consumed by business processes up and down to ensure their adaptation to the workload changes.

In this work, we deal with provisioning of horizontal elasticity of SBPs. This can be achieved by providing Cloud environments with elasticity mechanisms allowing scaling up and down deployed SBPs. To scale up a SBP, elasticity mechanisms must add new copies of some services of the considered SBP. To scale down a SBP, these mechanisms should remove the useless copies of services.

Many strategies can be used to manage SBPs elasticity. These strategies decide about when, where and how execute elasticity actions. Some of them are reactive and some others are predictive. Thus, it is necessary to evaluate these elasticity strategies before implementing them in real Cloud environments to ensure their effectiveness. In our work, we are interested on reactive strategies. Actually, we have already presented as a first step, formal model of SBPs elasticity based on queuing theory with a dynamic number of servers and metrics to calculate to evaluate elasticity strategies [13].

In this paper, we address the elasticity of SBPs in the Cloud and especially the evaluation of elasticity strategies. To do this, we proposed an analytical model for strategies evaluation. In the proposed model, services are modeled as queue, and a SBP is modeled as a network of queues. We use queuing theory with variable number of servers to represent SBPs adaptation to demands' variation. We consider a queuing model as Markov chain to evaluate elasticity strategies, and calculate performance metrics. Finally, we show the results of experiments. The proposed analytical model allows Cloud providers to evaluate and decide about the elasticity strategy to consider before it deployment and use in real environments.

The paper is organized as follows: Sect. 2 discusses related works. Then, Sect. 3 presents a formal model for SBPs elasticity. We present in Sect. 4, our analytical approach for the evaluation of SBPs elasticity. Section 5 shows the experimental results. Finally, Sect. 6 concludes this paper and gives future work.

2   Related Works

A number of research studies have addressed challenges of elasticity in cloud environments.

In [11], the authors consider scaling at both the service and application levels in order to ensure elasticity. They discuss the elasticity at the service level as we did in our approach. Nevertheless, the correctness of the proposed mechanisms is not proved.

In [6], the authors present a framework for modeling and reasoning about nonfunctional properties that should reflect elasticity of deployed business services. As defined, the elastic properties and mechanisms can tackle any application, since the characteristics of business processes are not considered in the proposed approach. Contrary to our approach, the elasticity mechanism serves all the deployed processes.

In [5], the authors present an approach that consists in producing a model for an elastic SBP which is the result of the composition of the SBP model with models of mechanisms for elasticity. Contrary to our approach, the proposed approach requires an effort from the designer. In addition, the proposed approach changes the nature of the considered SBP.

Replication mechanisms have been widely considered in the areas of service adaptation (in order to ensure QoS), service availability and fault tolerance [3, 12], but the proposed mechanisms allow the replication of the entire SBP, while the bottleneck may come from some services.

Cloud computing has attracted considerable research attention, but only a small part of the work done addressed performance issues, and rigorous analytical approach has been adopted by only a few. Authors of [4] model a cloud server as a $M/G/m/m + r$ and they propose an analytical technique based on an approximate Markov chain model for performance evaluation of a cloud computing center. Contrary to our approach, the number of server is fixed.

In [10], the authors propose a queue M/M/m that allows the performance study of the deployed applications in Cloud infrastructure under different rules of elasticity. In the proposed model, the number of servers is variable according to load variation.

In [8], the authors focus on ensuring elasticity for jobs highly paralleled on a cloud cluster. They present a queue M/G/1/K used to determine the optimal number of cloud resources necessary to satisfy the response time constraint. In [9], the authors proposed a provisioning system where they present a G/G/1 queuing model to determine the number of servers needed to serve expected workload over time. All these approaches allow to ensure elasticity at application level, but they do not allow to ensure elasticity at service level.

In [1], the authors propose a Petri net model for ensuring SBPs elasticity based on duplication and consolidation mechanisms. In [2] they provided a framework for the evaluation of elasticity strategies using model checking and simulation techniques.

In [13], we proposed to model SBPs elasticity using queuing model system with variable number of services copies to represent SBPs adaptation to demands variation and to provide a duplication and a consolidation mechanisms. In this work, the main idea is to propose an analytical model based on queuing model with variable number of servers to represent SBPs adaptation to demands' variation and to evaluate elasticity strategies.

3   A Formal Model for SBPs Elasticity

A SBP is a business process that consists in assembling a set of elementary IT-enabled services. These services carry out the business activities of the considered SBP. Assembling services into a SBP can be ensured using any appropriate service composition specifications (e.g. BPEL).

Elasticity of a SBP is the ability to duplicate or consolidate as many instances of the process or some of its services as needed to handle the dynamic of received requests. Indeed, we believe that handling elasticity does not only operate at the process level, but it should operate at the level of services too. It is not necessary to duplicate all the services of a considered SBP, while the bottleneck comes from some services of the SBP.

In our work, we are interested in the evaluation of SBPs elasticity. In this context, queuing models seem to be an interesting model that allows modeling and performance evaluation of SBPs elasticity. However, since we aim in this work to deal with SBP adaptation according to load variation, the classical queuing models are not suitable. In fact, these models use a fixed number of servers and do not allow the variation of the number of servers. To resolve this, we proposed in [13] to use a queuing model system with a dynamic number of servers to model SBPs elasticity. The proposed model allows changing the number of used servers depending on some metrics (queue length, etc.), in order to have the minimum and sufficient number of servers that ensure the required QoS. To do this, new servers are added only, when needed and removed once they are useless.

In our model, each basic service of the SBP is represented by a queue. The SBP will be represented by a network of queues. When an invocation of a service arrives, it is directed to the service queue. When a service has a lot of invocations, it will be overloaded and this can leads to degradation of QoS. A solution to this overflow problem is to duplicate the service in order to increase service capacity and maintain the desired QoS despite the increased load. When a service has few invocations, it will use more resources than required for the same QoS. A solution to that is to consolidate the service in order to avoid under utilization of resources. Note here, that when we have more than one copy of a service, we have to define a load balancing strategy that decides about the way a service call is transferred over the set of service copies (Round Robin, Random, etc.).

Duplication and consolidation operations are executed as many times as necessary, in order to ensure a proper working of the deployed SBP. The duplication of a service consists in the creation of a new copy of this service, ensuring the QoS. The consolidation of a service is the removing of an unnecessary copy of this service, in order to avoid under utilization of resources.

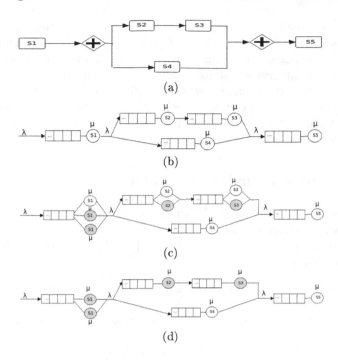

Fig. 1. An example of the elasticity of SBPs using queuing model.

The example of Fig. 1 presents a SBP for an online computer shopping service composed of five services and modeled in BPMN:

- Requests Service ($S1$): receives requests to purchase a computer.
- Components assembly Service ($S2$): performs the assembly of computer components according to the desired characteristics.
- Test Service ($S3$): performs tests of the computer.
- Invoice Service ($S4$): creates the invoice related to the purchased computer.
- Delivery Service ($S5$): delivers the computer with its invoice to the customer.

In this example, we propose to model the SBP example shown in Fig. 1(a). The queuing model of this SBP is represented in Fig. 1(b). In Fig. 1(c) we have the resulted model after the duplication of services S1, S2, S3. In Fig. 1(d), we have the resulted model after the consolidation of services S1, S2, S3. As mentioned previously, in order to manage SBPs elasticity (i.e., execution of duplication/consolidation operations), many strategies can be used. A strategy is responsible for making decisions on the execution of the duplication/consolidation mechanisms (i.e., deciding when, where and how to execute these operations). The abundance of possible strategies require their evaluation before using them in a real Cloud environment, in order to guarantee their efficiency in enhancing SBP's performance. Defining an elasticity strategy is a key challenge, since it requires to choose the appropriate metrics and values, in order to maintain the QoS while reducing operational costs.

Elasticity strategies can be reactive or proactive. Reactive strategies are based on rules mechanisms (e.g. Event-Condition-Action rules), while predictive strategies are based on predictive-performance models and load forecasts. Generally, these strategies use performance metrics to make their decisions (i.e., elasticity indicators). In our model, we can use different performance information as metrics in order to take elasticity decisions. For example, we can use information about the length of the queue, the average waiting time, the number of arrivals (invocations), the number of clients, etc.

4   The Proposed Analytical Model

As introduced in [13], we model SBPs using a queuing model $M/M/N/r + N$, its specificity is the dynamic number of servers.

In our model, each basic service of the SBP will be represented by a queue $M/M/N/r + N$, where:

- M: the interarrival time of requests is exponentially distributed with average value of λ.
- M: the services processing time follows an exponential law with the average value of μ.
- N: the service under consideration contains N servers, which represents the number of copies of the considered service (initially there is a single copy of each service), in order to handle request arrivals (First Come First Served).
- $r + N$: the service capacity which means that the buffer size for invocations is equal to r.

Using this model, we can represent elasticity adaptation of SBPs by adding or removing copies of services. In our model, the number of copies of services is controlled by an elasticity strategy that uses the length of the queue as an elasticity metric. On one hand, when the number of invocations in the queue exceeds k ($k =$ threshold), we add a copy of service, when it exceeds $2k$, we add another copy of service, when it exceeds ik we add $(i + 1)^{th}$ copy of service ($i = 0, 1, 2, ..., n$). On the other hand, when the number of invocations in the queue decreases and is less than ik, the $(i + 1)^{th}$ copy of the service is removed. Considering this strategy, we can represent the length of the queue in this form: $ik + j$ ($j = 0, ..., k$), and the number of invocations in the system in this form: $ik + j + (i + 1)$.

In order to allow the evaluation of elasticity strategies, a queuing system $M/M/N/r + N$ can be considered as a Markov process, which can be analyzed by exploiting the Markov chains. We model the number of invocations in the system (those in service and those waiting to be served); if these invocations are enumerated as: $0, 1, 2, ... r + N$, a homogeneous Markov chain is obtained. Therefore, the Markov chain observed the state of the system.

Let, P_i be the steady state probability to have i invocations in the system.

Our queuing model $M/M/N/r + N$ is represented by the graph with transition rates (in Fig. 2) associated to the markov chain to our system, where each arrival of a new invocation is assimilated to a birth, and each departure of an invocation being served assimilated to a death.

4.1   Calculations of Probabilities

To derive various performance indices of the model in the steady state, we must first calculate the stationary probabilities. The corresponding Markov chain to the graph transition rates, shown in Fig. 2, is aperiodic and irreducible, therefore, the Markov chain is ergodic and consequently, it admits a steady state where stationary probabilities exist. At steady state, the inflow of each state of the chain is equal to the outflow of this state (the principle of **Chapman-Kolmogorov**). Applying this rule, the equations system is obtained as follows, it is assumed that: $\rho = \dfrac{\lambda}{\mu}$, then:

$$P_1 = \rho P_0, \; P_2 = (\rho + 1)P_1 - \rho P_0, \cdots P_{k+1} = (\rho + 1)P_1 - \rho P_0,$$

$$P_{k+2} = \frac{1 + \rho}{2}\, P_{k+1} - \frac{\rho}{2}\, P_k,$$

$$P_{ik+j+(i+1)} = \left(\frac{\rho}{(i+1)} + 1 \right) P_{ik+(j-1)+(i+1)} - \left(\frac{\rho}{(i+1)} \right) P_{ik+(j-2)+(i+1)}$$

We solved these equations by recurrence in general case of a process of birth and death, birth rates and dead respective λ and μ, the formula of probability is:

$$P_{ik+j+(i+1)} = \frac{\rho^{ik+j+(i+1)}}{(i!)^{k+1}\,(i+1)^{j+1}}\, P_0$$

The sum of the probabilities is equal to 1, from this we can calculate P_0:

$$P_0 = \left(1 + \sum_{i=0}^{n} \sum_{j=0}^{k} \frac{\rho^{ik+j+(i+1)}}{(i!)^{k+1}(i+1)^{j+1}} \right)^{-1}$$

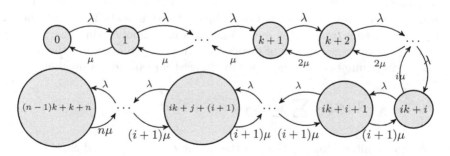

Fig. 2. Process describing the state of the queue $M/M/N/r + N$

Simplifying, we obtain:

$$\sum_{i=0}^{n}\sum_{j=0}^{k}\frac{\rho^{ik+j+(i+1)}}{(i!)^{k+1}(i+1)^{j+1}} = \sum_{i=0}^{n}\left(\frac{\rho^i}{i!}\right)^{k+1}\cdot\frac{1-\left(\frac{\rho}{i+1}\right)^{k+1}}{i+1-\rho}\cdot\rho$$

First case: $\rho \neq i+1$

$$P_0 = \left(1+\sum_{i=0}^{n}\left(\frac{\rho^i}{i!}\right)^{k+1}\cdot\frac{1-\left(\frac{\rho}{i+1}\right)^{k+1}}{i+1-\rho}\cdot\rho\right)^{-1}$$

Second case: $\rho = i+1$

$$P_0 = \left(1+e^{\rho(k+1)}(k+1)\sum_{i=0}^{n}(P(\mathcal{P}(\rho)=i))^{k+1}\right)^{-1}$$

4.2 Fundamental Parameters of Performance of the Queuing Model

Once we have the stationary probabilities, we calculate the performance indices of the model of each queue of SBP.

Average Number of Copies of Services S. It is an important parameter of our analyze. This parameter is about the number of copies of services in our system. It will allow us to evaluate how efficient is the resources allocation by the strategy to face the variation of the SBP solicitations.

$$S = \sum_{i=0}^{n}\sum_{j=0}^{k}(i+1)P_{ik+j+(i+1)}$$

Average Response and Waiting Time. The average waiting time will allows us to evaluate the influence of the implemented strategy on the invocations waiting time according to the evolution of invocations arrival. Before calculating the average waiting time in the queue and average response time, we start by calculating the average number of invocations in the system and in the queue.

The average number of invocations in the system can be obtained as:

$$E\{N\} = \sum_{i=0}^{n}\sum_{j=0}^{k}(ik+j+(i+1))P_{ik+j+(i+1)}$$

The average number of invocations in the queue can be obtained as:

$$E\{N_q\} = \sum_{i=0}^{n}\sum_{j=0}^{k}(ik+j+(i+1))P_{ik+j}$$

The average time spent in the system and average waiting time are obtained by the formula of Little. Let W be average time spent in the system in the steady state, and similarly let W_q be the average waiting time in the queue.

$$W = \frac{E\{N\}}{\lambda}, W_q = \frac{E\{N_q\}}{\lambda}$$

Rate of Lost Invocations. As we have a finite capacity system (i.e., there is blocking, etc.), let us define the rate of lost invocations R_c. When the capacity of the queue or system is reached, invocations which came later are rejected, the rate of lost invocations can be obtained as follows:

$$R_c = \sum_{i=0}^{n} \sum_{j=0}^{k} (ik + j + (i+1)) P_{ik+j+(i+1)+1}$$

5   Experimentation

In order to study the performance of elasticity strategies, we performed several experiments. We apply our approach on the service of SBP. The described experiments are performed using the values which are shown in the following. We used an exponential process to define a scenario of calls arrival on the service and the service processing time follows an exponential law. In Fig. 3, we assume that "$\lambda = 0, 5$" and "$\mu = 0, 25$" and in Fig. 4 "$\lambda = 0, 2$" and "$\mu = 0, 25$". The equations of performances parameters presented above have been solved numerically using a program written in C.

To evaluate performances, we vary the threshold k. We study the evolution of several metrics from obtained steady-state probabilities. To evaluate the efficiency of the strategy, we focused on the following metrics:

1. Number of calls arrival in a time unit.
2. Number of copies of services S.
3. Average calls waiting time.
4. The cost of waiting time, resources that would let us identify which strategy is the best. Assuming that the best strategy is the one with the lowest cost.

When we take $k = 1$, a new copy is created for each invocation, so the waiting time and the number of waiting invocations are equal to zero.

Figures 3(a) and 4(a) show the scenario of calls arrival according to λ (respectively 0, 5 and 0, 2). The number of copies of services depends on the number of arrival. It varies according to the arrival of the invocations. In some cases, we can say that a strategy is better than another. For example in Figs. 3(d) and 4(d) the strategy with $k = 2$ is better than others, and that is true whatever the arrival law. Also we can find for each arrival law a better strategy. In Fig. 3(g), the strategy with $k = 7$ is better in contrast to the Fig. 4(g), where the best strategy is the one with $k = 10$.

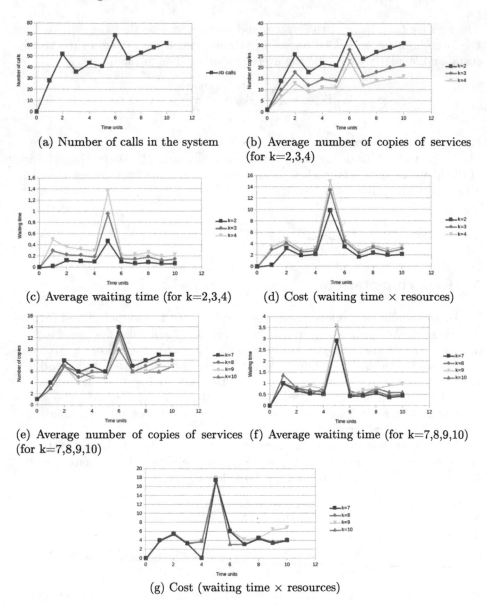

(a) Number of calls in the system

(b) Average number of copies of services (for k=2,3,4)

(c) Average waiting time (for k=2,3,4)

(d) Cost (waiting time × resources)

(e) Average number of copies of services (for k=7,8,9,10)

(f) Average waiting time (for k=7,8,9,10)

(g) Cost (waiting time × resources)

Fig. 3. Numerical results for the queuing system ($\lambda = 0, 5$)

From this, we can say that the best strategy depends on the arrival law and the time of service.

Regardless of the number of arrival, the small threshold k provides better performance standpoint response time, waiting time, ... , but we can see in our study that many resources have been provided when the threshold is small. The QoS is affected because of execution of duplication/consolidation process

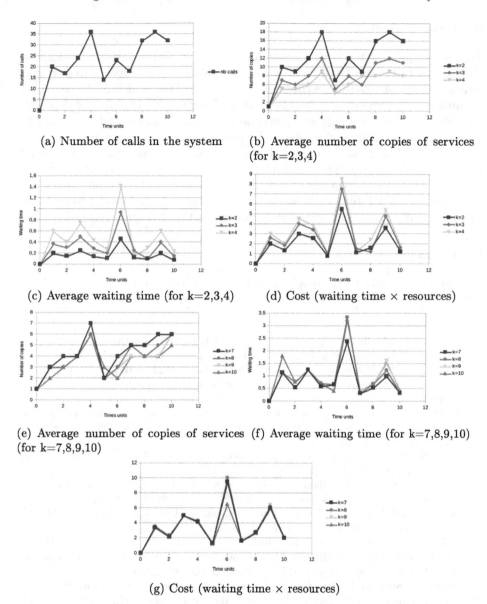

(a) Number of calls in the system

(b) Average number of copies of services (for k=2,3,4)

(c) Average waiting time (for k=2,3,4)

(d) Cost (waiting time × resources)

(e) Average number of copies of services (for k=7,8,9,10)

(f) Average waiting time (for k=7,8,9,10)

(g) Cost (waiting time × resources)

Fig. 4. Numerical results for the queuing system ($\lambda = 0, 2$)

many times. The threshold should be chosen according to the resources that the provider can deploy and also their capacities. When we have a large number of arrival and we use strategies with a small k, there may have a loss of calls because of the unavailability of necessary resources.

6 Conclusion

This paper proposed a formal model for evaluating SBPs elasticity strategies. Our goal is to be able to evaluate the performance of elasticity strategies, and forecast the best strategy according to the case. The modelling is based on queuing model system with variable number of servers. The number of deployed services is dynamically adjusted based on demands variation and according to the implemented elasticity strategy. To evaluate the performance parameters of elasticity strategies, we proposed also an analytical approach. The model was evaluated and experimental results show the performance variations under different values of the threshold k and the influence of the arrival process on the strategy. As a future work, we plan to propose a formal model to evaluate elasticity while considering different strategies and performance metrics.

References

1. Amziani, M., Melliti, T., Tata, S.: A generic framework for service-based business process elasticity in the cloud. In: Barros, A., Gal, A., Kindler, E. (eds.) BPM 2012. LNCS, vol. 7481, pp. 194–199. Springer, Heidelberg (2012). doi:10.1007/978-3-642-32885-5_15
2. Amziani, M., Melliti, T., Tata, S.: Formal modeling and evaluation of service-based business process elasticity in the cloud. In: WETICE (2013)
3. Chrysoulas, C., Kostopoulos, G., Haleplidis, E., Haas, R., Denazis, S., Koufopavlou, O.: A decision making framework for dynamic service deployment. In: ISTMWC (2006)
4. Khazaei, H., Misic, J.V., Misic, V.B.: Performance analysis of cloud computing centers using M/G/m/m+r queuing systems. IEEE Trans. Parallel Distrib. Syst. **23**(5), 936–943 (2012)
5. Klai, K., Tata, S.: Formal modeling of elastic service-based business processes. In: IEEE SCC, pp. 424–431 (2013)
6. Lê, L.S., Truong, H.L., Ghose, A., Dustdar, S.: On elasticity and constrainedness of business services provisioning. In: IEEE SCC, pp. 384–391 (2012)
7. NIST: Final Version of NIST Cloud Computing Definition Published (2011). http://www.nist.gov/itl/csd/cloud-102511.cfm
8. Salah, K.: A queueing model to achieve proper elasticity for cloud cluster jobs. In: Proceedings of the 2013 IEEE Sixth International Conference on Cloud Computing (CLOUD 2013), pp. 755–761. IEEE Computer Society (2013)
9. Singh, R., Sharma, U., Cecchet, E., Shenoy, P.J.: Autonomic mix-aware provisioning for non-stationary data center workloads. In: Parashar, M., Figueiredo, R.J. (eds.) ICAC, pp. 21–30. ACM (2010)
10. Suleiman, B., Venugopal, S.: Modeling performance of elasticity rules for cloud-based applications. In: EDOC 2013, Washington, DC, pp. 201–206 (2013)
11. Tsai, W.T., Sun, X., Shao, Q., Qi, G.: Two-tier multi-tenancy scaling and load balancing. In: ICEBE, pp. 484–489 (2010)
12. Weissman, J.B., Kim, S., England, D.: A framework for dynamic service adaptation in the grid: next generation software program progress report. In: IPDPS. IEEE Computer Society, Los Alamitos (2005)
13. Yataghene, L., Amziani, M., Ioualalen, M., Tata, S.: A queuing model for business processes elasticity evaluation. In: IWAISE, pp. 22–28. IEEE (2014)

A Brokerage Architecture: Cloud Service Selection

Hela Malouche$^{(\boxtimes)}$, Youssef Ben Halima, and Henda Ben Ghezala

RIADI Labs, National School of Computer Science,
Manouba University, Tunis, Tunisia
Malouchehela8@gmail.com, Youssef.benhalima@gmail.com,
Hhbg.hhbg@gmail.com

Abstract. Due to the various benefits of cloud computing such as flexibility and ease of management, several organizations decided to adopt its services. However, with the large number of available cloud services, the selection of services which meets the specific requirements of the user becomes a complex task. This paper proposes a cloud brokerage architecture which allows selecting cloud services based on functional and non-functional requirements identified by the user. Before selecting the best cloud service which satisfies the user, it is important to know the significance of each parameter that characterizes the cloud service. For this reason, we will use the objective ranking of attributes approach based on rough set theory. In this paper, the selection of cloud service by the broker is done using a developed version of the CM-factory algorithm which takes into account the organization cross-cutting concerns.

Keywords: Cloud computing · Brokerage architecture · Service selection · CM-factory algorithm · Rough set theory

1 Introduction

The main objective of every organization is to maximize its profit and minimize its costs. For this reason, organizations are always looking for new technologies that can achieve this goal. Among the most promising emerging technologies is the cloud computing, which became the most popular model for organizations. Cloud computing is a pay-as you-go model that enables organizations to significantly reduce costs by migrating their IT hardware and software to cloud environment. However, the existence of several cloud service providers makes the selection of a cloud service a complicated task for the organization.

One of the promising solutions to address this problem is the use of cloud broker. The need for cloud broker has been proved by many organizations in the field of cloud like Gartner and NIST [1].

Cloud Broker plays the role of a mediator between the cloud user and the cloud provider, and its main function is to free users from the complexity of finding the best cloud provider. It also allows managing services and cloud resources without showing the technical details of the various platforms Cloud. This paper presents a cloud brokerage architecture which contains several components such as: access manager,

© Springer International Publishing AG 2017
K. Drira et al. (Eds.): ICSOC 2016 Workshops, LNCS 10380, pp. 45–55, 2017.
https://doi.org/10.1007/978-3-319-68136-8_4

matching service, deployment service. We are interested in this paper to detail the role of the matching service component. To accomplish its task, the matching service component must follow an algorithm that we have proposed in this paper which is a developed version of the CM-factory algorithm [2]. Each cloud service is characterized by a set of attributes. Thus, before selecting the most suitable cloud service for the user requirements, it is important to identify the significance of each cloud service attribute. A correct assignment of weights for different attributes helps the user to select the most suitable cloud service to its requirements. However, the evaluation of the importance of each attribute based only on subjective choices of the user can make the service selection process arbitrary, unreliable, and unable to make the right selection that matches the user requirements. For this reason, the weight assignment for the various attributes must take into account the subjective judgment of the user and the objective judgment of other users which have the same service requirements. For this reason, we have used in this paper the objective ranking of attributes approach based on rough set theory [3] which allows to calculate the significance of each service attribute, put them in order, and identify the objective weight of each one.

The remainder of this paper is structured as follows: in Sect. 2, we will present related work related to service selection in the web services and cloud computing areas. In Sect. 3, we will describe the cloud broker architecture and its various components. In Sect. 4, we will present a developed version of the CM-factory algorithm and we will present the objective ranking of attributes approach based on rough set theory that we will use in this algorithm. Finally, in Sect. 5 we will conclude the paper and we will describe our future work.

2 Related Work

Recently, the problem of SLA-based service selection and the resource allocation have been widely studied in the web services and cloud computing areas. We will present in this section some works dealing with this problem. In [4], the authors focused on broker-based Web service architecture which is based on the use of broker as an intermediary between clients and servers. Two algorithms for resource allocation, HQ and HR, have been proposed. The role of the broker is based on these algorithms and allows helping the servers to assign services to clients according to their QoS needs. The authors in [5] presented an Intelligent Cloud Resource Allocation Service (ICRAS) to help users find the most appropriate cloud service offer. ICRAS allows discovering the existing resource configurations in order to select the configuration that meets the user requirements. [6] proposed an approach for the specification of configurable Web service requests and offers, with different pricing and preference functions, and a framework for optimal service selection. The proposed service selection algorithm can support several service configurations and features. In [7], the authors presented a framework named CloudGenius which allows selecting an adequate infrastructure service and VM image to support Web application migration to the cloud. CloudGenius help to automate the selection process based on analytic hierarchy process (AHP). Thus, the user must give a detailed description of the service requirements using a weighted criteria catalogue. The evaluation in the current version of the prototypical implementation is restricted to quantitative criteria and supports only migration to Amazon Web Services (AWS).

[8] presented a declarative decision support system named CloudRecommender in order to automatically select a cloud service. The functionalities and QoS parameters of the infrastructure services are described in a formalized domain model. The cloud service selection in this approach is based on already existing service information and does not allow a runtime selection based on dynamic QoS information such as throughput and latency.

To ensure resource allocation, the authors in [9] presented an SLA-based cloud computing framework. Two parameters are considered in this allocation: the workload and data centers geographical location. This framework presents SLA negotiation mechanism to support the preparation of SLA which satisfies users and providers requirements. However, this framewok can be improved by adding other properties as support for resources allocation such as cost, availability, and so on.

[10] proposed a new scheduling heuristic based on various SLA parameters for deploying user applications in the cloud environment. This proposed heuristic can efficiently distribute applications on the cloud resources, however it focuses on fulfillment of functional properties of the services such as required CPU and storage, and does not support non-functional properties.

In [11], the authors proposed resource allocation algorithms which allows to satisfy consumers, while minimizing the cost and SLA violation, and maximize the SaaS providers profit by optimizing the resources allocation. These algorithms do not take into consideration customers profile for resource allocation. This problem has been resolved in [12] by proposing an extended version of these algorithms which aims to support SaaS providers and consumers simultaneously. The new version of these algorithms takes into account the QoS parameters required by both customers and SaaS providers. However, the proposed algorithms do not support the SLA negotiation process which can improve the level of consumer satisfaction and maximize their utility.

The authors in [13] presented an architecture which allows a QoS-aware deployment of applications on the most suitable cloud service provider. An ontology-based discovery of cloud services is proposed in order to make it easy for users to select the best cloud provider. Thus, this architecture can meet the requirements of users (software and hardware requirements). This approach is validated by a case study which approves its efficiency and effectiveness.

[14] presented a cloud service selection model named CloudEval, to meet the requirements of users in terms of specified service levels based on the non-functional properties evaluation of candidate services. This model is based on multi-attribute decision making technique in order to facilitate the selection of the optimal service for the user.

A migration framework is presented in [15]. One of the features proposed in this framework is the selection of the most suitable cloud provider based on pre-defined requirements specifically related to SMEs. This task is performed in the selection platform which is a component of this framework. The proposed solution lack of flexibility since it is based on predefined requirements and conditions.

The authors in [16] proposed an automated approach which allows the user select the cloud storage services that meets its requirements. For this reason, the authors have defined an XML schema containing a description of the capabilities of each cloud storage system. This approach allows satisfying user requirements and estimating the performance and cost. However, the manual update of the XML schema is time-consuming and can lead to several errors. This problem can be solved by making the XML descriptions updated automatically.

The authors in [17] proposed a decision-making model based on a fuzzy analytic hierarchy process (AHP) allowing companies' users to select the suitable IaaS provider which meets their goals. Cloud service providers are assessed using multiple comparison criteria. In this model, the selection of IaaS providers is based only on the goals of the company, and the specified service level are neglected.

A cloud service selection model is presented in [18]. This model proposed the aggregation of subjective and objective criteria of a cloud service based on a fuzzy simple additive weighting system. This model requires the participation of users in the evaluation process.

In [19], the authors presented a systematic comparator named Cloudcmp to help users select the cloud provider that satisfies their needs by making a classification in terms of performance and cost. The results presented in [19] shows that it is still difficult to choose one provider, since each provider has its strengths. This model can give better results by applying it to specific applications.

A step-by-step decision process called *Cloudstep* is proposed in [20]. This process uses template-based profiles describing the organization, target application and cloud provider profiles. The application profile activity extracts its functional and non-functional proprieties, and the technologies required to use this application. The cloud provider profile activity allows specifying the characteristics of each cloud provider to verify whether it is appropriate to the application and the organization profiles. This process may not select any cloud provider if it does not find any provider who meets the constraints identified in the application and organization profiles.

The authors in [2] proposed a cloud-migration factory (CM-factory) framework. The main component of this framework is the service definition model which is composed of three parts: service-description to describe the functional properties of the service, service-parameters to describe non-functional properties and service-migration to describe the migration specific parameters. In order to indicate the importance of each parameter a weight indicator is used when describing the target service. Then, a cloud provider is selected based on these properties and the weight indicator.

[21] introduced an approach called HS4MC. This approach is composed of two phases: SLA construction and service selection. In the first phase, a set of SLAs are prepared according to the requirements of the SaaS provider. In the second phase, a selection algorithm is used to calculate the satisfaction score for a cloud service based on prospect theory.

In [22], the authors proposed a broker-based framework which allows to select cloud services by following an automatic matching process. The cloud provider that best meets the user requirements is considered as selection candidate. A utility-based matching algorithm is developed in order to maximize the user utility.

These works present different solutions for the selection of cloud services. However, they do not offer solutions to deal with the complexity of assigning weights for each parameter of cloud service. A correct attribution of weights helps user to rank the various cloud service providers and to select the most suitable one to its requirements. The assignment of weights based on subjective information of the user or the decision maker can make the service selection process unreliable and arbitrary. Thus, in the algorithm presented in this paper, the assignment of weight is based on the subjective preferences of the user and the collected objective information from other users.

3   Cloud Broker Architecture

The cloud broker is a very important concept related to the cloud computing technology and it is considered as key concern for its future [1]. The main function of the cloud broker consists in helping the user to find the cloud service provider that meets their functional and non-functional requirements. Thus, it plays the role of an intermediary between the user and the cloud provider. Figure 1 shows the general architecture proposed for the brokerage system.

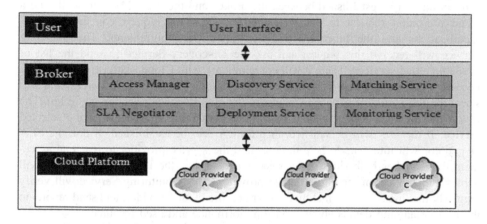

Fig. 1. Architecture of cloud broker

The different components of the cloud broker architecture are:

- *User Interface:* allows user to access to the brokerage platform, submit its service request, describe its functional and non-functional requirements and describe the desired service level agreement (SLA). From this interface, the user can also control the quality of service provided. The user can connect to Drools to store new knowledge.
- Access manager: It seeks to prevent unauthorized access and protect data and all the brokerage system from hackers, virus, or malware.
- *Discovery service:* this component allows to periodically discovering new cloud services that are available on the cloud market.
- *Matching service:* this component represents the main task of the cloud service broker. It selects the best cloud service that meets the functional and non-functional

requirements of the user by following the algorithm proposed in this paper. Then, a connection is established between the user and the selected cloud provider.

- *SLA negotiator:* allows user and cloud provider to reach an agreement that satisfies both sides. Upon arriving at an agreement, an SLA is established.
- *Deployment service:* This is the component responsible for deploying user applications after choosing the most suitable cloud service for its requirements.
- *Monitoring service:* this component verified that the SLAs are respected by the user and the cloud service provider and that there are no cases of violence of these agreements. Similarly, the resources used for each application are checked and daily, weekly and monthly reports are sent to users to allow them to verify costs of the various cloud services provided.
- *Cloud platforms:* communication between the broker and the cloud providers is ensured by standard interfaces.

The communication between components of this architecture is described as follows: the user will connect to the brokerage system via the user interface by using username and password. The Access Manager will verify the identity of the user and a connection will be established between the broker and the user. The latter will send a cloud migration request to the Matching Service. This request contains the task specifications and the functional and non-functional requirements. The Matching Service will receive this request and ask the Discovery Service to send the list of available cloud services. Then, it will communicate with Cloud platform to collect the necessary data concerning the cloud services available (e.g. SLAs, resources) and will select the most suitable service by applying the cloud service selection algorithm. The user will receive a response from the broker containing the details of the selected service. If the user will be satisfied, then a SLA will be established. If not, the SLA Negotiator will intervene to help the user and the service provider to reach an agreement that satisfies both sides. After selecting a service, the Deployment Service will deploy the service on the chosen cloud provider. The Monitoring Service will verify regularly that the SLAs are met by the user and the cloud provider, and send reports to the user containing details about service performance and used resources.

In the following, we present the service selection algorithm which allows the matching service component to select the cloud service that meets the functional and non-functional requirements of the user.

4 Service Selection Algorithm

The purpose of the service selection algorithm is to help user to choose the best cloud service that meets its requirements. The definition of weights of different attributes is a complex task for users. Thus, before presenting this algorithm, we will introduce the method that we will use to solve the weight assignment problem.

4.1   Evaluation of Service Attributes

A cloud service is defined by a set of parameters and attributes. However, user envisages a difficulty in the evaluation of the importance of each attribute. The objective ranking of attributes approach based on rough set theory [3] is a solution which is proposed to assess the importance of each attribute and put them in order. This method can help, on the one hand, users to select the best cloud service, and on the other hand, the cloud providers by insisting them to improve the quality of their services. The attributes are evaluated by taking into consideration the subjective preferences of the user and objective evaluations from other users who have the same requirements and expectations from cloud service.

The ranking attributes of cloud services algorithm proposed in [3], put in order the different attributes of cloud services by calculating the significance of each attribute.

Based on this algorithm, the weight of each parameter α can be calculated as follows [3]:

$$w_\alpha = \frac{Sig_\alpha(\alpha)}{\sum_{c \in C} Sig_c(c)} \tag{1}$$

Where, 'Sig_α' represent the significance of the attribute 'α', calculated by following the ranking attributes of cloud services algorithm. It is calculated as follows:

$$Sig(\alpha) = \frac{|card\,(Pos_{\,c}(D))| - |card\,(Pos_{\,c-\{\alpha\}}(D))|}{|U|} \tag{2}$$

With:

U represents the cloud services set. D represents the decision attribute set. 'C' represents the set of condition attributes of a cloud service, and $c = \{C - \alpha\}$. $Pos_c(D)$ is the positive region of the partition U/D with respect to the condition attributes C [3]. If $Pos_c(D) = Pos_{c-\{\alpha\}}(D)$, then the attribute α is unnecessary to select the best cloud service and may be reduced.

The comprehensive weight is calculated by taking into consideration the subjective preferences of user and the objective assessments of cloud service, as follows [3]:

$$I(w) = \beta W_o(w) + (1 - \beta) W_{so}(w); \; 0 \leq \beta \leq 1 \tag{3}$$

Where, $W_o(w)$ and $W_{so}(w)$ are the calculated weight of each attribute respectively based on objective data and subjective preferences [3]. 'β' represents the user preference for objective and subjective weights of attributes when selecting the best cloud service. 'β' is identified by the user. If the user chooses to give more importance to the subjective information, then $\beta = 0$. If these attributes depend only on the objective information, then $\beta = 1$.

4.2 Proposed Algorithm

A service S is defined as following:

$$S = \begin{cases} fct = (x_1, x_2, \ldots, x_d) \\ Nfct = (y_1, y_2, \ldots, y_p) \end{cases}$$

Where, 'fct' and '$Nfct$' represents respectively the functional and non-functional parameters of a service S.

Similarly, an offered service O_i can be defined with two parameters:

$O_i = \{x^{Oi}, y^{Oi}\}$, where x^{Oi} is the functional parameter of a service O_i and y^{Oi} is its non-functional parameter.

Let 'n' be the number of offered services to be treated by the broker. $O = \{O_1, O_2, \ldots, O_n\}$ is the set of all treated offers.

A target service 'T' is defined as follows:

$$T = \begin{cases} \{(x_1, min_{x1}, max_{x1}, I_{x1}(w)), (x_2, min_{x2}, max_{x2}, I_{x2}(w)), \ldots (x_d, min_{xd}, max_{xd}, I_{xd}(w))\} \\ \{(y_1, min_{y1}, max_{y1}, I_{y2}(w)), (y_2, min_{y2}, max_{y2}, I_{y2}(w)), \ldots (y_p, min_{yp}, max_{yp}, I_{yp}(w))\} \end{cases}$$

Where, (min_x, max_x) represents the required boundaries for a functional parameter x, and (min_y, max_y) represents the required boundaries for a non-functional parameter y. $I_x(w)$ and $I_y(w)$ are the comprehensive weights calculated respectively for the functional and non-functional parameters by using the objective ranking of attributes approach based on rough set theory. For example, for the attribute 'availability', the minimum value required by the user is 94 (% /month), the maximum value is 99 (% /month) and the comprehensive weight of this attribute is "0.65". These values can be presented in the target service as follows: (availability, 94, 99, 0.65).

Let 'd' and 'p' represents respectively the number of attributes of the functional parameters and the non-functional parameters of a service S.

For a given service, we can find parameters which the largest value is the desirable value for the user as well as parameters which the smallest value is the desirable value. For example, for parameters like cost, the desirable value for user is the smallest value. As against for the throughput, the desirable value is the highest value. For this reason, non-functional parameters of a given service must be normalized before the ranking of cloud services. By applying the normalization equation presented in [21], desirable values for all parameters will be the highest values.

The normalization is done by applying this formula:

$$norm(y_k^{Oi}) = \begin{cases} \dfrac{y_k^{Oi} - min_{yk}}{max_{yk} - min_{yk}} & \text{If the largest value of the attribute } k \text{ is the desirable value} \\ \dfrac{max_{yk} - y_k^{Oi}}{max_{yk} - min_{yk}} & \text{If the smallest value of the attribute } k \text{ is the desirable value} \end{cases}$$

We consider an operator *'Inc'* which allows verifying that a value of a given parameter j is included in the desirable range proposed by the user.

$$Inc\left(x_j^O\right) = \begin{cases} 1 \text{ if } min_j \le x_j^O \le max_j \\ 0 \text{ if } x_j^O < min_j \text{ or } x_j^O > max_j \end{cases}$$

Let $W_{max}(y)$ the highest weight of the non-functional parameters obtained by applying the objective ranking of attributes approach based on rough set theory.

Let $U(O_i)$ the assessment score of the offered Service O_i. A list *'Selectedlist'* is used to group the resultant offered services with their evaluation score.

This algorithm is described using the following pseudo-code:

```
1   For i vary from 1 to n Do;
2    For j vary from 1 to d Do;
3     If    ( Inc(x_j^oi)= 0 )    Then
4      O' ← (O-O_i) and n' ← (n-1)
5     Endif
6    Endfor
7   Endfor
8   For i vary from 1 to n' Do;
9    For k vary from 1 to p Do;
10    If  (I_yk(w) = W_max(y) )  Then
11     If   (Inc(y_k^oi)= 0)      Then
12      O" ← (O'-O_i ) and n" ← (n'-1)
13     Endif
14    Endif
15   Endfor
16  Endfor
17  For i vary from 1 to n" Do;
18   For k vary from 1 to p Do;
19    U (O_i) ← U (O_i)+ (norm (y_k^oi) × I_yk(w))
20   Endfor
21   Insert U (O_i) in Selectedlist(O_i,U(O_i))
22  Endfor
23  If sizeof (Selectedlist) > 0 Then
24   Sort Selectedlist by U Values in descending order
25   return k = key of the highest U in Selectedlist
26  Else
27   return k = null
28  Endif
```

In a first step, the algorithm filters the offered services and keeps only those which satisfy all the functional parameters. The result of this step is a set of filtered services offered O' with n' elements (lines 1 to 7). Then, all the non-functional parameters which have the highest weight should be satisfied. For this reason, the algorithm filters again the resultant offered services O' and the result is a new set of offered services O'' with n'' elements (lines 8 to 16). After that, the algorithm calculates the assessment score of the filtered offered service and inserts it in the *Selectedlist* (lines 17 to 22). In the next step (lines 23 to 28), the algorithm sorts the calculated scores by a descending order and returns the key of the offered service with the highest score which represents the most suitable offered service for the user.

This algorithm allows taking into account the functional and non-functional proprieties of the user during the cloud provider selection process, based on objective weights assignment for all properties of cloud services. Thus, this algorithm can complement the CM-factory algorithm.

5   Conclusion and Future Work

In this paper, we have presented the architecture and various components of the brokerage system. The matching service is a component of the brokerage architecture which allows selecting the best cloud provider for the user.

The selection process presented in this paper is based on an algorithm which takes into consideration the functional and non-functional requirements of the user. This algorithm is a developed version of CM-factory algorithm. The assignment of weights for each parameter of a cloud service is a complex task for the user. If this assignment is based only on subjective preferences of the user, the selected cloud provider may not be the best one that meets its needs. For this reason, we have used the objective ranking of attributes approach based on rough set theory, in order to take into consideration the subjective information of the user and the objective information when assigning the weights of different parameters.

In our future works, we will solve other problems encountered during the selection of cloud service process, for example, when there is no service that meets user requirements.

References

1. Fowley, F., Pahl, C., Zhang, L.: A comparison framework and review of service brokerage solutions for cloud architectures. service-oriented computing, ICSOC 2013 Workshops 8377, pp. 137-149 (2014)
2. ElHoussaini, C., Hafiddi, H., Nassar, M., Kriouile, A.: CM-factory for enabling enterprise migration to cloud. Int. J. Cloud Comput. **4**(3), 211–233 (2015)
3. Liu, Y., Esseghir, M., Boulahia, L.M.: Evaluation of parameters importance in cloud service selection using rough sets. Appl. Math. **7**, 527–541 (2016)
4. Yu, T., Lin, K.J.: The design of QoS broker algorithms for QoS-capable web services. Int. J. Web Serv. Res. (IJWSR) **1**(4), 33–50 (2004)
5. Clark, K., Warnier, M., Brazier, F.M.T.: An intelligent cloud resource allocation service. In: Proceedings of the International Conference on Cloud Computing and Services Science (CLOSER2012), pp. 37–45 (2012)
6. Lamparter, S., Ankolekar, A., Studer, R., Grimm, S.: Preference-based selection of highly configurable web services. In: Proceedings of the 16th International Conference on World Wide Web, pp. 1013–1022. ACM, New York (2007)

7. Menzel, M., Ranjan, R.: Cloudgenius: decision support for web server cloud migration. In: Proceedings of the 21st International Conference on World Wide Web, pp. 979–988. ACM, New York (2012)
8. Zhang, M., Ranjan, R., Nepal, S., Menzel, M., Haller, A.: A declarative recommender system for cloud infrastructure services selection. In: Vanmechelen, K., Altmann, J., Rana, O.F. (eds.) GECON 2012. LNCS, vol. 7714, pp. 102–113. Springer, Heidelberg (2012). doi:10.1007/978-3-642-35194-5_8
9. Son, S., Jung, G., Jun, S.C.: An sla-based cloud computing that facilitates resource allocation in the distributed data centers of a cloud provider. J. Supercomput. **64**(2), 606–637 (2013)
10. Emeakaroha, V.C., Brandic, I., Maurer, M., Breskovic, I.: SLA-aware application deployment and resource allocation in clouds. computer software and applications conference workshops (COMPSACW), 2011. IEEE 35th Annual, pp. 298–303 (2011)
11. Wu, L., Garg, S.K., Buyya, R.: SLA-based resource allocation for software as a service provider (SaaS) in cloud computing environments. In: 11th IEEE/ACM International Symposium on Cluster, Cloud and Grid Computing (CCGrid), pp. 195-204. IEEE (2011)
12. Wu, L., Garg, S.K., Versteeg, S., Buyya, R.: SLA-based resource provisioning for hosted software-as-a-service applications in cloud computing environments. IEEE Trans. Serv. Comput. **7**(3), 465–485 (2014)
13. Dastjerdi, A.V., Tabatabaei, S.G.H., Buyya, R.: An effective architecture for automated appliance management system applying ontology-based cloud discovery. 2010. In: 10th IEEE/ACM International Conference on Cluster, Cloud and Grid Computing (CCGrid), pp. 104–112 (2010)
14. Hsu, C.L.: A cloud service selection model based on user-specified quality of service level. computer science & information technology (CS & IT), pp. 43–54 (2014)
15. Nussbaumer, N., Liu, X.: Cloud migration for SMEs in a service oriented approach. computer software and applications conference workshops (COMPSACW), 2013. IEEE 37th Annual, pp. 457–462, 22-26 July 2013 (2013)
16. Ruiz-Alvarez, A., Humphrey, M.: An automated approach to cloud storage service selection. In: Proceedings of the 2nd Workshop on Scientific Cloud Computing (Science Cloud 2011), pp. 39–48. ACM, New York (2011)
17. Kwon, H.K., Seo, K.K.: A decision-making model to choose a cloud service using fuzzy AHP. Adv. Sci. Technol. Lett. Cloud Super Comput. **35**, 93–96 (2013)
18. Qu, L., Wang, Y., Orgun, M.A.: Cloud service selection based on the aggregation of user feedback and quantitative performance assessment. In: Proceedings of the IEEE 10th International Conference on Services Computing (SCC 2013), pp. 152–159 (2013)
19. Li, A., Yang, X., Kandula, S., Zhang, M.: CloudCmp: comparing public cloud providers. In: Proceedings of the 10th ACM SIGKCOMM Conference on Internet Measurement, IMC2010, pp. 1–14. ACM (2010)
20. Beserra, P.V., Camara, A., Ximenes, R., Albuquerque, A.B., Mendonça, N.C.: Cloudstep: a step-by-step decision process to support legacy application migration to the cloud. In: Proceedings of IEEE 6th International Workshop on the Maintenance and Evolution of Service-Oriented and Cloud-Based Systems (MESOCA), pp. 7–16. IEEE, Trento (2012)
21. Farokhi, S., Jrad, F., Brandic, I., Streit, A.: HS4MC-hierarchical SLA-based service selection for multi-cloud environments. In: Proceedings of the 4th International Conference on Cloud Computing and Services Science (CLOSER 2014), pp. 722–734. Barcelona, Spain (2014)
22. Jrad, F., Tao, J., Streit, A., Knapper, R., Flath, C.: A utility-based approach for customised cloud service selection. Int. J. Comput. Sci. Eng. **10**(1/2), 32–44 (2015)

Service Virtualization for Self-adaptation in Mobile Cyber-Physical Systems

Amir Taherkordi[1,2]([✉]), Peter Herrmann[1], Jan Olaf Blech[3],
and Álvaro Férnandez[1]

[1] NTNU, Trondheim, Norway
{amirhost,herrmann,alvarof}@item.ntnu.no
[2] University of Oslo, Oslo, Norway
amirhost@ifi.uio.no
[3] RMIT University, Melbourne, Australia
janolaf.blech@rmit.edu.au

Abstract. Mobile Cyber-Physical Systems (mCPS) consist of cooperating units that often operate in an unpredictably changing environment. Thus, they need to adapt quickly to varying *spatial* and *temporal* conditions during operation, e.g., to avoid collisions. The control software of the mobile units has to reflect this complex dynamics, and traditional device-level adaptation models are usually not efficient enough to engineer them smoothly. We address this challenge by proposing a *Virtual Adaptation Services Framework (VASF)*. It provides a virtualized application-level view to adaptation requirements, enabling adaptation coordination between cooperative mCPS devices. In particular, VASF allows us to describe the contextual conditions of mCPS by abstract rules that are analyzed at runtime by the tool-set BeSpaceD. Based on this analysis, the control systems of the involved mCPS units are automatically reconfigured using the OSGi framework. The approach is demonstrated with DiddyBorg robots that are operated by Raspberry Pi boards.

Keywords: Mobile CPS · Spatiotemporal reasoning · Virtualized adaptation services

1 Introduction

A *Cyber-Physical System* (CPS) integrates a physical mechanism with a computer-based control and monitoring system. Usually, it contains feedback loops in which the physical processes affect embedded computer systems and vice versa [11]. Being tightly integrated with physical processes, a CPS is not always predictable and does not necessarily operate in a controlled environment [25]. Therefore, it needs to respond and adapt quickly to changes during operation, such as hardware and software defects, changes in resource use efficiency and surrounding environments, unexpected conditions, and non-continual feature usage.

© Springer International Publishing AG 2017
K. Drira et al. (Eds.): ICSOC 2016 Workshops, LNCS 10380, pp. 56–68, 2017.
https://doi.org/10.1007/978-3-319-68136-8_5

This concern is particularly important for *mobile Cyber-Physical Systems* (mCPS), in which a unit moves freely in its environment and may cooperate with other units, e.g., in mobile robotics and smart vehicles [37]. The mCPS essentially run in highly dynamic environments (e.g., coordination of autonomous vehicles). In consequence, they need to adapt their behavior in a collaborative manner at runtime. The kind of adaption that mCPS software systems may perform can be the dynamic allocation of resources [22], content adaptation [26] (e.g., multimedia content), or the adaptation of the structure and functionality of software, to name the most significant ones. Among these, dynamic and autonomous adaptation of mCPS software is considered the most difficult aspect to implement. It involves the deployment of software modules and reconfiguration of networks and software architectures at runtime, as well as the adaptation of mCPS control software parameters (e.g., the speed of a unit) [14].

To coordinate a bunch of mCPS units and adapt them to a varying environment in a timely manner, we need efficient *context reasoning* solutions that guide the reconfigurations carried out in the various devices. The control systems of the involved mCPS have to consider numerous *spatial* and *temporal* contextual conditions (e.g., humans in the vicinity). This and the potentially large number of cooperating units makes context processing and self-adaptation of mCPS software a non-trivial design problem for which traditional device-centric adaptation approaches are hardly suited [36].

The challenge to create adaptable mCPS software systems has received growing attention by the research community. Existing work addressed this challenge within specific application domains, e.g., robotics and smart automotive systems [14]. Most proposed solutions are either devoted to low-level reconfiguration issues for adaptation (e.g., component-based frameworks [12]) or focus on specifying the CPS adaptable behavior through high-level language abstractions, such as Domain-Specific Languages (DSL) [33,34]. However, the state-of-the-art has not sufficiently addressed the aforementioned complexity issues in modeling and developing adaptive mCPS.

We propose a self-adaptation service framework for mCPS addressing the complexity in modeling and adapting to highly dynamic location and time aspects of cooperative mCPS, called *Virtual Adaptation Services Framework* (VASF). In contrast to device-oriented approaches, it allows us to define adaptation requirements for a whole system of cooperating mCPS units, while adhering to the principles of the MAPE-K adaptation loop [9]. In particular, we can model spatiotemporal system properties using a set of rules that relate contextual aspects to reconfiguration and other change tasks. VASF uses the tool-set BeSpaceD [4] to reason about which rules to apply in a certain context. The result of this analysis is a number of adaptation actions that are automatically executed at the involved mCPS units. The provision of a rule-based reference context model eases the modeling of simultaneous and complicated contextual conditions, while the automatic runtime operation of VASF facilitates software reconfigurations on cooperating mCPS devices. We demonstrate the framework implementation on DiddyBorg robots [30] operated by Raspberry Pi boards.

The rest of this paper is organized as follows: In Sect. 2, we introduce a motivating scenario followed by the proposed adaptation framework in Sect. 3. We present related work in Sect. 4 and conclude in Sect. 5.

2   Motivating Scenario

Autonomous mobile robots are getting popular in various application domains ranging from healthcare to warehousing and transport (e.g., autonomously operating cars and stellar rovers). Like mCPS in general, the robots operate collaboratively in varying physical environments that may have different contextual properties. For instance, transport robots can face changing indoor and outdoor environments ranging from sterile "highways" in which they are protected from conflicting obstacles to areas crowded by humans, stationary barriers, and other robots which may be on conflicting courses. The differing environments aggravate the construction of a correct and timely working control software since, for example, the sensors to be used need to change constantly. In the following, we list some typical contextual environment properties:

- **Surface:** The state of the surface, a mobile robot operates on, may effect relevant control parameters (e.g., braking distances are larger on wet surfaces than on dry ones). Further, the surface may influence the sensors to be used since, for instance, some sensors tend to provide wrong readings when the robot movement is bumpy.
- **Network access:** Larger distances and obstacles may impede the communication between robots operating in the same area which, e.g., may lead to a delayed reaction when two robots are on a conflicting course (see [18]).
- **Self-localization:** For many tasks, it is important for a robot to know where it is (see, e.g., [24]). The way to find the current position, however, depends on various aspects (for example, GPS can only be used outdoors; for triangulation, a number of beacons have to be located at the right spots).
- **Coordination and collision prevention:** For the control, it is relevant whether a robot operates alone in a sterile environment or if it has to coordinate with other robots. A relevant use case is, of course, the protection of humans that may be severely hurt when colliding with a robot.
- **Energy consumption:** Many robots are run by batteries, and for a sustainable operation it is often relevant to keep energy consumption as low as possible. For instance, it may be useful to switch off sensors at the side and the back of a robot if it operates straight ahead for a while.

When a robot moves between locations for which the above mentioned contextual properties differ, it has to adapt its control software. If, moreover, several robots collaborate, the adaptations may embrace the control systems of all of them.

Our testbed consists of DiddyBorg robots [30], see Fig. 1. That are affordable and easily manageable demonstrators, each consisting of six motors that are controlled by a Raspberry Pi. To use DiddyBorg robots in practice, we provided them with sensors in order to enable self-localization and to avoid collisions

(a)   (b)

Fig. 1. (a) A DiddyBorg robot and (b) its testing environment

with fixed and moving obstacles. In our current arrangement, we test the use of infrared and ultrasound sensors combined with an accelerometer and a magnetic sensor determining the direction of the robot. Moreover, the robots are provided with sensors for temperature and air pressure which enables us to adapt their behavior in, e.g., icy conditions. Infrared sensors are suitable for very close distances until 80 cm. They fit nicely to the ultrasound sensors which cannot render precise measures to obstacles closer than 60 cm but provide good distance sensing of more distant objects of up to about 5 m. Using all these sensors, we have to prevent straining the batteries of a DiddyBorg robot. Its motors are operated by 10 AA cells connected in series while we use a rechargeable 5V battery to drive the Raspberry Pi and the sensors. We consider the following dynamic adaptations beneficial:

- To save energy, it seems sensible not to use all sensors at once but to start and stop them according to the environment, the robot operates in, and to adapt the control software accordingly.
- Typical controller parameters like maximum speed and protective braking distances shall be adjusted depending on the physical location and other properties of the environment. For instance, when the robot operates in a long and empty corridor, and the ultrasound sensor detects no obstacle within three meters, the robot can operate with full speed. When enclosing an obstacle, the speed may be reduced depending on the distance to the obstacle.
- We also consider special constructional features which might affect the quality of the sensor readings (e.g., we found out that the heating pipes in one of our labs falsify the readings of the ultrasound sensors which render wildly shaking values when the pipes are approached).
- Temporary conditions in an environment can occur, e.g., due to spills or accidents, that afford extra caution or to avoid an area entirely.

Our VASF-based solution introduced below, shall address these adaptation types.

3   Adaptation Framework

The main goal of VASF is to provide a unified abstraction for adaptation in mCPS in order to reduce the complexity of modeling spatiotemporal-related contextual changes of the control software of mCPS. In particular, it allows us to express the contextual aspects of a mCPS that may consist of various cooperating units, with a set of easily understandable rules. Each rule allows the user to relate contextual information to context change tasks. Based on sensor inputs and other existing context data, a *context reasoning system* driven by BeSpaceD [4] analyzes the rules and sorts out potential conflicts between them. The result of the analysis is a set of reconfigurations that VASF automatically forwards to the involved units. They may vary from basic parameter-based software reconfiguration (e.g., switching from one localization sensor type to another type) to software service-level changes (e.g., replacement of a energy-draining localization software service with a less powerful but more energy-efficient one).

Figure 2 illustrates the main design elements of VASF. That includes: (i) the context modeling space which represents the mCPS operation environment; (ii) the software framework which resides on the software system of mCPS devices and offers the context monitoring and processing, and reconfiguration functionality. Reconfiguration is performed through services relying on the Java-based OSGi framework [28]. From the developer's viewpoint, VASF provides a unified virtualized view to the mCPS-level adaptation needs which will be further detailed for each mCPS device. The different design aspects of VASF are introduced below.

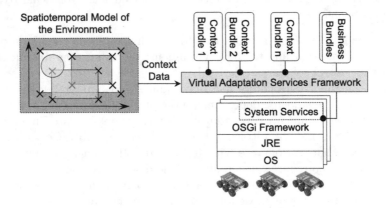

Fig. 2. Overview of our virtualization-based approach for self-adaptation in mCPS

3.1 Spatiotemporal Context Modeling and Reasoning

For context modeling and reasoning, we propose the use of our BeSpaceD language and tool [4] for spatiotemporal modeling and reasoning. Spatiotemporal models provide a formal view of the context modeling space that robots are operating in. Such models can include *geometric* information like obstacles, regions with specific operating conditions as well as *topological* information such as interconnection information between different regions that do not depend on a specific geometry. Temporal aspects are used to describe the change of geometry and topology over time, and the appearance and disappearance of structures and other robots. Furthermore, BeSpaceD formalizes conditions under which a change may occur.

BeSpaceD is implemented in Scala and its core functionality runs in a Java environment. It has been successfully applied in different contexts such as decision support for factory automation [3] and for verification of spatiotemporal properties of industrial robots [19]. Besides of basic logical operators (e.g., AND), BeSpaceD offers special constructs for space, time, and topology. For instance, OccupyBox refers to a rectangular two-dimensional space parameterized by its left lower and its right upper corner points while constructs like TimeInterval make the modeling of temporal aspects possible. For example, the following formula expresses that the rectangular space with the corner points $(1050, 2056)$ and $(1502, 2603)$ will be temporary closed between the time points 200 and 600:

```
IMPLIES(AND(TimeInterval(200,600),Owner("TemporaryClosure")),
    OccupyBox(1050,2056,1502,2603))
```

BeSpaceD formulas can be efficiently analyzed for spatiotemporal and other properties. For instance, we can specify a point of time and a predicate and derive the spatial implications from these definitions. Likewise, logical quantifiers can be applied to specify and check the existence of a spatiotemporal condition in a specification, or to prove that a certain property holds for a distinct time and space area. In addition, algorithms and tools such as external SMT solvers (e.g., we have a connection to z3 [8]) can help to resolve geometric constraints such as the overlapping of different areas in time and space. A variety of different operators (for instance, breaking geometric constraints on areas down to geometric constraints on points) exist which facilitates the reasoning about geometric and topological constraints.

We decided to utilize BeSpaceD for reasoning about the context rules since it addresses their spatiotemporal nature well. The BeSpaceD language is used to specify the rules while the efficient automatic analysis of BeSpaceD makes it suitable to find out which rules have to be triggered in a certain context. Moreover, the expressibility of BeSpaceD allows us to define prioritization schemes in order to find out which of two or more contradicting rules to prefer.

3.2 Software Reconfiguration

The control software of an mCPS unit shall support runtime changes in the configuration parameters as well as in the software structure, e.g., through software component replacement. In addition, the mCPS software has to support *plugability of context data provider* components. Such general-purpose components are dynamically loaded and unloaded from the mCPS device, providing contextual information such as sensor data.

The software reconfiguration mechanism is built on the Java-based OSGi (formerly known as Open Service Gateway initiative) platform [28]. We chose this framework as resource-efficiency has been one of the core design goals of OSGi and therefore it does not impose high resource overhead on mCPS devices. Some existing implementations, such as Concierge [32], exhibit a reasonable memory footprint for resource-constraint devices (80 kB). Our testbed, the Raspberry Pi node used to control a DiddyBorg, can host the Eclipse OSGi framework, called Equinox [10]. OSGi offers a class-loading mechanism to dynamically load and unload Java packages, so-called *business bundles* that, in our context, may implement a service like listening to a sensor or controlling an activator. For that, OSGi offers functions to activate, deactivate, and replace a business bundle. In particular, it preserves automatically the dependencies of a system when some of its bundles are installed, uninstalled or reconfigured.

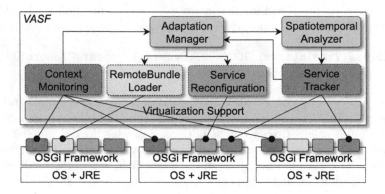

Fig. 3. Architecture of virtualization-based adaptation using the OSGi framework

Figure 3 shows the architecture of VASF. The core idea of the proposed architecture is to provide a virtualization layer supporting access to the collaborating units. Thus, it allows abstract services like Context Monitoring to interact with one or more actual services on selected devices in order to perform part of an adaptation process, e.g., loading a bundle on devices.

Service *properties* are the main source of information for determining the filtering, i.e., which data to consider. They enable the association of additional metadata with services, in addition to the service name. We propose two types of properties for services in order to achieve adaptation: (i) generic properties that describe the functionally of a service, e.g., localization.ultrasound; (ii) properties describing the non-functional aspects of services, e.g., accuracy.distance.high or energy.low. For example, if the functional property for filtering is decided to be localization.shortrange, another level of filtering can be performed by including the non-functional property energy.low in order to select a short range localization service that demands less energy. If there is more than one bundle implementing a service, the service.ranking property, a standard OSGi property, is defined for such services in order to select a single service with the highest ranking.

VASF can either be implemented and deployed on a network node (e.g., a gateway) or reside on an mCPS unit that is powerful enough to perform the context processing and communicate with other devices for performing the adaptation actions. In the latter case, we need a leader selection protocol (see, e.g., [29]) to compensate for the failure of the leading unit. The key component of VASF, Virtualization Support, handles the communications between VASF and the mCPS units, in our case, the Raspberry Pi devices. The WiFi capability of devices along with the socket-based data transmission between the VASF device and robots will be used, e.g., to perform service tracking and load remote bundles.

Adaptation Manager receives the current system context retrieved by the Context Monitoring service from the corresponding actual services on the units. Adaptation Manager forwards the context space information to Spatiotemporal Analyzer, running the BeSpaced-based analysis. Based on its results, Spatiotemporal Analyzer selects the OSGi mechanism to execute, as well as the new property settings and notifies Service Tracker. This service is used to detect services of a specific type, e.g., sending notifications when a service is started or stopped. Its instance at the VASF level is in charge of communicating with the equivalent services on selected mCPS devices to perform service tracking. Thanks to OSGi, we can build our own Service Tracker based on OSGi's service tracking component. Specifically, when Spatiotemporal Analyzer suggests a new service for update, Service Tracker will perform investigations regarding the current status of the old service and ensure that other bundles using this service can continue their execution safely during reconfiguration.

After the new service is located by Spatiotemporal Analyzer and Service Tracker, Adaptation Manager will initiate the service reconfiguration phase using the dynamic service reconfiguration feature of OSGi. If no service with the specified filtering criteria is found, Adaptation Manager invokes RemoteBundle Loader to download the bundle that implements the requested service and load it to the OSGi runtime system. This service is also used to load Context Bundles (see Fig. 2) that are dynamically added to the system in order to collect new context information based on the available sensors of the robot. Like Service Tracker, Service Reconfiguration on VASF communicates with the actual equivalent services on selected mCPS devices to perform the configuration process.

3.3 Combining Context Reasoning and Software Reconfiguration

The business bundles in our DiddyBorg testbed comprise functionality like path planning, the control of the six engines, reading the various sensors, and special tasks necessary in a certain environment (e.g., a detector for unstable sensor readings close to heating pipes). Depending on the reconfigurations selected in the current context, bundles may change in one or more robots. For example, in the case of an area temporarily closed for an mCPS, a new path planning algorithm may be loaded and replace the previous one. Furthermore, once BeSpaceD identifies the approach of an uncritical area, we may temporarily unload bundles that control some sensing devices if these are not needed for the uncritical area. This can result in energy savings.

Table 1. Context change rules for the test bed

No	Location	Other context aspects	Reconfigurations	Other changes
1	Hallways	US sensor detects no obstacle within 300 cm	Switch off IR sensor	
2	Everywhere	US sensor detects obstacle between 100 and 300 cm	Switch on IR sensor	Reduce speed to 50%
3	Everywhere	US or IR sensors detect obstacle within 100 cm		Reduce speed to 25%
4	Everywhere	US or IR sensors detect obstacle within 70 cm	Rely on IR sensor only	
5	Room B216	Magnetic sensor detects course towards the heating pipes	Switch on detector for unstable readings of the US sensor	
6	Room B216	Detector shows unstable readings of the US sensor		Reduce speed to 25%
7	Outdoors	Temperature sensor shows a temperature below 3°C		Reduce speed to 50%
8	Hallways	Time is between 00 and 15 of the hour (lecture break)	Switch on IR sensor	Reduce speed to 50%
9	Everywhere	Two or more robots within 10 m	Switch on IR sensor at all effected robots	Reduce speed to 50% at all effected robots
10	Everywhere	Two or more robots within 5 m		Reduce speed to 25% at all effected robots

To clarify our approach, we list in Table 1 a set of rules[1] guiding context reasoning and software reconfiguration for our DiddyBorg robot testbed. The rules depend on the current robot location and other contextual aspects like sensor readings, input from collaborating units, time properties, or reports about other robots being in the same room. They are described as BeSpaceD formulas and guide the context reasoning. The results of a rule may be software reconfigurations and other changes, e.g., the adjustment of control parameters. For instance, rule 5 defines that if the robot is in room B216 and the magnetic sensor detects that it heads towards the heating pipes which may effect the reading of the ultrasound sensor, an OSGi-bundle containing a detector function is added which constantly checks the readings of the ultrasound sensor. If the detector finds out that the readings get unstable, i.e., start to jump ferociously, this is an indication that the robot approaches the heating pipes. In this case, following rule 6, the control parameter determining the robot speed is changed such that the speed is reduced to 25% preventing the robot crashing against the pipes.

As discussed above, rules may be contradictory. For instance, rule 1 demands to switch off the infrared sensor saving energy when the robot is operated in one of the hallways and the ultrasound sensor does not detect any obstacles within 3 m. In contrast, according to rule 8 the infrared sensor has to be kept operating between 00 and 15 of the hour since then there is a break between lectures and many people are expected in the hallways. Thus, the likelihood of somebody

---

[1] In Table 1, *US* stands for *ultrasound* and *IR* for *infrared*.

encountering the robot from the side leaving a room is significantly higher and the infrared sensor may provide a better reading of the exact distance. The context reasoning shall, of course, guarantee the safest possible solution which, in our case, means prioritizing rule 8 keeping the infrared sensor on. Using its prioritization scheme which, for instance, may determine that a sensor has to be active if desired by one of the contradicting rules, BeSpaceD decides that rule 8 will be applied and not rule 1.

The Diddyborg demonstrator is currently under development, thereby we cannot provide reliable measures on the time needed for the various adaptations of the control systems of the robots. First tests of OSGi on a Raspberry Pi, however, give the impression that the typical OSGi reconfiguration functions like starting or changing business bundles are quite resource-efficient, expecting no major performance penalties of our approach. Of course, that has to be analyzed more in-depth when the full demonstrator is running. Likewise, we have to determine the impact of the BeSpaceD-based analysis on the overall performance. As discussed in [21], BeSpaceD proved to run efficiently for similar approaches such that we do not expect a serious penalty here either.

4   Related Work

Self-adaptation of CPS software systems has received great attention because of their inherent unpredictability and high dynamicity. In the following, we discuss the related work with respect to context modeling techniques for mCPS and the solutions for enabling self-adaptation of mCPS software system.

Spatiotemporal specifications and means to reason about them, are an important part of our work. A variety of different specification mechanisms such as a process algebra-like formalism and a related type system for concurrency and resource control exists [6]. In the SPEEDS project [2,17], contracts between components are used to model behavior in the form of transition systems. Means to reason about spatial and geometric constraints are described in, e.g., [1,20]. Additional logic approaches for hybrid systems (e.g., [13,31]) provide comprehensive languages and tools for describing CPS including time and space. In contrast to these works, our system combines the Java basis of the OSGi context with spatiotemporal reasoning at runtime that can take place on the robot controller to support runtime adaptivity of CPS.

Other work addresses the large amount of information available for context processing [7,23]. This also includes the diversity of application variants for software reconfiguration [5,27]. However, the view to diversity in these types of approaches is different from what we envisage for mCPS applications, i.e., growing and diverse *spatiotemporal* contextual changes. Another aspect of context processing is to address uncertainty in adaptation. In [15,16], meta-adaptation strategies are proposed that extend the adaptability of a system by constructing new tactics at runtime reflecting the changes in the environment.

With respect to dynamic software adaptation models for CPS, a framework for mapping the large component model Kevoree into micro controller-based architectures is discussed in [12]. The main goal of this work is to push dynamics and elasticity concerns directly into resource-constrained devices, based on the notion of models@runtime. The proposed dynamic component model is benchmarked against certain key criteria such as memory usage and reliability, on an Arduino board with an ATMEL AVR 328P microcontroller. The main focus of this work is on efficient development of dynamic components for resource-constrained CPS, which is different from the goal of this paper, i.e., modeling contextual aspects in a scalable manner and adopting a service-based view to adaptation instead of the device-level view. In [33], an approach is proposed for the development of adaptable software applications for embedded systems based on a Domain-Specific Language (DSL). The authors chose DSL-based adaptation to specify adaptation policies and strategies at a high-level, using rules that produce the necessary runtime reconfigurations independent from the application logic. In particular, they develop the adaptation framework of a Lego NXT Mindstorms robot exploring the environment. Similarly, PLASMA [35] and Sykes [34] utilize ADL and planning-as-model-checking technologies to enable dynamic replanning in the architectural domain in robots. The focus of these works is on specifying the adaptable behavior through DSL, while our work is characterized by a high-level service-oriented abstraction model, which is domain-independent and simplifies adaptation modeling and implementation in typical mCPS.

5   Conclusions and Future Work

Enabling efficient dynamic software adaptation is a key requirement of mCPS with respect to their high dynamicity and spatiotemporal contextual changes. The main goal of the framework, presented in this paper, is to facilitate the adaptation of mCPS software, referring to the support of complicated contextual changes in the spatiotemporal aspects of mCPS. Further, our approach supports the collaborative nature of mCPS for which we need an application- and high-level view to adapting the whole mCPS, rather than individual devices. We achieve this by introducing a new software architectural model, which is based on the idea of virtualizing the adaptation services at the application level through a Virtulization Services Adaptation Framework (VASF) and then interpreting the process to actual low-level adaptation actions performed on selected devices. We use BeSpaceD for modeling and reasoning, while the framework components and the self-configuration model are demonstrated for the DiddyBorg robots with Raspberry Pi boards using OSGi. As our future plan, we will develop a generic version of VASF and use it in a variety of mCPS environments. As an demonstrator, we will apply the adaptation framework to a bottling plant deployed in the RMIT's advanced manufacturing precinct. In addition, as an adaptation solution for CPS, we plan to study the reliability of VASF when faults occur during the service reconfiguration.

References

1. Bennett, B., Cohn, A.G., Wolter, F., Zakharyaschev, M.: Multi-dimensional modal logic as a framework for spatio-temporal reasoning. Appl. Intell. **17**(3), 239–251 (2002)
2. Benveniste, A., et al.: Multiple viewpoint contract-based specification and design. In: Formal Methods for Components and Objects (2008)
3. Blech, J.O., et al.: Efficient incident handling in industrial automation through collaborative engineering. In: 2015 IEEE 20th Conference on Emerging Technologies Factory Automation (ETFA) (2015)
4. Blech, J.O., et al.: BeSpaceD: towards a tool framework and methodology for the specification and verification of spatial behavior of distributed software component systems. ArXiv e-print abs/1404.3537 (2014)
5. Brataas, G., Hallsteinsen, S.O., Rouvoy, R., Eliassen, F.: Scalability of decision models for dynamic product lines. In: SPLC, vol. 2, Kindai Kagaku Sha (2007)
6. Caires, L.: Spatial-behavioral types for concurrency and resource control in distributed systems. Theoret. Comput. Sci. **402**(2–3), 120–141 (2008)
7. Conan, D., Rouvoy, R., Seinturier, L.: Scalable processing of context information with COSMOS. In: Indulska, J., Raymond, K. (eds.) DAIS 2007. LNCS, vol. 4531, pp. 210–224. Springer, Heidelberg (2007). doi:10.1007/978-3-540-72883-2_16
8. de Moura, L., Bjørner, N.: Z3: an efficient SMT solver. In: Ramakrishnan, C.R., Rehof, J. (eds.) TACAS 2008. LNCS, vol. 4963, pp. 337–340. Springer, Heidelberg (2008). doi:10.1007/978-3-540-78800-3_24
9. Dobson, S., et al.: A survey of autonomic communications. ACM Trans. Auton. Adapt. Syst. **1**(2), 223–259 (2006)
10. Eclipse: Eclipse Equinox Framework (2016). http://www.eclipse.org/equinox/
11. Eidson, J., Lee, E., Matic, S., Seshia, S., Zou, J.: Distributed real-time software for cyber-physical systems. Proc. IEEE **100**(1), 45–59 (2012)
12. Fouquet, F., et al.: A dynamic component model for cyber physical systems. In: Proceedings of 15th ACM Symposium on Component Based Software Engineering (CBSE 2012). ACM (2012)
13. Frehse, G., Le Guernic, C., Donzé, A., Cotton, S., Ray, R., Lebeltel, O., Ripado, R., Girard, A., Dang, T., Maler, O.: SpaceEx: scalable verification of hybrid systems. In: Computer Aided Verification (CAV) (2011)
14. Fritsch, S., et al.: Time-bounded adaptation for automotive system software. In: ACM/IEEE 30th Conference on Software Engineering, ICSE 2008 (2008)
15. Gerostathopoulos, I., et al.: Meta-adaptation strategies for adaptation in cyber-physical systems. In: Software Architecture: 9th European Conference, ECSA 2015 (2015)
16. Gerostathopoulos, I., et al.: Self-adaptation in software-intensive cyber-physical systems: from system goals to architecture configurations. J. Syst. Softw. **122**, 378–397 (2016)
17. Graf, S., et al.: Contract-based Reasoning for Component Systems with Rich Interactions. In: Sangiovanni-Vincentelli, A., Zeng, H., Di Natale, M., Marwedel, P. (eds.) Embedded Systems Development. EMSY, vol. 20, pp. 139–154. Springer, New York (2014). doi:10.1007/978-1-4614-3879-3_8
18. Han, F., et al.: Model-based engineering and analysis of space-aware systems communicating via IEEE 802.11. In: 2015 IEEE 39th Annual Computer Software and Applications Conference (COMPSAC), vol. 2 (2015)

19. Herrmann, P., et al.: A model-based toolchain to verify spatial behavior of cyber-physical systems. Int. J. Web Serv. Res. (IJWSR) **13**(1), 40–52 (2016)
20. Hirschkoff, D., Lozes, É., Sangiorgi, D.: Minimality results for the spatial logics. In: Pandya, P.K., Radhakrishnan, J. (eds.) FSTTCS 2003. LNCS, vol. 2914, pp. 252–264. Springer, Heidelberg (2003). doi:10.1007/978-3-540-24597-1_22
21. Hordvik, S., et al.: A methodology for model-based development and safety analysis of transport systems. In: 11th International Conference on Evaluation of Novel Approaches to Software Engineering (ENASE) (2016)
22. Huber, N., et al.: Model-based self-adaptive resource allocation in virtualized environments. In: SEAMS 2011 (2011)
23. Kang, S., Lee, J., Jang, H., Lee, H., Lee, Y., Park, S., Park, T., Song, J.: SeeMon: scalable and energy-efficient context monitoring framework for sensor-rich mobile environments. In: MobiSys 2008. ACM (2008)
24. Lauer, M., Lange, S., Riedmiller, M.: Calculating the perfect match: an efficient and accurate approach for robot self-localization. In: Bredenfeld, A., Jacoff, A., Noda, I., Takahashi, Y. (eds.) RoboCup 2005. LNCS, vol. 4020, pp. 142–153. Springer, Heidelberg (2006). doi:10.1007/11780519_13
25. Lee, E.: Cyber physical systems: design challenges. In: 2008 11th IEEE International Symposium on Object Oriented Real-Time Distributed Computing (ISORC) (2008)
26. Lum, W.Y., Lau, F.C.M.: A context-aware decision engine for content adaptation. IEEE Pervasive Comput. **1**(3), 41–49 (2002)
27. Nallur, V., Bahsoon, R.: A decentralized self-adaptation mechanism for service-based applications in the cloud. IEEE Trans. Softw. Eng. **39**(5), 591–612 (2013)
28. OSGi Alliance: OSGi Service Platform (2016). http://www.osgi.org/. Accessed 22 Jan 2016
29. Patterson, S., Bamieh, B.: Leader selection for optimal network coherence. In: 49th IEEE Conference on Decision and Control, pp. 2692–2697 (2010)
30. PiBorg: DiddyBorg Raspberry Pi Robot (2016). http://www.piborg.org/diddyborg
31. Platzer, A.: Differential dynamic logic for hybrid systems. J. Autom. Reasoning **41**(2), 143–189 (2008)
32. Rellermeyer, J.S., Alonso, G.: Concierge: a service platform for resource-constrained devices. SIGOPS Oper. Syst. Rev. **41**(3), 245–258 (2007)
33. Santos, A.C., et al.: Specifying adaptations through a DSL with an application to mobile robot navigation. In: SLATE 2013 (2013)
34. Sykes, D., et al.: From goals to components: a combined approach to self-management. In: SEAMS 2008 (2008)
35. Tajalli, H., et al.: PLASMA: a plan-based layered architecture for software model-driven adaptation. In: Proceedings the IEEE/ACM Conference on Automated Software Engineering, ASE 2010 (2010)
36. Weyns, D., et al.: On decentralized self-adaptation: lessons from the trenches and challenges for the future. In: SEAMS 2010 (2010)
37. White, J., et al.: R&D challenges and solutions for mobile cyber-physical applications and supporting internet services. J. Internet Serv. Appl. **1**(1), 45–56 (2010)

IoT Systems Provisioning
and Management in Cloud Computing

Introduction to the Workshop on IoT Systems Provisionning and Management in Cloud Computing (ISyCC'16)

Sami Yangui[1], Mohamed Mohamed[2], and Diala Naboulsi[1]

[1] Concordia University, Montreal, QC, Canada
[2] IBM Research, San Jose, USA

1 Preface

The first International Workshop for IoT Systems Provisioning & Management in Cloud Computing (ISyCC'16) was held in conjunction with the 14th International Conference on Service Oriented Computing (ICSOC'16) on October 10–13, 2016 in Banff, Alberta, Canada.

This track offered an exciting and highly interactive opportunity to show research results in Cloud Computing, Internet of Things (IoT), and Service-oriented Computing. The presented papers focused on IoT applications provisioning processes, as well as, data management aspects of such applications in cloud setting.

We received 5 submissions, of which 4 were accepted. Below the list of the accepted papers.

- Jia Guo, Ing-Ray Chen, Jeffrey Tsai and Hamid Al-Hamadi, Trust-based IoT Participatory Sensing for Hazard Detection and Response
- Kutalmis Akpinar and Kien A. Hua, EQL: Event Query Language for the Sharing of Internet-of-Things Infrastructure and Collaborative Applications Development
- Habeeb Olufowobi, Robert Engel, Nathalie Baracaldo, Luis Angel Bathen, Samir Tata and Heiko Ludwig, Data Provenance Model for Internet of Things (IoT) Systems
- Nathalie Baracaldo, Luis Angel Bathen, Roqeeb O. Ozugha, Robert Engel, Samir Tata and Heiko Ludwig, Securing Data Provenance in Internet of Things (IoT) Systems

We would like to thank the authors for their submissions, the program committee for their reviewing work, and the organizers of the ICSOC 2016 conference for their support which made this workshop possible.

2   Organization

Workshop Chairs

Sami Yangui	Concordia University, QC, Canada
Mohamed Mohamed	IBM Research, USA
Diala Naboulsi	Concordia University, QC, Canada

Program Committee

Asma Trabelsi	University of Tunis, Tunisia
Rami Selami	Telecom SudParis, France
Carla Mouradian	Concordia University, Canada
Mohamed Abu-lebdeh	Concordia University, Canada
Sara Ayoubi	Concordia University, Canada
Hyame Alameddine	Concordia University, Canada
Walid Gaaloul	Telecom SudParis, France
Bruno Defude	Telecom SudParis, France
Sami Bhiri	University of Monastir, Tunisia
Ahmed Samet	University of Campiegne, France
Samir Tata	IBM Research, USA
Khaled Gaaloul	Luxembourg Institute of Science and Technology, Luxembourg
Wided Guedria	Luxembourg Institute of Science and Technology, Luxembourg
Nejib Belhadj-Alouane	University Tunis El-Manar, Tunisia

EQL: Event Query Language for the Sharing of Internet-of-Things Infrastructure and Collaborative Applications Development

Kutalmış Akpınar[✉] and Kien A. Hua

Department of Computer Science,
University of Central Florida, Orlando, FL 32826, USA
kutalmis@knights.ucf.edu, kienhua@cs.ucf.edu

Abstract. A user-friendly and functional query language for complex events in an IoT environment, along with the query processing techniques involved therein, are introduced in this paper. In an IoT environment which smart services provide a uniform Boolean abstraction to handle massive device heterogeneity, the proposed query language, EQL (Event Query Language), allows application developers to access event streams from smart services. Our approach allows application developers without domain knowledge to more intuitively formulate queries using temporal and logical operators. The processing of EQL queries takes into account the soft real-time event response requirement of the IoT environment.

Keywords: ThingStore · Event query language · Internet of things · Complex event processing · Service marketplaces

1 Introduction

With recent advancements in IoT technologies, a new ecosystem of Internet-capable physical objects that sense, compute and communicate without human intervention is being formed. ThingStore [1] is a collaborative platform that brings several actors of this ecosystem together by providing service interface definitions, APIs and query processing servers. This study presents Event Query Language (EQL) and a query processing service that resides within ThingStore for real-time event queries in an IoT environment.

Service definitions and event query language contribute to the field of IoT as a part of standardization efforts in service hosting and application development. The previous study on ThingStore [1] gives a shorter definition for EQL, but focuses on the complete system design. In contrast, the current study not only details smart services, event query language and query processing environment, but also renews them. Studies on temporal and logical operators also exist among CEP research [3,4]; however, they are not able to support heterogeneous nature of IoT environment. The contributions of this study are as follows:

© Springer International Publishing AG 2017
K. Drira et al. (Eds.): ICSOC 2016 Workshops, LNCS 10380, pp. 73–78, 2017.
https://doi.org/10.1007/978-3-319-68136-8_6

– An event model and a set of event processing operators are introduced to the field of Complex Event Query Processing. Unlike the previous study on Thing-Store, the new operator and smart service definitions are not constrained by any system-specific parameters such as event sampling intervals.
– A new event query processor is designed to provide immediate response to event occurrences. Unlike the previous study, events are modelled in continuous-time rather than discrete-time, which relies on sampling events.

2   Event Query Language

For the convenience of application developers, EQL is designed to be a user-intuitive SQL-like language. An example of a query is given below:

SELECT Event-handler
FROM   Camera3.Intrusion AS Service1,
                    Sensor4.Temperature("[sub-query text here]")
                    AS Service2
WHERE Before(Service1, Service2)
WITHIN 30 s
UNTIL   5 min

In this study, we present a new set of complex event definitions for $WHERE$ section of the language. The other sections are similar to the previous work [1].

Definition 1. *A **smart service** is a software program that performs a computation over a data stream to produce and deliver a useful approximation to a boolean function of continuous time, where the description of the function is some phenomena in the physical domain.*

The boolean function $f(t) : \mathbb{R} \rightarrow \{0,1\}$ can be defined as:

$$f(t) = \begin{cases} 1, & \textit{Physical phenomena exists at time } t \\ 0, & \text{otherwise} \end{cases}$$

Using the function above, we can transfer information from a smart service to the query processing framework in real-time by delivering a boolean value and a timestamp at the time of each state change. This sends a $\{1, t_0\}$ signal at some time t_0 such that $f(t_0) = 1 \; \wedge \; \lim_{\delta t \rightarrow 0} f(t_0 - \delta t) = 0$. Similarly, it sends a $\{0, t_1\}$ signal at some time t_1 such that $f(t_1) = 0 \; \wedge \; \lim_{\delta t \rightarrow 0} f(t_1 - \delta t) = 1$. The ideal method assumes existence of a global timestamp among all smart services.

Using the data transport method given above, any boolean, continuous-time function of the physical world can be re-constructed by the query processor. Assume a query processor receives some sequence of tuples $F = F_1, F_2, F3...,$ where $F_n = (v_n, t_n) \; \forall n \in \mathbb{N}$ and v_n represents the boolean state value at timestamp t_n. The re-construction of function $f(.)$ is defined as:

$$f'(t) = \begin{cases} 1, & \exists \, n : (t_n < t < t_{n+1}) \wedge (v_n = 1) \\ 0, & \text{otherwise} \end{cases}$$

Although this function and the transport method outlined above represent the complete functionality desired from a smart service, smart services can only deliver an approximation of these features due to the limitations of available sensing and software technologies and lack of global timestamp. As an approximation, the system assumes arrival time of information as the occurrence time, and it does not retrieve timestamp from the sensing environment.

Definition 2. *Given $f(.)$ as the re-constructed continuous-time function of smart service A, an **event instance** of A is a time interval defined as a tuple (t_{start}, t_{end}) such that:*

$$t_{start} \leq t_{end}$$
$$\forall t_0 : t_{start} \leq t_0 < t_{end} \implies f(t_0) = 1$$
$$\lim_{\delta t \to 0} f(t_{start} - \delta t) = 0$$
$$f(t_{end}) = 0$$

In other words, any continuous time interval between two state changes in which function f(.) remains true between are considered to be event instances.

Definition 3. *A **complex event** is a set of time intervals, where a time interval is defined as a tuple of timestamps (t_{start}, t_{end}) such that $t_{start} \leq t_{end}$.*

Every smart service can be expressed as the set of all event instances associated with their continuous-time functions. Thus, smart services may be regarded as complex events. Some smart service A can be represented as: $A = \{a_1, a_2, a_3...\}$ where $a_n = (a_{sn}, a_{en})$.

Definition 4. *A **smart service operator** is a function that takes one or more smart services as input, and outputs another smart service.*

Definition 5. *A **complex event operator** is a function that takes one or multiple complex events as input, and generates another complex event according to a pre-defined pattern.*

It is important that operator outputs are the same type as their input so that they can be called and processed by other operators in a nested manner. The difference between a smart service and a complex event is that event instances in smart services cannot overlap, but a complex event may have overlapping event instances. In these terms, smart services can be processed by smart service and complex event operators, but the output of complex event operators can only be processed by the same class.

The proposed query language supports three smart service operators which are derived from boolean algebra. These are AND, OR and NOT. Assume that f_A, f_B and f_C are continuous-time boolean functions of smart services A, B and C that are $\mathbb{R} \to \{0, 1\}$, smart service operators are defined as:

$$C = \boldsymbol{AND}(A, B) \iff \forall t : f_C(t) = f_A(t) \land f_B(t)$$
$$C = \boldsymbol{OR}(A, B) \iff \forall t : f_C(t) = f_A(t) \lor f_B(t)$$
$$C = \boldsymbol{NOT}(A) \iff \forall t : f_C(t) = 1 - f_A(t)$$

The proposed query language supports seven complex event operators: *BEFORE, MEETS, OVERLAPS, STARTS, DURING, FINISHES, EQUAL.* These operators are derived from Allen's temporal event logic [2]. Given two complex events, $A = \{a_1, a_2, a_3...\}$ and $B = \{b_1, b_2, b_3...\}$ where each element of A and B indicates time interval tuples $a_n = (a_{sn}, a_{en})$ and $b_k = (b_{sk}, b_{ek})$, the temporal operators are defined as below:

$$(a_{sn}, b_{ek}) \in \boldsymbol{BEFORE}(A, B) \iff a_{en} < b_{sk}$$
$$(a_{sn}, b_{ek}) \in \boldsymbol{MEETS}(A, B, \sigma) \iff |a_{en} - b_{sk}| < \sigma$$
$$(a_{sn}, b_{ek}) \in \boldsymbol{OVERLAPS}(A, B) \iff (a_{sn} < b_{sk} < a_{en} < b_{ek})$$
$$(a_{sn}, b_{ek}) \in \boldsymbol{STARTS}(A, B, \sigma) \iff (|a_{sn} - b_{sk}| < \sigma) \wedge (a_{en} < b_{ek})$$
$$(a_{sn}, b_{ek}) \in \boldsymbol{DURING}(A, B) \iff (a_{sn} < b_{sk}) \wedge (a_{en} > b_{ek})$$
$$(a_{sn}, b_{ek}) \in \boldsymbol{FINISHES}(A, B, \sigma) \iff (a_{sn} < b_{sk}) \wedge (|a_{en} - b_{ek}| < \sigma)$$
$$(a_{sn}, b_{ek}) \in \boldsymbol{EQUAL}(A, B, \sigma) \iff (|a_{sn} - b_{sk}| < \sigma) \wedge (|a_{en} - b_{ek}| < \sigma)$$

From the definitions above, as the constant σ goes to zero, the operators *MEETS, STARTS, FINISHES* and *EQUAL* define simultaneous start or end points as constraints. The detection of simultaneousness in measures of milliseconds normally requires a hardware real-time environment. However, the proposed language allows one to define a vicinity of time for this. This is enabled using the parameter σ.

3   Event Query Processing

A query that is received by the query processor is parsed into an execution tree whose nodes are smart services, operators and event handlers. An example of an execution tree is given in Fig. 1. Smart services are the leaves of execution tree. They provide event state changes (*OnEventAStart, OnEventAEnd, OnEventB-Start, OnEventBEnd*) to the upper branches. Upper branches are smart service operators and complex event operators. While smart services, smart service

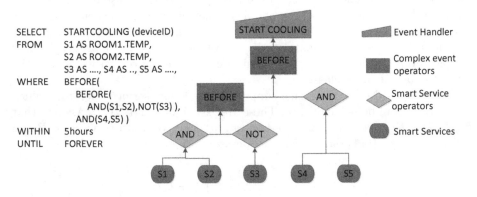

Fig. 1. An example of an execution tree for an event query.

Algorithm 1. Procedures for BEFORE(A,B) node

$ListA$: List of event instances of branch A. Sorted by end times.
$IdCnt$: an integer counter.
$DictAB$: Dictionary of incomplete event instance lists of current node. Indexes are
    id values of event B.
$Next$: upper node.
function ONEVENTASTART($newA$)
    Do nothing.
function ONEVENTAEND($newA$)
    Delete expired events from $ListA$ by comparing end times with $newA$.end.
    Insert $newA$ into $ListA$.
function ONEVENTBSTART($newB$)
    $newEvents$: Empty list
    Delete expired events from $ListA$ by comparing end times with $newB$.start.
    for all $a \in ListA$, $newB$.start $> a$.end **do**
        ev: {start: a.start; id: $idCounter$++},
        Insert ev into $newEvents$ and $DictAB[newB$.id];
    for all $ab \in newEvents$ **do** Signal $Next$ for new event ab.
function ONEVENTBEND($newB$)
    $list = DictAB[newB$.id]
    $DictAB[newB$.id] = null
    for all $ab \in list$ **do**
        Signal $Next$ for event end: {start: ab.start, end: $newB$.end, id:ab.id}.

---

operators and complex event operators can be leaves of complex event operators,
only smart services and smart service operators can be leaves for smart service
operators.

Operators perform with soft real-time requirements. Each event change is
handled with a procedure call which is described within the node. A sample procedure to handle events in a complex event operator node is given in Algorithm 1.

4   Experimental Study

For experimental studies, the same setup as the previous study of *ThingStore*
[1] is built. The differences obtained clearly proves the effectiveness of the new
system. First, while the previous system performs computation on every discrete
time step of the *ThingStore* query processor, *New EQL* computes only in the case
of state changes from smart services. Since the average state change frequency in
an environment will be significantly smaller than the discrete sampling frequency,
the new proposed system always performs with fewer operations. In the case of
our test, each new service changes its state once, so the throughput is 1 for each
new query subscription added to the system. To perform the same functionality,
our previous system calculates and delivers output for every internal sampling
clock, which reaches above 40000 computations per second when 1000 queries
are present in the system. Comparison with the previous experiment is shown on
Fig. 2a. *ThingStore* data is re-used and shows a median value of 10 experiments.

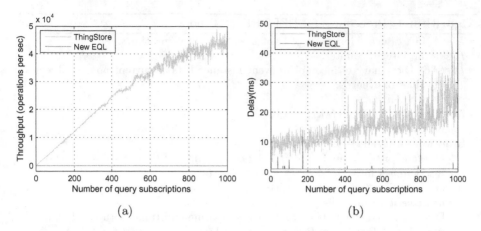

Fig. 2. Performance analysis of event query execution. Throughput (b) and delay (a) of the system under different system loads.

The new system also delivers a fast response to event instances. Figure 2b shows the end-to-end delay between smart service and the client under different loads. As in the previous paper, the median value of 10 simulations is used for *ThingStore*. The median delay of 10 simulations for the new system is a constant value of 1ms, so delay values for a single simulation are directly shown in the graph. As also indicated in the previous study, when a small number of queries are subscribed, the delay value of *ThingStore* will be at least a random value around 1ms to 15ms, which is the sampling frequency. On the contrary, the new system has a robust performance of around 1ms or 2ms for almost every event instant in this setup. It can also be observed that *ThingStore*'s delay increases as the subscriptions increase and computations get delayed.

References

1. Akpınar, K., Hua, K.A., Li, K.: Thingstore: a platform for internet-of-things application development and deployment. In: Proceedings of the 9th ACM International Conference on Distributed Event-Based Systems, DEBS 2015, pp. 162–173. ACM, New York (2015). http://doi.acm.org/10.1145/2675743.2771833
2. Allen, J.F.: Maintaining knowledge about temporal intervals. Commun. ACM **26**(11), 832–843 (1983)
3. Bui, H.L.: Survey and comparison of event query languages using practical examples. Ludwig-Maximilians Universität München thesis (2009)
4. Wang, F., Liu, S., Liu, P., Bai, Y.: Bridging physical and virtual worlds: complex event processing for RFID data streams. In: Ioannidis, Y., et al. (eds.) EDBT 2006. LNCS, vol. 3896, pp. 588–607. Springer, Heidelberg (2006). doi:10.1007/11687238_36

Trust-Based IoT Participatory Sensing for Hazard Detection and Response

Jia Guo[1], Ing-Ray Chen[1(✉)], Jeffrey J.P. Tsai[2],
and Hamid Al-Hamadi[3]

[1] Virginia Tech, Blacksburg, USA
{jiaguo,irchen}@vt.edu
[2] Asia University, Taichung, Taiwan
jjptsai@gmail.com
[3] Kuwait University, Kuwait City, Kuwait
hamid@cs.ku.edu.kw

Abstract. The physical world can be monitored by ubiquitous Internet of Things (IoT) devices through participatory sensing by which a huge amount of data is collected and analyzed in the cloud for hazard detection and response. In this paper, we propose a Trust as a Service (TaaS) cloud utility leveraging a cloud hierarchy for assessing service trustworthiness of IoT devices so as filter out untrustworthy sensing data before hazard detection and response are taken. We demonstrate that our TaaS utility achieves accuracy, convergence, and resiliency compared with contemporary IoT/P2P distributed trust protocols while achieving scalability to cope with a huge number of IoT devices. We demonstrate the feasibility with an air pollution detection and response application.

Keywords: Internet of Things · Trust · Participatory sensing · Cloud computing

1 Introduction

The physical world can be monitored by ubiquitous Internet of Things (IoT) devices through participatory sensing by which a huge amount of data is collected and analyzed for hazard detection and response [1]. One possible IoT participatory sensing application is environmental monitoring where IoT devices (e.g., smart phones carried by humans) collect environmental data (noise, air pollution, temperature, humidity, light, etc.) and submit via wireless data communication links to a processing center located in the cloud for environmental data analysis [2]. In return, a user (e.g., emergency response personnel) can send a query to the cloud to query a location's air pollution levels of CO, NO_2, SO_2, and O_3. Another possible application is road/traffic monitoring by which traffic flows, pot-holes, bumps, braking, and honking information reported from IoT devices (smart phones carried by passengers/drivers in a car) are aggregated by a data processing center located in the cloud to unveil traffic patterns previously unobserved with existing monitoring infrastructure. This is especially useful in disaster response situations after the occurrence of a public hazard such as a hurricane or a terrorist attack.

© Springer International Publishing AG 2017
K. Drira et al. (Eds.): ICSOC 2016 Workshops, LNCS 10380, pp. 79–84, 2017.
https://doi.org/10.1007/978-3-319-68136-8_7

The major challenges for detection and response participatory sensing applications are scalability and selection of trustworthy participants [3]. Scalability is needed considering that the number of IoT devices will grow exponentially in the next decade. Selection of trustworthy participants is needed because not all IoT devices will be trustworthy and some IoT devices may behave maliciously to disrupt the network or service (e.g., in a terrorist attack scenario) or just for their own gain (e.g., in an evacuation scenario following a disaster).

While selection of trustworthy participants has attracted some attention [4–9], scalability remains an open problem. In this paper, we develop a "Trust as a Service" (TaaS) cloud utility leveraging a cloud hierarchy so as to cope with a huge number of IoT devices to address the scalability issue. We also demonstrate that as an added benefit, TaaS addresses the selection of trustworthy participants issue better than existing distributed IoT trust protocols because it is able to aggregate broad evidence from all nodes having interaction experiences with a target IoT device.

The rest of the paper is organized as follows. Section 2 discusses how TaaS is implemented leveraging a cloud hierarchy. Section 3 demonstrates the utility of TaaS with an air pollution detection and response IoT application for which TaaS is shown to outperform existing non-scalable distributed IoT trust protocols. Section 4 summarizes the paper and outlines future work.

2   TaaS Cloud Utility Leveraging a Cloud Hierarchy

Our TaaS cloud utility leverages a cloud hierarchy as illustrated by Fig. 1 for integrated mobility, service, and trust management of a huge number of IoT devices [10]. We label the clouds from top to bottom as nation, state, county, and city clouds as would be needed in a federal emergency assessment, management, and response system. The city and county clouds can be base stations and routers owned by mobile network operators, while state and nation clouds can be mini and big data centers owned by cloud service providers. Each city cloud at the bottom layer can be just a base station covering a geographical region, providing a communication path for IoT devices (e.g., sensors, smart phones, vehicles) in a region to interact with the cloud via wireless communication.

Each user is associated with a family of "home" clouds, starting from the home city cloud (base station) at the bottom layer, home county cloud (router) at the second bottom layer, home state cloud at the second top layer, and home nation cloud at the top layer. These home clouds are assigned based on the "home" geographical location of an IoT device similar to the home location register (HLR) in mobile networks [11, 12]. When an IoT device moves from one region to another region (if the IoT device is mobile), a "mobility handoff" ensues by which the city cloud which the IoT device just roams into will inform all home clouds of the IoT device of the new location.

An IoT device will only interact with its current city cloud for service invocation to minimize energy consumption and service latency. There are two standard cloud computing operations to be performed by a city cloud, *store-process-forward* and *forward-wait-reply*, described as follows. The local city cloud will examine a service request from an IoT device. If the service request is to report new service data such as a feedback or a sensing outcome, the current city cloud will follow the

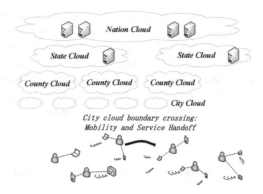

Fig. 1. Hierarchical cloud architecture for hazard detection and response.

store-process-forward procedure. i.e., it will store a replicated copy of the service data, process it locally as needed, and pass the new service data to the home clouds of the IoT device. If the service request is a query regarding a target IoT device, then the current city cloud will follow the *forward-wait-reply* procedure. That is, the query will be forwarded to the least common "home" cloud of the requesting IoT device and the target IoT device. If the service request involves several IoT devices some of which are not under the current city cloud, then the city cloud will pass the request to the least common "home" cloud of these IoT devices for processing because the least common "home" cloud will store location and service data of these IoT devices. Then it will wait for a reply to return to it after which it will forward the reply to the requesting IoT device. A "service handoff" is triggered when an IoT device goes to a new city cloud, necessitating the migration of the virtual machine for cloud computing.

Our TaaS cloud utility is implemented utilizing the standard *store-process-forward* and *forward-wait-reply* procedures described above. Specifically, IoT device i (acting as a service requester) can simply report to its current city cloud a *user satisfaction* report of its service trustworthiness assessment toward IoT device j who just completed a sensing service of a specific air pollutant level (e.g., sensing CO air pollution) in the form of $(i, j, T_{ij}, apt_s, l_s, t_s)$ where T_{ij} (in [0, 1]) is the sensing result trustworthiness of j as assessed by i, apt_s is the air pollutant type (e.g., apt_s = "CO"), l_s is the location at which sensing is perform, and t_s is the time of sensing. T_{ij} can be assessed after fact, i.e., after i itself experiences it or verifies it after reading official reports about the level of this particular air pollutant at the particular location and particular time. If neither is accessible, T_{ij} can be assessed by the discrepancy between j's sensing result from the average sensing result from all sensing results received by i for the same location at the same time. T_{ij} is set to 1 and can go down to 0 proportional to the amount of discrepancy detected. The city cloud upon receiving a user satisfaction report would follow the standard *store-process-forward* procedure described earlier to store the user satisfaction report to all home clouds of IoT device i.

An IoT device (on behalf of its owner) can simply query its local city cloud about the trustworthiness of a target IoT device for providing sensing service of a specific pollutant type. The current city cloud would follow the standard *forward-wait-reply* procedure described earlier. The least common home cloud of the requesting IoT device and the target IoT upon receiving the query will simply use all user satisfaction reports stored in its local store and apply a trust computation method such as Beta Reputation [5] or Adaptive IoT Trust [9] to assess the trustworthiness of the target node. When the trust assessment is completed, the home cloud will return the response (i.e., the trustworthiness of the target IoT device for providing service) to the city cloud who received the query who in turn will forward the response to the requesting IoT device for decision making.

3   Case Study: Air Pollution Detection and Response

The case study is for the *Fairfax County Hazard Detection and Response Team* charged to monitor the pollution levels of CO, NO_2, SO_2, and O_3 for all cities under the county so as to take appropriate actions if the air pollution level is above a tolerance threshold. Since the area to be covered is rather large, the county officials only install a few county-sensors in more strategic and populated areas to collect air pollution data. To cover the whole county area air quality detection, the county officials also encourage environment-health-conscious civilians driving or carrying air pollution detection capable vehicles or smartphones [2] to report air pollution data.

In case of emergency, the county officials can request IoT devices in a particular location to immediately report their sensing results to their respective city clouds, as the cloud hierarchy knows the locations of all home county IoT devices. Also the county officials send queries via TaaS to get the trustworthiness scores of these IoT devices. To know if a location has acceptable air quality, the county officials (running as node i) accept results (S_j) from 200 most trustworthy IoT devices (which have the highest T_{ij} trust values) for the air quality detection service out of a total of 2000 nodes, and compute a trust-weighted average $\sum_{j=1}^{200}(T_{ij}/\sum_{j=1}^{200}T_{ij}) \times S_j$ for each air pollutant (e.g., CO). If the level exceeds a minimum threshold (e.g., above 70 ppm for CO), the county officials push alerting text to IoT devices in the affected area.

We simulate the above system populated with 2000 IoT devices capable of detecting and reporting CO air pollutant levels using the ns3 simulator. The CO level is simulated to be in the range of [60, 70 ppm] in various locations. The percentage of bad nodes is set at P_M in the range of [0, 30%]. A malicious node always reports CO readings above 70 ppm in the range of [70, 120 ppm] regardless of location in order to confuse the county official. It can perform attacks on and off in order to evade detection. We simulate this by a random attack probability P_a in the range of [0, 100%]. Also a malicious node always performs bad-mouthing attacks (saying a good node's sensing result is not trustworthy in the user satisfaction report) and ballot-stuffing attacks (saying a bad node's sensing result is trustworthy).

We compare our cloud hierarchy based TaaS with existing non-scalable distributed IoT/P2P management protocols including EigenTrust [6], PeerTrust [7], ServiceTrust [8], and Adaptive IoT Trust [9] for which each IoT device keeps own trust data based on own experiences and service satisfaction feedbacks from its peers that it encounters.

For fair comparison, the environment is setup as in [9] and we also adopt Adaptive IoT Trust in [9] for trust computation. We measure two performance metrics for performance analysis: (a) the trust-weighted average CO reading vs. ground truth (i.e., the actual CO level at a specific location and a particular time); (b) the accuracy of selecting trustworthy participants.

Figure 2 shows the trust-weighted average CO readings vs. time (each time point is a CO detection service request) with the percentage of bad nodes P_M set at 30% and P_a set at 100%. We observe TaaS (red line) levering the proposed cloud hierarchy can provide CO readings very close to ground truth (black line) as time progresses. Further, our TaaS cloud utility outperforms EigenTrust, PeerTrust, ServiceTrust, and Adaptive IoT Trust in terms of accuracy, convergence, and resiliency due to its ability to effectively aggregate trust evidence from all nodes in the system through the simple standard store-process-forward and forward-wait-reply cloud computing paradigms.

Figure 3 shows the percentage of bad nodes selected to provide sensing results.

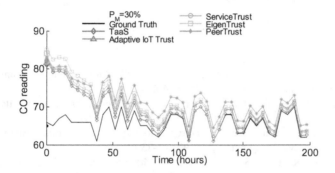

Fig. 2. Performance comparison of trust-weighted average CO readings of the air pollution detection and response application. (Color figure online)

TaaS outperforms EigenTrust, PeerTrust, ServiceTrust, and Adaptive IoT Trust as time progresses because unlike Adaptive IoT Trust [9], TaaS can leverage cloud service to aggregate broad evidence from all nodes having service experiences with IoT devices reporting sensing results.

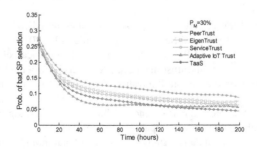

Fig. 3. Percentage of Bad IoT devices selected to provide CO sensing service for the air pollution detection and response application.

4 Conclusion

In this paper we developed a scalable TaaS cloud utility leveraging a cloud hierachy that can provide integrated mobility, service, and trust management of a huge number of IoT devices. Through an air pollution detection and response IoT application, we demonstrated that our TaaS cloud utility outperforms existing distributed IoT/P2P trust protocols while achieving scalability and accuracy of selecting trustworthy participants, because it can leverage simple yet powerful store-process-forward and for-ward-wait-reply cloud computing paradigms to aggregate broad service evidence from all nodes in the system.

In this paper we only conducted performance comparison of TaaS against existing distributed IoT trust protocols in terms of the accuracy of selecting trustworthy participants. In the future, we plan to conduct more experiments to quantify the gain of our scalability design in terms of performance metrics such as resource overhead, energy consumption, and service latency.

References

1. Khan, W.Z., Xiang, Y., Aalsalem, M.Y., Arshad, Q.: Mobile phone sensing systems: a survey. IEEE Commun. Surv. Tutorials **15**, 402–427 (2013)
2. Devarakonda, S., et al.: Real-time air quality monitoring through mobile sensing in metropolitan areas. In: UrbComp, Chicago, Illinois, USA (2013)
3. Mousa, H., et al.: Trust management and reputations systems in mobile participatory sensing applications: a survey. Comput. Netw., 90, 49–73 (2015)
4. Amintoosi, H., Kanhere, S.S., Allahbakhsh, M.: Trust-based privacy-aware participant selection in social participatory sensing. J. Inform. Secur. Appl. **20**, 11–25 (2015)
5. Jøsang, A., Ismail, R.: The beta reputation system. In: Bled Electronic Commerce Conference, Bled, Slovenia, pp. 1–14 (2002)
6. Kamvar, S.D., Schlosser, M.T., Garcia-Molina, H.: The EigenTrust algorithm for reputation management in P2P networks. In: 12th International Conference on World Wide Web, Budapest, Hungary (2003)
7. Xiong, L., Liu, L.: PeerTrust: Supporting reputation-based trust for peer-to-peer electronic communities. IEEE Trans. Knowl. Data Eng. **16**, 843–857 (2004)
8. Su, Z., Liu, L., Li, M., Fan, X., Zhou, Y.: ServiceTrust: trust management in service provision networks. In: IEEE International Conference on Services Computing, Santa Clara, pp. 272–279 (2013)
9. Chen, I.R., Guo, J., Bao, F.: Trust Management for SOA-based IoT and its application to service composition. IEEE Trans. Serv. Comput. **9**, 482–495 (2016)
10. Chen, I.R., Guo, J., Tsai, J.J.P., Al-Hamadi, H.: A hierarchical cloud architecture for integrated mobility, service, and trust management of service-oriented IoT systems. In: 6th IEEE International Conference on Innovative Computing Technology, Dublin, Ireland (2016)
11. Chen, I.R., Chen, T.M., Lee, C.: Performance evaluation of forwarding strategies for location management in mobile networks. Comput. J. **41**, 243–253 (1998)
12. Chen, I.R., Verma, N.: Simulation study of a class of autonomous host-centric mobility prediction algorithms for wireless cellular and ad hoc networks. In: 36th Annual Symposium Simulation (2003)

Data Provenance Model for Internet of Things (IoT) Systems

Habeeb Olufowobi[2], Robert Engel[1(✉)], Nathalie Baracaldo[1],
Luis Angel D. Bathen[1], Samir Tata[1], and Heiko Ludwig[1]

[1] Almaden Research Center IBM Research, San Jose, CA, USA
{engelrob,baracald,bathen,stata,hludwig}@us.ibm.com
[2] Howard University, 2300 Sixth Street NW, Washington, DC 20059, USA
habeeb.olufowobi@bison.howard.edu

Abstract. Internet of Things (IoT) systems and applications are increasingly deployed for critical use cases and therefore exhibit an increasing need for dependability. *Data provenance* deals with the recording, management and retrieval of information about the origin and history of data. We propose that the introduction of data provenance concepts into the IoT domain can help create dependable and trustworthy IoT systems by recording the lineage of data from basic sensor readings up to complex derived information created by software agents. In this paper, we present a data provenance model for IoT systems that is geared towards providing a generic mechanism for assuring the correctness and integrity of IoT applications and thereby reinforcing their trustworthiness and dependability for critical use cases.

1 Introduction

The Internet of Things (IoT) [7] has received significant attention in industry and in the academic community in recent years. As IoT applications are increasingly deployed for critical use cases, the importance of designing dependable and verifiable IoT systems that can be "trusted" with critical decision-making processes and corresponding automated actions becomes more prevalent.

Consider, for instance, the case of a "smart home" equipped with sensors to monitor the health of an elderly individual living in that home. The readings from the sensors are used in conjunction with a real-time analytics engine in order to notify relatives and health professionals when a medical emergency, such as heart attack, is automatically detected by the system. In order to take appropriate action, it is important that the recipients of such a notification of an emergency can trust in the reliability and accuracy of the information reported by the health monitoring system. However, without further *verifiable information* about which sensor data led to the detection of the heart attack it remains unclear on which grounds the system's decision to notify about an emergency is based upon. This lack of transparency impedes the (manual or automated) verification of the correctness of the system's decision. Moreover, if

© Springer International Publishing AG 2017
K. Drira et al. (Eds.): ICSOC 2016 Workshops, LNCS 10380, pp. 85–91, 2017.
https://doi.org/10.1007/978-3-319-68136-8_8

the circumstances that led to the emergency notification (or the lack thereof) are unclear it may not be possible to rule out that the system's decision is an outcome of a malicious attack tampering with the system or a result of otherwise corrupted data, e.g., from a defective sensor.

Data provenance deals with the recording, management and retrieval of information about the origin and history of data [2]. This may include information about agents that created or modified some piece of data, processes and/or transformations that it has been subjected to (i.e., activities), as well as dependencies between particular data items in the form of derivation histories [13]. We propose that the introduction of data provenance concepts into the IoT domain can help create dependable and trustworthy IoT systems. This is achieved by recording the lineage of data, starting from the most basic entities of information in the IoT system (e.g., a sensor reading) up to complex derived information (e.g., a notification of an emergency created by a real-time analytics engine and based on various sensor readings). Data provenance is *metadata* and as such requires a data model that describes which specific information is collected.

In this paper, we present a data provenance model for IoT systems. Note that in order to reliably prevent tampering and/or fully verifying information integrity of an IoT system, cryptographic methods such as encryption, hashing, or *blockchaining* need to be applied in combination with a data provenance model; however, this is beyond the scope of this paper.

Additional use cases for data provenance in the IoT domain include:

1. *Auditing* and *Digital Forensics*, in which the status of an IoT system or a sequence of events in an IoT system at some time or in some time period of the past needs to be determined (e.g., for investigating the circumstances that were causal for a particular action performed by an IoT application);
2. *Privacy* and *Data Sovereignty*, in which the origin and lineage of data is instrumental for enabling fine-grained access control for sensitive information collected in IoT applications (e.g., access control for health-related data).

In the following, we present a data provenance model for the IoT domain, depict its preliminary implementation, compare it with existing works in current literature and provide a conclusion and outlook on future work.

2   Data Provenance Model

In this section, we describe a general data provenance model as well as a preliminary concretization of this model for typical IoT environments.

2.1   General Data Provenance Model

We define a *data point* (dp) as a uniquely identifiable and addressable piece of data (i.e., a value) in the context of an IoT system. Examples for dps in the context of IoT systems include sensor readings such as discretized audio/video streams, complex analytics results derived from sensor readings, actuator commands, etc. A dp distinguishes itself specifically from other data flowing in the system (e.g., bulk sensor readings that are of no further interest, ephemeral inter-mediary analytics results, etc.) in that it is addressable, i.e., it has an ID that is unique in the context of the IoT system. A dp may be based on other dps that have contributed to its creation or modification. We refer to these related dps as *input data points* (input dps). We introduce the *addr(dp)* and *inputs(dp)* functions providing the address/ID of a dp and the set of input dps, respectively.

While our proposed model is independent of a specific execution model of IoT applications (e.g., event-driven, workflow-driven, etc.), the execution logic of an IoT application is responsible for defining *when (if)* provenance information needs to be collected for a particular dp. We refer to the specific state of an IoT system in which the collection of provenance data for a particular dp is deemed necessary by the execution logic as a *provenance event*.

We define *context* of a dp as information about state of an IoT system that is of interest for provenance when a corresponding provenance event occurs; we write *context(dp)* to denote a corresponding function. Context is the "core" of the provenance information for a dp and its specific contents may vary for different IoT applications. For instance, context may include information about agents involved in the computation of the dp, time and location information, execution context (e.g., triggering events), etc. While the specific contents of context are not defined in this general data provenance model, we show a possible concretization of context for IoT applications in Sect. 2.2.

We define a *provenance record* as a tuple associating the address of a dp with the set of provenance records of its input dps and the specific context of the corresponding provenance event. We introduce the *provenance function* $prov(dp)$ providing the provenance record for some dp as

$$prov : dp \mapsto \langle addr(dp), \{prov(idp)|idp \in inputs(dp)\}, context(dp)\rangle.$$

Note that this definition of provenance allows for the description of both *creation* and *modification* of dps. In the latter case, the set of input dps contains the provenance record of the dp before modification, i.e.,

$$prov(dp') = \langle addr(dp'), \{prov(dp), ...\}, context(dp')\rangle.$$

2.2 Context

Specific context for provenance may vary for different IoT applications. We propose an early-stage data model for context in typical IoT environments comprising the concepts of *Agents, Execution Context*, as well as *Time* and *Location* information (cf. Fig. 1).

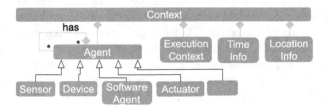

Fig. 1. Class diagram of a possible model for *context*

An *Agent* is an entity that creates and/or modifies data points (e.g., sensor, software agent, device, person, organization, etc.). It is recursively defined such that an agent may contain other agents (e.g., a device containing several sensors). This recursion allows for defining agents in a hierarchy, and may be used as fine-grained as required. For instance, an agent hierarchy may span from the concept of a particular function in a software library running over a virtualization container on a particular device to a particular IoT network.

Execution Context provides information related to the provenance event at hand, such as events or dps that triggered the creation/modification of the dp; this information may be particularly required for auditing and digital forensics. *Time* and *Location* information may be added to the provenance information.

2.3   Example

Consider, for instance, an IoT application responsible for computing the average temperature in a room over some time period. There are three readings from a temperature sensor: $dp_1 = 77F, dp_2 = 55F, dp_3 = 63F$. According to the definition in Sect. 2.1, their provenance records are given as follows:

$prov(dp_1) = \langle addr(dp_1), \emptyset, \langle agent = sensor1@raspPi1, time = 5am, ... \rangle \rangle$
$prov(dp_2) = \langle addr(dp_2), \emptyset, \langle agent = sensor1@raspPi1, time = 6am, ... \rangle \rangle$
$prov(dp_3) = \langle addr(dp_3), \emptyset, \langle agent = sensor1@raspPi1, time = 7am, ... \rangle \rangle$

A fourth datapoint dp_4 is created by a software agent calculating the average temperature, i.e., $dp_4 = (dp_1 + dp_2 + dp_3)/3 = 65F$. Hence it follows

$prov(dp_4) = \langle addr(dp_4), \{prov(dp_1), prov(dp_2), prov(dp_3)\},$
$\langle agent = averager@cloudvm1, time = 8am, ... \rangle \rangle.$

Thus far, the provenance events for dp_1 to dp_4 were related to the *creation* of new dps. In other cases dps may be *modified*, such as a software agent converting units of the calculated average temperature: $dp'_4 = 17.78C$. This results in

$prov(dp'_4) = \langle addr(dp'_4), prov(dp_4),$
$\langle agent = converter@cloudvm1, time = 9am, ... \rangle \rangle.$

3   Implementation

IoT systems are composed of sensors, actuators, devices, and gateways that are possibly connected to a Cloud. Managing provenance in such a system requires the provisioning of mechanisms that collect, store and query provenance data. To do so, we are currently implementing provenance mechanisms based on the MQTT[1] broker which should be deployed in any IoT component where provenance data should be managed. Those IoT components are clients and providers of provenance data. They are provided with a simple, lightweight, publish/subscribe messaging protocol as well as system and local provenance data stores. Each IoT component can subscribe for any provenance data topic coming from any other IoT component. IoT components are also responsible for sending provenance data for all registered (and authorized) IoT components.

---

[1] http://docs.oasis-open.org/mqtt/mqtt/v3.1.1/mqtt-v3.1.1.html.

As mentioned before, our proposed model for data provenance is independent of a specific execution model of IoT applications. The execution logic is responsible for defining when (if) provenance information needs to be collected. To support that, we are implementing declarative provenance management policies to describe what provenance data should be collected. Moreover, such policies control how the provenance data is disseminated and stored in the IoT system.

4   State of the Art

Data provenance has been a research topic for many years and has been broadly researched in e-science [13], file systems [12], databases [2,14] and sensor networks [8]. Groth et al. [6] presented a logical architecture for provenance systems identifying key roles (i.e., actors) and their interactions. An unpublished work [1] describes an architectural model for data provenance in the IoT domain defining components for provenance event handling, such as collection, verification, etc.

As of today there is no generally accepted form of representing provenance information. Existing approaches for modeling data provenance include the Open Provenance Model (OPM) [10] and the Provenance Data Model (PROV-DM) [11]. OPM provides an ontology for modeling provenance as an annotated graph based on three types of nodes: Artifacts, Processes, and Agents. The edges of these nodes are directed and represent causal dependencies. PROV-DM is a refinement of OPM and aims at covering a broader range of application domains than OPM. PROV-DM models are based on *Agents*, *Activities*, and *Entities*. In addition, PROV-DM provides predefined relations for different application domains and a rich ontological infrastructure for representing different types of Activities. Models based on OPM and PROV-DM have been used for capturing provenance in workflow systems (e.g., ProvONE [4], D-PROV [9], P-PLAN [5]).

OPM and PROV-DM adopt a largely document-centric view that is centered on expressing actions performed on documents and the causal relationships between such actions. However, data provenance for dependable IoT systems requires focusing on infrastructures of agents such as sensors, devices, software agents, etc. and the data exchanged. Moreover, in the context of IoT systems where agents are typically represented by software agents, the distinction between *Agents* and *Activities/Processes* put forward in PROV-DM and OPM can be neglected: a sufficiently fine-grained specification of *Agent* inherently describes the activity performed on a dp (e.g., the specification of a particular function of a software library operating on a dp sufficiently describes the applied transformation if the source code is known and verified through secure code provisioning; cf. Sect. 5). Hence, we argue that in IoT environments it is sufficient to record the lineage of a dp in terms of its creation and modification by agents. In other words, as discussed in Sect. 2 our proposed data provenance model captures activities in a highly expressive *Agent* concept and distinguishes between creation and modification of dps using self-referential sets of *input dps*.

Other works on data provenance in the IoT domain include the Semantic Sensor Network Ontology (SSN) [3] describing sensors and corresponding observations/values. However, it falls short of modeling other actors in IoT systems, such as devices, software agents, persons or organizations.

5   Conclusion

In this paper, we presented a data provenance model for IoT systems. The model describes the context of the creation or modification of datapoints, including information about involved agents, execution context, time, and location information. Moreover, the model captures dependency relationships between datapoints and is independent of execution models of IoT applications.

Our future work will focus on integrating the proposed data provenance model with secure methods for code provisioning on IoT devices and with cryptographic methods for verifying the integrity of provenance metadata. By recording the lineage of data as well as metadata about agents in a secure fashion we aim at providing a generic mechanism for assuring the integrity of IoT systems and thereby reinforcing their trustworthiness and dependability for critical use cases.

References

1. Bauer, S., Schreckling, D.: Data provenance in the internet of things. In: EU Project COMPOSE, Conference Seminar (2013)
2. Buneman, P., Khanna, S., Wang-Chiew, T.: Why and where: a characterization of data provenance. In: Van den Bussche, J., Vianu, V. (eds.) ICDT 2001. LNCS, vol. 1973, pp. 316–330. Springer, Heidelberg (2001). doi:10.1007/3-540-44503-X_20
3. Compton, M., et al.: The ssn ontology of the w3c semantic sensor network incubator group. Web Semant. Sci. Serv. Agents WWW 17, 25–32 (2012)
4. Cuevas-Vicenttín, V., et al.: Provone: a prov extension data model for scientific workflow provenance (2015)
5. Garrijo, D., Gil, Y.: P-plan ontology (2012)
6. Groth, P., Jiang, S., Miles, S., Munroe, S., Tan, V., Tsasakou, S., Moreau, L.: An architecture for provenance systems. Technical report (2006)
7. Gubbi, J., Buyya, R., Marusic, S., Palaniswami, M.: Internet of things (iot): a vision, architectural elements, and future directions. Future Gener. Comput. Syst. 29(7), 1645–1660 (2013)
8. Lim, H.S., Moon, Y.S., Bertino, E.: Provenance-based trustworthiness assessment in sensor networks. In: Seventh International Workshop on Data Management for Sensor Networks, pp. 2–7. DMSN 2010. ACM, New York (2010)
9. Missier, P., Dey, S., Belhajjame, K., Cuevas-Vicenttín, V., Ludäscher, B.: D-prov: extending the prov provenance model with workflow structure. In: 5th USENIX Workshop on the Theory and Practice of Provenance (TaPP 13) (2013)
10. Moreau, L., et al.: The open provenance model core specification (v1. 1). Future Gener. Comput. Syst. 27(6), 743–756 (2011)
11. Moreau, L., et al.: Prov-dm: the prov data model. w3c recommendation (2013)
12. Muniswamy-Reddy, K.K., Holland, D.A., Braun, U., Seltzer, M.I.: Provenance-aware storage systems. In: USENIX Annual Technical Conference, pp. 43–56 (2006)

13. Simmhan, Y.L., Plale, B., Gannon, D.: A survey of data provenance in e-science. SIGMOD Rec. **34**(3), 31–36 (2005)
14. Tan, W.C., et al.: Provenance in databases: past, current, and future. IEEE Data Eng. Bull. **30**(4), 3–12 (2007)

Securing Data Provenance in Internet of Things (IoT) Systems

Nathalie Baracaldo[1]([envelope]), Luis Angel D. Bathen[1], Roqeeb O. Ozugha[2],
Robert Engel[1], Samir Tata[1], and Heiko Ludwig[1]

[1] Almaden Research Center, IBM Research, San Jose, CA, USA
{baracald,bathen,engelrob,stata,hludwig}@us.ibm.com
[2] Dakota State University, 820 N Washington Ave., Madison, SD, USA
roqeeb.ozugha@trojans.dsu.edu

Abstract. The Internet of Things (IoT) promises to yield a plethora of new innovative applications based on highly interconnected devices. In order to enable IoT applications for critical and/or sensitive use cases, it is important to (i) foster their dependability by assuring and verifying the integrity and correctness of data processed in such applications, and (ii) adequately account for privacy and confidentiality concerns. For addressing these requirements, IoT systems can be equipped with *data provenance* mechanisms for maintaining information on the lineage and ownership of data. However, in order to provide secure and dependable IoT systems, provenance data needs to be sufficiently protected against tampering and unauthorized access. In this paper, we present a novel framework for cryptographic provenance data protection and access control based on blockchain technology and confidentiality policies.

Keywords: IoT · Provenance · Security · Blockchain · Keyless signature · Access control

1 Introduction

The Internet of Things (IoT) [8] has received significant attention in industry and in the academic community in recent years. Gartner forecasts that 6.4 billion connected things will be in use worldwide in 2016 [6]. They also predict that by 2020, more than 25% of identified attacks in enterprises will involve IoT [6], yet less than 10% of organizations' budget is dedicated to security.

IoT environments create an opportunity to collect information, run analytics and make important decisions that range from modifying the dosage of medicines for elderly patients to distributing budget for different projects in smart cities. Given the distributed nature of IoT systems, it is important to ensure that data used for analytics is actually generated by the expected entities. Failing to do so creates an opportunity for adversaries to manipulate decision making processes. For example, an adversary may fabricate data to ensure a smart city invests money in a targeted location or project.

© Springer International Publishing AG 2017
K. Drira et al. (Eds.): ICSOC 2016 Workshops, LNCS 10380, pp. 92–98, 2017.
https://doi.org/10.1007/978-3-319-68136-8_9

In this context, maintaining the history of data creation, modification and transfer, a.k.a. *provenance*, has become an increasingly important requirement in IoT environments. *Data provenance* deals with the recording, management and retrieval of information about the origin and history of data [5]. In the smart city use case, provenance data may include information about the devices that collected information such as model and serial number, their location as well as the timestamp when observations are collected.

By recording and verifying the history of data, provenance data provides the ability to assure the integrity and correctness of systems, but also enables *auditing* and *digital forensics* and can help enforce *privacy* and *data sovereignty*. For the latter, the origin and lineage of data is instrumental for enabling fine-grained access control for sensitive information collected in IoT applications (e.g., health-related data).

In this paper, we present a framework to maintain and protect IoT provenance data. Our framework is designed for IoT environments and provides the following functionality: (i) Ensure provenance data integrity is protected using a fully distributed lightweight keyless blockchain component. (ii) Ensure confidentiality of provenance data by providing custom access control to multiple stakeholders when necessary. Our solution allows the enforcement of fine-grained access control policies over provenance data. Because in IoT environments data and its provenance data flow is not easy to control, our solution makes use of cryptographic techniques to ensure confidentiality. (iii) Finally, our architecture is designed to allow high availability of provenance data.

In the following, we present the state of the art and then we introduce the proposed framework.

2   State of the Art

Multiple researchers have recognized the need to provide protection against forgery, fabrication and leakage of private information in provenance systems. Braun *et al.* present multiple scenarios in which data and its associated provenance information require different protection [2]. Muniswamy-Redd *et al.* highlight the necessity of protecting provenance data generated in cloud environments against forgery, fabrication and leakage of private information [12].

Cryptographic techniques have been proposed to protect forgery and confidentiality of provenance data [1,9,14,17]. Hasan *et al.* propose the use of broadcast encryption to ensure the confidentiality and integrity of provenance records and their related provenance chains [9]. The model defined in [14] utilizes a mutual agreement signature-based approach to provide confidentiality, integrity and availability of links between provenance data records. The model captures digital acyclic graph provenance and information sharing between users. Other approaches [1,17] use private-public key infrastructure to prevent forgery and confidentiality leakage of provenance data.

The above mentioned approaches uniquely focus on the cryptographic primitives and do not provide an architecture suitable for IoT environments. Additionally, they do not explicitly integrate access control policies to protect provenance data, making it difficult to manage changes in access control policies. Moreover, because provenance data is not stored in a distributed fashion, adversaries may be able to repudiate their latest creation or modification of data. To address these drawbacks, in this paper we integrate access control policies with cryptographic enforcement to protect the confidentiality and privacy of provenance data in a easy to manage fashion, and provide an architecture suitable for IoT environments.

3   Terminology and Requirements

In this section we present the requirements that led to the design of our system, but first, we present the terminology used throughout the paper. We assume a provenance model that describes the lineage of *data points*. A data point is a *uniquely identifiable* and *addressable* value in the context of the IoT system. A data point is specifically different from basic readings or other data flowing in the system in that it is addressable. The provenance information describes the context of the creation or modification of data points, including information about involved agents (e.g., a device containing several sensors), execution context, time, and location information.

We identify the following requirements for secure provenance in IoT environments:

1. Adversaries should not be able to tamper, fabricate provenance data or link valid provenance data to a different data point.
2. Provenance data should be highly available to entities that need to verify it.
3. The architecture should adapt to meet resource constraints in different environments.
4. The framework should allow the specification of policies that define the stakeholders or entities that may access certain provenance data. The goal here is to provide fine-grained confidentiality protection of provenance data by limiting the access to pre-defined stakeholders, e.g., auditors.

Based on these requirements, we now introduce the proposed architecture.

4   Secure Provenance Framework

In this section, we present the proposed framework depicted in Fig. 1. We make the following assumptions:

1. Devices and sensors are registered and authenticated with their assigned gateway(s). Similarly, gateways and other analytic services use best practices to communicate (SSL) and store data (data-at-rest encryption).
2. Gateways and agents that may modify or create information have assigned a cryptographic asymmetric key pair.
3. Provenance data may have different confidentiality protection requirements. These requirements are specified using an attribute-based access control policy, e.g., [7], which defines who may access different types of provenance data.

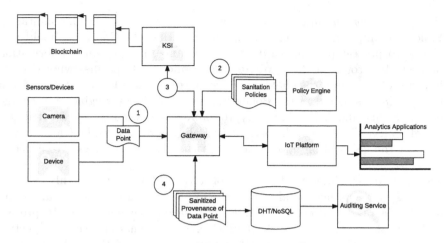

Fig. 1. Secure Provenance System Architecture

Our framework is composed of the following modules: a *Policy Engine*, *Keyless Signature Infrastructure Module (KSI)*, an *IoT Platform Module* and an *Auditing Service*.

The *Policy Engine* is used to maintain the policies that define how to protect provenance data. These policies are enforced through attribute-based encryption (ABE) [16] to ensure only authorized users can gain access to protected provenance data. In this scheme, protected provenance data is stored encrypted and each ciphertext is associated with a combination of attributes and private keys of authorized users. Users may decrypt a ciphertext (in this case provenance data) only when their private keys and their associated set of attributes "match" the ciphertext.

The *KSI* Module is used to provide provenance integrity, and the *IoT Platform Module* serves as the management point for our applications. This follows very closely the implementation of IBM's Bluemix IoT Platform-as-a-Service model [10]. We provide an *Auditing Service*, which interacts with the storage backend, and can build provenance graphs for data points by linking the data points to their provenance data.

Figure 1 shows how provenance data flows through our architecture:

1. Sensors (e.g., cameras) or Devices (e.g., phones) may generate a data point, which is initially sent to the Gateway. In order to provide scalability, we assume sensors and devices keep a list of peer Gateway nodes.
2. Gateways are the point of entry into our provenance framework, so it is of utmost important to maintain their availability. Gateways are managed in a decentralized manner akin to the way traditional P2P systems operate (e.g., BitTorrent). Gateways constantly publish their IPs and services to peers so that any one node that needs to subscribe may interact with it. Sensors may send their data to any of their peer Gateways. Once data is received by a Gateway, it polls the Policy Engine and requests the *Sanitation Policy* mapped to

the specific *type of data* it needs to process (and caches it). The Sanitation Policy contains the set of cryptographic keys that the Gateway should use, if any, to protect provenance data. For instance, if geographic information needs to be protected, an attribute-based policy that specifies what entities in terms of attributes they hold may access geographic information for a given type of data is stored in the Policy Engine. The Policy Engine is in charge of generating and maintaining cryptographic keys used for each attribute-based policy. Thus, when the Sanitation Policy is retrieved, the Gateway will encrypt the geolocation information with the right set of keys. We call this *sanitized provenance data.*

3. We provide data integrity by means of a *KSI* [3,4] as it is highly scalable and has been mathematically proven to protect against several tampering attacks. We use a *blockchain* [11,13] as a second layer in order to protect and publish the top root of the *KSI* tree. Data points and their respective provenance data are linked through unique identifiers (*UUIDs*) derived from the hash of their contents in a similar fashion as transaction IDs [13]. Once the metadata has been sanitized, it is sent to one (or several) KSI peer(s) to sign and enter the provenance data into the ledger. This step ensures the integrity protection of the provenance data, thereby preventing any sort of tampering from happening. As with KSI systems, validation of data integrity is a straight forward and inexpensive task.

4. Finally, the sanitized provenance data along with the KSI signature is persisted onto a DHT (in the event of a peer-to-peer storage model) or a NoSQL DB hosted in a cloud provider. The DHT model allows for gateways to participate in a peer-to-peer distributed storage model, where they may all share some of their storage. This allows us to provide high availability by distributing the data across multiple peers. We use erasure coding to minimize the amount of storage consumed by the DHT as in [15]. Similarly, we could leverage the high availability of traditional storage backends (e.g., NoSQL DBs, DHTs, etc.) promised by cloud providers (over 5–9s reliability service level agreements) [15]. We use the provenance data's *UUIDs* as storage keys when sent to our storage backend.

Finally, we note that any entity that uses as input or transforms data produced by the IoT environment, such as analytic services that aggregate information, can also maintain provenance information of their observations using our architecture.

5   Conclusions

In this paper, we presented a framework for protecting provenance data in IoT environments that addresses the requirements of (i) tamper prevention, (ii) high availability and (iii) access control for provenance data while ensuring that (iv) even constrained devices can be part of the system. Using a fully distributed, lightweight and keyless signature infrastructure in conjunction with attribute-based encryption and blockchain, the framework allows for the enforcement of fine-grained access control policies while assuring and enforcing the integrity of the provenance data. To the best of our knowledge, our proposed framework is the first to provide a lightweight, scalable architecture for protecting provenance data that enforces confidentiality of provenance data at the point of transmission in IoT systems.

Our ongoing research efforts focus on implementing and evaluating the aforementioned framework as well as combining it with mechanisms for secure deployment and verification of code in IoT environments (i.e., for verifying the integrity of producers of provenance data).

References

1. Gadelha, J., et al.: Kairos: an architecture for securing authorship and temporal information of provenance data in grid-enabled workflow management systems. In: eScience 2008 (2008)
2. Braun, U., Shinnar, A., Seltzer, M.I.: Securing provenance. In: HotSec (2008)
3. Buldas, A., Kroonmaa, A., Laanoja, R.: Keyless signatures' infrastructure: how to build global distributed hash-trees. In: Riis Nielson, H., Gollmann, D. (eds.) NordSec 2013. LNCS, vol. 8208, pp. 313–320. Springer, Heidelberg (2013). doi:10. 1007/978-3-642-41488-6_21
4. Buldas, A., Truu, A., Laanoja, R., Gerhards, R.: Efficient record-level keyless signatures for audit logs. In: Bernsmed, K., Fischer-Hübner, S. (eds.) NordSec 2014. LNCS, vol. 8788, pp. 149–164. Springer, Cham (2014). doi:10.1007/978-3-319-11599-3_9
5. Buneman, P., Khanna, S., Wang-Chiew, T.: Why and where: a characterization of data provenance. In: Van den Bussche, J., Vianu, V. (eds.) ICDT 2001. LNCS, vol. 1973, pp. 316–330. Springer, Heidelberg (2001). doi:10.1007/3-540-44503-X_20
6. Gartner: Gartner says worldwide IoT security spending to reach $348 million in 2016 (2016). http://www.gartner.com/newsroom/id/3291817
7. Goyal, V., Pandey, O., Sahai, A., Waters, B.: Attribute-based encryption for fine-grained access control of encrypted data. In: Proceedings of the 13th ACM Conference on Computer and Communications Security, pp. 89–98. ACM (2006)
8. Gubbi, J., Buyya, R., Marusic, S., Palaniswami, M.: Internet of Things (IoT): a vision, architectural elements, and future directions. Future Gen. Comp. Sys. 29(7), 1645–1660 (2013)
9. Hasan, R., Sion, R., Winslett, M.: The case of the fake picasso: preventing history forgery with secure provenance. FAST 9, 1–14 (2009)
10. IBM: IBM bluemix (2016). https://console.ng.bluemix.net
11. Linux Foundation: The Hyperledger Project (2016). https://www.hyperledger.org
12. Muniswamy-Reddy, K.K., Seltzer, M.: Provenance as first class cloud data. ACM SIGOPS Oper. Syst. Rev. 43(4), 11–16 (2010)
13. Nakamoto, S.: Bitcoin: a peer-to-peer electronic cash system (2008). https://bitcoin.org/bitcoin.pdf
14. Rangwala, M., Liang, Z., Peng, W., Zou, X., Li, F.: A mutual agreement signature scheme for secure data provenance. Environments 13, 14
15. Rodrigues, R., Liskov, B.: High availability in DHTs: erasure coding vs. replication. In: Castro, M., van Renesse, R. (eds.) IPTPS 2005. LNCS, vol. 3640, pp. 226–239. Springer, Heidelberg (2005). doi:10.1007/11558989_21

16. Sahai, A., Waters, B.: Fuzzy identity-based encryption. In: Cramer, R. (ed.) EURO-CRYPT 2005. LNCS, vol. 3494, pp. 457–473. Springer, Heidelberg (2005). doi:10.1007/11426639_27
17. Wang, X., Zeng, K., Govindan, K., Mohapatra, P.: Chaining for securing data provenance in distributed information networks. In: MILCOM 2012, pp. 1–6 (2012)

Big Data Services
and Computational Intelligence

Introduction to the Second International Workshop on Big Data Services and Computational Intelligence (BSCI'16)

Zhangbing Zhou[1], Patrick C.K. Hung[2], Yucong Duan[3], and Richard Lomotey[4]

[1] China University of Geosciences, Beijing, China
[2] University of Ontario Institute of Technology, Oshawa, Canada
[3] Hainan University, Haikou, China
[4] The Pennsylvania State University, Beaver, USA

1 Preface

The pervasive nature of big data technologies as witnessed in industry services and everyday life has given rise to an emergent, data-focused economy stemming from many aspects of industrial applications. The richness and vastness of these services are creating unprecedented research opportunities in a number of industrial fields including public health, urban studies, economics, finance, social science, and geography. These services can be formed a high-level computational intelligence based on emerging analytical techniques such as big data analytics and web analytics. We are moving towards the, which are deployed in a multi-scale complex distributed architecture. In this context, computational intelligence employs software tools from advanced analytics disciplines such as data mining, predictive analytics, and machine learning. At the same time, it becomes increasingly important to anticipate technical and practical challenges and to identify best practices learned through experience. At the era of Big Data Services, BSCI'16 is in conjunction with the International Conference on Service Oriented Computing (ICSOC) 2016, October 10–13, 2016, Banff, Alberta, Canada. It aims to offer a new platform for contributions and discussions related to the topics covered by ICSOC 2016. It focuses on exploring and discussing emerging topics dealing with big data services and computational intelligence, which is complementary with the established ICSOC topics of interest. In this special session, among 4 submissions we accepted 2 of them. One is "Enhancing UML Class Diagram Abstraction with Page Rank Algorithm and Relationship Abstraction Rules". Through integrating existing practice in system modeling in traditional software engineering, it presents complexity alleviation solutions to model service systems with capability of abstract transformation among huge volume of specific modeling details. The other is "Energy-Aware Composition for Service-Oriented Wireless Sensor Networks". It proposes a service oriented wireless sensor network framework featured with energy-aware optimization from particle swarm algorithm and genetic algorithm.

2 Organization

Workshop Chairs

Zhangbing Zhou   China University of Geosciences (Beijing), China
Patrick C.K. Hung   University of Ontario Institute of Technology, Canada
Yucong Duan   Hainan University, Haikou, China
Richard Lomotey   The Pennsylvania State University, Beaver, USA

Program Committee

Chan N. Nguyen   Universite de Lorraine, France
Wei Tan   Thomas J. Watson Research Center, USA
Sami Yangui   Concordia University, QC, Canada
Lu Liu   University of Derby, UK
Shizhan Chen   Tianjin University, China
Brahmananda Sapkota   Samsung Electronics, South Korea
Joel J.P.C Rodrigues   University of Beira Interior, Portugal
Jianwei Niu   Beihang University, China
Keman Huang   Tianjin University, China
Beihong Jin   Institute of Software Chinese Academy of Sciences, China
Yunchuan Sun   Beijing Normal University, China
Junsheng Zhang   Institute of Scientific and Technical Information of China,
                        China
Jin Liu   Wuhan University, China

Enhancing UML Class Diagram Abstraction with Page Rank Algorithm and Relationship Abstraction Rules

Liang Huang[1], Yucong Duan[1(✉)], Zhangbing Zhou[2], Lixu Shao[1],
Xiaobing Sun[3], and Patrick C.K. Hung[4]

[1] State Key Laboratory of Marine Resource Utilization in the South China Sea,
College of Information Science and Technology,
Hainan University, Haikou, China
1512460987@qq.com, 751486692@qq.com,
duanyucong@hotmail.com
[2] China University of Geosciences, Beijing, China
zhangbing.zhou@gmail.com
[3] School of Information Engineering, Yangzhou University, Yangzhou, China
xbsun@yzu.edu.cn
[4] Institute of Technology, University of Ontario, Oshawa, Canada
patrick.hung@uoit.ca

Abstract. Model-Driven Engineering (MDE) alleviates the cognitive complexity and effort through the refinement and abstraction of consecutive models. In MDE, models should accurately and completely accommodate the expected data, information and knowledge in requirement specification following a series of refinement and abstraction. Proper abstraction starting from Class Diagrams lays the foundation for effective reuse and efficient manipulation of contained data, information and knowledge. Most current model abstraction approaches assume the scenarios with interaction of stakeholders for providing the key entities and thereafter focus on the relationship abstraction. However few work is done on unguided abstraction where stakeholders don't know the key entities. Towards resolving the abstraction covering both automatic locating of representative entities and abstracting of link among these entities in Class Diagrams, we proposed a combination of class rank algorithm which prioritizes classes and relationship abstraction rules which heuristically determine the representative semantics of relationships towards improving the efficiency and effectiveness of class abstraction.

Keywords: Correlations · UML · Relationships · Page rank algorithm

1 Introduction

Models and modeling are essential parts of every engineering endeavors [1]. Unified Modeling Language (UML) is a nonindustrial standard for object-oriented modeling [2]. UML Class Diagram is used to describe the static structure of a system. A Class Diagram could be very large if a system is huge and complex. Designers easily become

© Springer International Publishing AG 2017
K. Drira et al. (Eds.): ICSOC 2016 Workshops, LNCS 10380, pp. 103–116, 2017.
https://doi.org/10.1007/978-3-319-68136-8_10

overwhelmed with details when dealing with large Class Diagrams. Model transformation is an essential part of MDE [15]. UML Class Diagram abstraction transforms a low-level class diagram to a high-level Class Diagram [3]. Well-designed Class Diagrams can lead to an eased development process towards a more ensured result system since they can be understood by stakeholders easily. Most existing model abstraction approaches fit for the scenario that stakeholders decide a few key entities usually according to their understanding of the significance of the entities. These key entities are used to represent the other entities. Then the main task of the abstraction is to expose the direct relationships among the key entities through mostly relationship abstraction. However this scenario is not always true especially when stakeholders are not familiar with the modeling techniques and the global perspective of a project. Then abstract need to be done without input of key entities. We can this scenario as unguided abstraction. Towards resolving the abstraction covering both automatic locating of representative entities and abstracting of link among these entities in Class Diagrams, we proposed a combination of class rank algorithm which prioritizes classes similar to page rank algorithm [14]. Page rank algorithm works by counting the number and quality of links to a page to determine a rough estimate of how important the website is. The underlying assumption is that more important websites are likely to receive more links from other websites. We regard classes as pages, relationships between classes as hyperlinks between pages, so we can apply page rank algorithm to compute the importance of a class in a Class Diagram. After the locating of the key entities, we introduce the heuristic relationship abstraction rules from Dr. Egyed [4] which heuristically determine the representative semantics of relationships towards improving the efficiency and effectiveness of class abstraction. We validate our approach with case studies.

In the rest of this paper, we give an overview of this paper in Sect. 2 firstly. Then we elaborate class rank algorithm to compute class ranks in Sect. 3 and a method to compute correlations between classes in Sect. 4. Approaches to compute relationships between classes are represented in Sect. 5. The related works are elaborated in Sect. 6. We give our conclusions in Sect. 7.

2   Overview

We propose a method to abstract class diagrams based on a class rank algorithm and relationship abstraction rules as Fig. 1 shows. We map a Class Diagram to a graph with nodes and edges. Nodes in a graph stand for classes in a Class Diagram and edges stand for relationships. On a mapped graph we implement abstraction through following operations.

(1) Compute ranks of classes: A rank of a class represents the importance of the class in a Class Diagram. Class with a high rank is important in a Class Diagram. We use class rank algorithm to calculate ranks of classes in a Class Diagram. Then we obtain a one-dimensional class rank vector R. We suppose that classes ranked in the top thirty percent are important classes and abstracted Class Diagram should only contain important classes. We need to get relationships between important classes and decide which relationships should be presented in the abstracted Class Diagram.

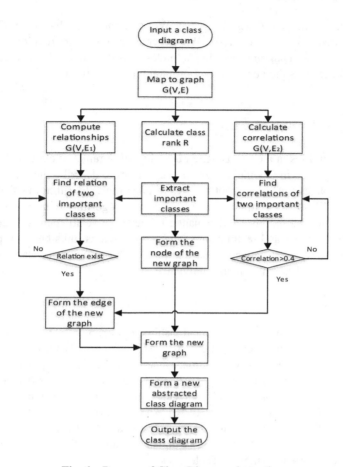

Fig. 1. Process of Class Diagram abstraction

(2) Compute correlations between classes: Correlation between two nodes is used to judge whether a strong association exists between them. If there is a strong association between two nodes, they can be connected through a line. We calculate correlations of two nodes based on the distance and relationships between them. Then we get a weighted graph $G(V,E_1)$. V is a node set and E_1 is an edge set with weighted correlations. Relationship between two classes can be presented in an abstracted Class Diagram if the correlation between two classes is bigger than 0.4.

(3) Compute the direct relationship between two classes: If there is a path between two classes, a direct relationship may exist between them. We use relationship abstraction rules to get the direct relationship. Then we can obtain a weighted graph $G(V,E_2)$. E_2 is an edge set with weighted relationships.

(4) Generate the abstracted graph: According to $G(V,E_1)$, $G(V,E_2)$ and R, we abstract $G(V,E)$ and get the abstracted graph $G_1(V,E)$ which is the abstraction of original graph $G(V,E)$. $G_1(V,E)$ only contains nodes that represent important classes and relationships between them.

(5) Generate abstracted Class Diagram: We generate an abstracted Class Diagram based on graph $G_1(V,E)$. We generate classes and relationships of the abstracted Class Diagram according to nodes and edges in $G_1(V,E)$. The abstracted Class Diagram is the abstraction of original Class Diagram.

3   Calculate Ranks of Classes

We locate key entities in a Class Diagram by calculating ranks of classes. The concept of rank is firstly used in Google's page rank algorithm to describe the importance of a page and rank pages [14]. We adopt the idea of page rank algorithm to calculate ranks of classes in a Class Diagram and name it class rank algorithm. Class rank algorithm works by counting the number and semantic influence of relationships of classes. We regard classes as pages and relationships between classes as links between pages. But there are some differences between links and relationships. Different relationships have different ranks and different semantic influence.

3.1   Definitions

Table 1 shows logograms of relevant relationships. For example, AG is an abbreviation for aggregation. An expression such as "A × AG × B" stands for "A aggregate B". Class rank (Rc) is represented with a float value between [0, 1000]. The value of Rc stands for the importance of a class in a Class Diagram. A class is deemed as more important if the class is labeled with a greater value. Relationship rank (Rr) is represented with an integer value between [0, 10]. The value of Rr stands for the semantic influence of a relationship in a Class Diagram. For example, if the rank of GL is larger than that of AS, it indicates that GL is of higher semantic influence than AS. We set ranks for different relationships as Table 2 shows.

Table 1. Logograms of relationships

AG	Aggregation	AGr	Aggregation reverse
DP	Dependency	DPr	Dependency reverse
GL	Generalization	GLr	Generalization reverse
AS	Association		

Transition probability (*TP*) represents the probability of a rank transition from one class to another. Transition probability between class i and class j is defined according to Eq. 1. $Rr(i,j)$ is the relationship rank of edge (i,j). For example, $Rr(i,j)$ is equal to 7 if the relationship of edge (i,j) is AG. Transition probability matrix represents all transition probabilities of class ranks from one class to another in a Class Diagram.

$$\mathrm{TP}(i,j) = \frac{R_r(i,j)}{\sum_{(i,k)\in E} R_r(i,k)}. \tag{1}$$

Table 2. Ranks of relationships

Relationship type	AG	DP	GL	AS	AGr	DPr	GLr
Rank	7	8	10	5	7	8	10

3.2   Calculate Class Ranks

We calculate the rank of a class based on its adjacent classes' ranks and transition probabilities from the class to its adjacent classes. We calculate a class rank according to Eq. 2:

$$Rc(i) = \sum_{(i,j)\in E} Rc(j) \bullet TP(j,i) = \sum_{(i,j)\in E} Rc(j) \bullet \frac{Rr(j,i)}{\sum_{(j,k)\in E} Rr(j,k)} \qquad (2)$$

where $Rc(i)$ is the class rank of class i. (i,j) is the edge from class i to class j. $Rr(j,i)$ is the relationship rank of edge (j,i). The formulated rules of this article will be evaluated using class diagram of a shopping management system shown in Fig. 2 at the analysis phase. Process of computing class ranks is as following shows:

(1) Set an initial vector of class ranks: There are 11 classes in the Class Diagram of shopping management system. Class rank is initialized to the same value for all classes. We suppose that the initial rank of each class is equal to 1000/11.

(2) Calculate transition probability matrix (M): We construct transition probability matrix based on rank transition probabilities of any two different classes having relationship with each other.

(3) Iteration: We use the last class rank vector to multiply the transition probability matrix and obtain a new class rank vector which is represented as Eq. 3:

$$R_i = R_{i-1} \bullet M. \qquad (3)$$

where R_i is the class rank vector after iterating $i - 1$ times. M is a constant transition probability matrix. In each iteration, a class will transfer its value of rank to its adjacent classes. After iterating i times, rank of a class tends to be stable. R_i approximates R_{i-1}. We skip out of the iteration and get the final class rank R_i. A class is deemed as more important if the class is labeled with a greater value of rank. We suppose that classes ranked in the top 30% are important classes. After computing, rank values of the 11 classes in Fig. 2 are shown in Table 3. So important classes in the Class Diagram of shopping management system are *Order*, *Payment* and *Customer*.

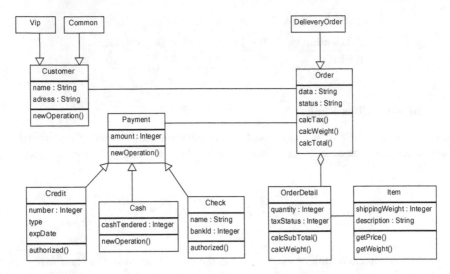

Fig. 2. A low-level Class Diagram of shopping management system

Table 3. Ranks values of classes in Fig. 2

Class	Customer	Order	Credit	Item	Payment	DelieveryOrder	Check	OrderDetail	Common	Cash	Vip
Rank	194	124	42	26	270	75	42	97	43	43	43

4 Compute Correlations Between Classes

In order to compute correlations between classes, we assume that two classes could be connected if the correlation between them is of high semantic influence. Correlation between two classes is related to the distance and relationships between them.

4.1 Definition

Correlation between two classes depends on paths between them. Paths between two classes contain intermediate classes and relationships between them. We use a line to connect two classes if the correlation between them is of high semantic influence. We suppose that correlation between classes is of high semantic influence if value of the correlation is bigger than 0.4. Strength of a relationship is similar to a relationship rank. We use strength of relationship to calculate the correlation of two classes. We give the strength of each relationship in Table 4. For example, correlation between class *Customer* and class *Order* is 0.5 because the relationship between them is *AS*.

Table 4. Strength of relationships

Relationship type	AG	DP	GL	AS	AGr	DPr	GLr
Strength	0.7	0.8	1.0	0.5	0.7	0.8	1.0

4.2   Calculate the Correlation Between Two Classes

We need to compute the correlation if two classes are not directly connected with each other. In Fig. 3, class A and class D are not directly connected with each other. There are two intermediate classes that are class B and class C between them. Steps of computing correlation between class A and class D are as follows:

(1) Find strength of intermediate relationships in the path: Correlation between class A and class B is 0.5 because the relationship between them is AS and strength of AS is 0.5. Correlation between class B and class C is 0.7 because the relationship between class B and class C is AG and strength of AG is 0.7. Correlation between class C and class D is 1.0 because the relationship between class C and D is GL and strength of GL is 1.0.

Fig. 3. Different relationships in a path between two classes

(2) Multiply the strengths: We multiply strengths of AS, AG and GL. Then we get the correlation between class A and class D which is $C(A,D)$. $C(A,D)$ is equal to 0.35. We need to compute correlation of two classes in each path if there are multiple paths between them according to Eq. 5:

$$C(i,j) = \underset{Path(n) \in (i,j)}{Max} \left\{ \prod_{k \in Path(n)} S(k) \right\} \tag{5}$$

where $Path(n)$ is a path between class i and j. K is a relationship in $Path(n)$ such as AG. $S(k)$ is the strength of relationship k. In Fig. 4, there are two paths between class A and class D. For *Path 1*, correlation between class A and class D is $C_1(A, D)$ which is equal to $0.5(1.0 * 0.5)$. For *Path 2*, correlation between class A and class D is $C_2(A,D)$ which is equal to $0.56(0.8 * 0.7)$. We choose $C_2(A,D)$ as the correlation between class A and class D because $C_2(A,D)$ is bigger than $C_1(A,D)$.

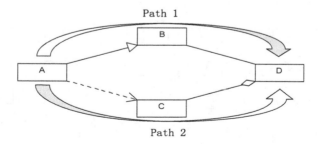

Fig. 4. Multiple paths between two classes.

(3) Calculate the correlation matrix of a Class Diagram: For any two classes in a Class Diagram, we compute the correlation between them and get a correlation matrix of the Class Diagram. Then we obtain graph $G(V,E1)$ of the Class Diagram based on the correlation matrix. $E1$ is an edge set with weighted correlations. In this way, we get correlations between classes in Fig. 2 as Table 5 shows. Correlation between classes is of high semantic influence if value of the correlation is bigger than 0.4 for instance correlation between class *Customer* and *Order*.

Table 5. Correlations between classes

	Customer	Order	Credit	Item	Payment	DeliveryOrder	Check	OrderDetail	Common	Cash	Vip
Customer	0.0	0.5	0.25	0.175	0.25	0.5	0.25	0.35	1	0.25	1
Order	0.5	0.0	0.5	0.35	0.5	1.0	0.5	0.7	0.5	0.5	0.5
Credit	0.25	0.175	0.0	0.175	1.0	0.5	1.0	0.35	0.25	1.0	0.25
Item	0.175	1.0	0.175	0.0	0.175	0.35	0.175	0.5	0.175	0.175	0.175
Payment	0.25	0.5	1.0	0.175	0.0	0.5	1.0	0.35	0.25	1.0	0.25
DeliveryOrder	0.5	1.0	0.5	0.35	0.5	0.0	0.5	0.7	0.5	0.5	0.5
Check	0.25	0.5	1.0	0.175	1.0	0.5	0.0	0.35	0.25	1.0	0.25
OrderDetail	0.35	0.7	0.35	0.5	0.35	0.7	0.35	0.0	0.35	0.35	0.35
Common	1.0	0.5	0.25	0.175	0.25	0.5	0.25	0.35	0.0	0.25	1.0
Cash	0.25	0.5	1.0	0.175	1.0	0.5	1.0	0.35	0.25	0.0	0.25
Vip	1.0	0.5	0.25	0.175	0.25	0.5	0.25	0.35	1.0	0.25	0.0

5　Compute Relationships Between Classes

Getting the direct relationship between two classes can ease the cognitive load of checking the consistency in a Class Diagram. If all intermediate relationships in the path between two classes are the same, it is easy to know the direct relationship between the two classes. On the left side of Fig. 5, class A inherits class C if class A inherits class B and class B inherits class C. Class A depends on class C if class A depends on class B and class B depends on class C. Class A aggregates class C if class A aggregates class B and class B aggregates class C. Class A associates with class C if class A associates with class B and class B associates with class C. However, it is not easy to obtain the direct relationship between class A and class C if different relationships are grouped together as shown on the right side of Fig. 5.

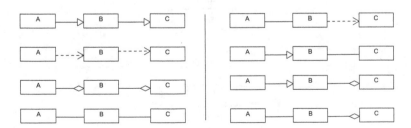

Fig. 5. Combination of relationships

5.1   Abstraction Rules

Dr. Egyed proposed a series of abstraction rules for automatically getting direct relationships from relationship combinations as Fig. 6 shows. The left side depicts the class input patterns and the right side (after "equals") depicts the class output patterns. Input and output patterns are allowed to be more complex as long as the output pattern is simpler than the input pattern. If not, the abstraction algorithm could be non-deterministic. We also analyzed the semantic dependencies between other classes and their relationships. Note that the direction of relations is indicated through their name. If the relation name is used with no add-on, then a forward relation (a relation from left to right) is meant. If the string "r" is added then a backward relation (a relation from right to left) is meant. The number following each rule indicates the reliability of result obtained from the implementation of this rule. For example, *rule(30){AS × Class × DP equals DP 50}* indicates that class *A* depends on class *C* if class *A* associates with class *B* and class *B* depends on class *C*. Value of the reliability of the result obtained from implementing *rule(30)* is equal to *0.5(50/100)*. According to *rule(15)*, class *A* associates with class *C* if class *A* inherits class *B* and class *B* associates with class *C*. Value of the reliability of the result obtained from implementing *rule(15)* is 1.

(1)AS x Class x AS equals AS 100	(15) GL x Class x AS equals AS 100	(29)AS x Class x AGr equals AS 70
(2)AS x Class x AG equals AS 100	(16) GL x Class x DP equals DP 100	(30)AS x Class x DP equals DP 50
(3)AS x Class x GLr equals AS 100	(17) GL x Class x AG equals AG 100	(31)AS x Class x DPr equals DPr 50
(4)AG x Class x AG equals AG 100	(18) GL x Class x GL equals GL 100	(32) DP x Class x AG equals DP 70
(5)AG x Class x GLr equals AG 100	(19)GL x Class x AGr equals AGr 100	(33) DP x Class x AS equals AS 50
(6)AGr x Class x AS equals AS 100	(20)GL x Class x DPr equals DPr100	(34) DP x Class x GL equals DP 50
(7)AGr x Class x DP equals DP 100	(21)GLr x Class x GLr equals GLr100	(35)DPr x Class x AS equals DPr 50
(8)AGr x Class x AGr equals AGr 100	(22)AG x Class x AS equals AS 90	(36)DPr x Class x GL equals DPr 50
(9)AGr x Class x GLr equals AGr 100	(23)AG x Class x DPr equals DPr 80	(37)DPr x Class x AGr equals DPr 50
(10) DP x Class x DP equals DP 100	(24)AGr x Class x GL equals AGr 80	(38)GLr x Class x AG equals AG 80
(11)DPr x Class x AG equals DPr 100	(25)AGr x Class x DPr equals DPr 70	(39)GLr x Class x AS equals AS 70
(12)DP x Class x GLr equals DP 100	(26)AG x Class x DP equals DP 50	(40)GLr x Class x AGr equals AGr 50
(13)DPr x Class x DPr equals DPr 100	(27)AG x Class x GL equals AG 50	(41)GLr x Class x DP equals DP 50
(14)DPr x Class x GLr equals DPr 100	(28) AS x Class x GL equals AS 70	(42)GLr x Class x DPr equals DPr 50

GL :generalization GLr :generalization reverse DP :dependency AS :Association
DPr :dependency reverse AG :aggregation AGr : aggregation reverse

Fig. 6. Rules for abstraction

5.2   Compute the Relationship Between Classes

(1)   Compute direct relationship between two classes in a path: We can get all intermediate relationships in the path between two classes and form a one-dimensional array of relationships. For any two adjacent relationships in a relationship array, we can abstract them if they satisfy a rule as shown in Fig. 6. In Fig. 3, relationship array that we got from the path is equal to *Arr = [AS, AG, GL]*. For any two adjacent relationships in Arr, we judge whether they satisfy a rule. For example, *AS* and *AG* meets *rule(2)*. *AG* and *GL* meets *rule(27)*. Then we need to consider which rule should be executed firstly and whether different execution orders of rules will lead to different results. We get the final relationship between class *A* and class *D* which is

AS if we execute *rule(2)* firstly following the first order shown in Fig. 7. Relationship array *A = [AS, AG, GL]* changes to *A1 = [AS, GL]* and relationship array *A1 = [AS, GL]* changes to *A2 = [AS]* if we execute *rule(28)* secondly. The final relationship between class *A* and class *D* is also equal to *AS* if we execute the rule (27) firstly following the second order shown in Fig. 7. Relationship array *A = [AS, AG, GL]* changes to *A3 = [AS, AG]* and relationship array *A3 = [AS, AG]* changes to *A4 = [AS]* if we execute rule(2) secondly.

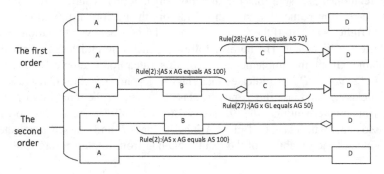

Fig. 7. Execution orders of abstraction rules

In Fig. 7, result of execution following the first order is *A2 = [AS]* and result of execution following the second order is *A4 = [AS]*. Value of the reliability of *A2 = [AS]* is equal to 0.7. Value of the reliability of *A4 = [AS]* is equal to 0.5. We choose the relationship with a higher reliability. We need to consider whether different execution orders will lead to different relationship results and find a way to get a relationship result with the highest reliability. For a relationship array *A = [X, Y, Z]* which contains only 3 relationships, there are 343(7 * 7 * 7) types of *A* (*e.g. [AS, AG, AS]*). For each type of *A*, we analyzed two execution orders of *A* like Fig. 7 shows. We found that results of two execution orders are the same regardless of the type. Table 6 gives the analysis results of 343 relationship array types.

Table 6. Analysis results of 343 types

Comparison of two results	Number	Percentage
Unequal	0	0%
Invalid	88	26%
Total	343	100%

Invalid result means that combination of the latter two relationships in array *A* does not conform to any of the abstraction rules. For relationship array *A[AS, GL, GLr]* shown in Fig. 8, there is no rule that meets the two adjacent relationships *GL* and *GLr*. Thus, there is only one order for *A* to choose which leads to a unique result. We will get

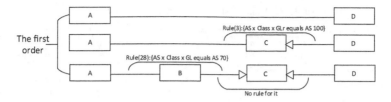

Fig. 8. Execution orders of relationship array *A[AS, GL, GLr]*

only one relationship result for the invalid type. We can conclude that there is only one relationship result no matter in which array type that contains 3 relationships. We apply heuristic abstraction rules to abstract relationships between two classes as algorithm 1 shows.

Algorithm 1 Applying heuristic abstraction rules to abstract relationships between two classes

Require: A path between class A and class B

Ensure: Relationships between intermediate classes in the path and values of the reliability

    While The final relationship between class A and class B is not found. **do**

        1:Find all relationship abstraction rules which are applicable for the path.

        2:Rank rules according to the descending order of their reliability.

        3: Choose the rule with the highest reliability and abstract the path.

end while

Output the relationship between class A and class B and the value of reliability

---

Compute direct relationship between two classes if there are two or more paths: We will get more than one relationship result if there are multiple paths between two classes. We should consider which result to choose. Our approach is to choose result with the highest reliability. We choose result with the highest relationship rank if reliabilities of two different results are equal.

(2) Calculate the relationship matrix of a Class Diagram: After computing direct relationship between any two classes in a Class Diagram, we create a relationship matrix of the Class Diagram and form graph *G(V,E2)*. We obtain relationships between classes in Fig. 2 as Table 7 shows.

We set the level of abstraction by controlling requirements for the number of important classes and strength of relationships. We get four important classes if we suppose that classes ranked in the top 40% are important. They are Payment, Customer, Order and OrderDetail. We reduce the number of important classes to three if the

Table 7. Relationship between classes in Fig. 2

	Customer	Order	Credit	Item	Payment	DeliveryOrder	Check	OrderDetail	Common	Cash	Vip
Customer	None	0.5	0.25	0.175	0.25	0.5	0.25	0.35	1	0.25	1
Order	0.5	None	0.5	0.35	0.5	1.0	0.5	0.7	0.5	0.5	0.5
Credit	0.25	0.175	None	0.175	1.0	0.5	1.0	0.35	0.25	1.0	0.25
Item	0.175	1.0	0.175	None	0.175	0.35	0.175	0.5	0.175	0.175	0.175
Payment	0.25	0.5	1.0	0.175	None	0.5	1.0	0.35	0.25	1.0	0.25
DeliveryOrder	0.5	1.0	0.5	0.35	0.5	None	0.5	0.7	0.5	0.5	0.5
Check	0.25	0.5	1.0	0.175	1.0	0.5	None	0.35	0.25	1.0	0.25
OrderDetail	0.35	0.7	0.35	0.5	0.35	0.7	0.35	None	0.35	0.35	0.35
Common	1.0	0.5	0.25	0.175	0.25	0.5	0.25	0.35	None	0.25	1.0
Cash	0.25	0.5	1.0	0.175	1.0	0.5	1.0	0.35	0.25	None	0.25
Vip	1.0	0.5	0.25	0.175	0.25	0.5	0.25	0.35	1.0	0.25	None

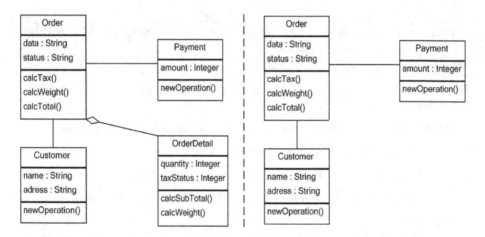

Fig. 9. Abstracted Class Diagram of different levels

standard that is set for the important classes is ranked in top 30%. We locate key entities by using class rank algorithm. From Tables 5 and 7 we can know the correlations and relationships between important classes. Therefore, we can get abstracted Class Diagrams of different levels of shopping management system as Fig. 9 shows which only contains important classes and relationships between them. The Class Diagram on the right side has a higher abstraction than the one on the left.

6   Related Work

It is more and more difficult for people to program, understand, and modify software with the increasingly complexity of a software system [13]. Dr. Eyged proposed a series of abstraction rules for Class Diagram which contain class abstraction rules and relationship abstraction rules. Direct relationship between any two classes in a Class Diagram can be calculated by using heuristic abstraction rules [4]. His abstraction method supports the scenario when key entities such as classes or instances are identified by stakeholders before an abstraction process or during interactions of a process. The pattern matching not only is costly [5] but also depends on the experience or project knowledge of the stakeholders in identifying the key entities/relationships. The scenario of abstraction without relying on the experience of stakeholders is a more challenging situation which need to be explored but not well addressed in existing literature. The first obstacle for unguided abstraction is to create or find the representative entities which can represent the trivial data, information and knowledge which are distributed in the mess of the trivial elements in model diagrams. Based on our hypothesis that some existing classes can represent the others properly, we uses class rank algorithm to calculate ranks of classes in a Class Diagram and use the ranks to represent the importance of the entities. During the implementation of the visualization [12], we adopted the hierarchical layout by Sugiyama to display our layered abstraction of UML Class Diagrams [6, 8] and also referred to the rank-direct layout method [9] which centers on higher ranked classes and clusters lower ranked classed to higher ranked classes. Harald found that various factors like layout quality, modeler experience, and diagram type led to significant differences in diagram reading strategies [10, 11]. Helen investigated the preference of UML modelers and found that joined inheritance arcs and directional indicators were preferred for Class Diagrams [7].

7 Conclusion

Well designed hierarchical abstraction can provide an effective means to efficiently understand and maintain complex models. Most existing model abstraction approaches assume that target classes are provided ahead. Thereafter the abstraction focuses on the abstraction at relationship level. Dr. Egyed had proposed a series of heuristic rules which are capable to efficiently fulfill the relationship abstraction. However unguided abstraction which doesn't come with guided information such as predetermined target classes is not fully studied in existing literature. We analyzed that unguided abstraction requires automated recognition of target classes which represent important entity concepts of abstracted models. Then based on the hypothesis that some existing classes fit well to represent other classes, we proposed a class prioritizing algorithm to recognize these representative classes through ranking them with different values. We further integrate the entity abstraction with the heuristic relationship abstraction to form an approach of unguided automatic abstraction of models. In the future, we propose to explore the entity abstraction scenario where no existing classes fit as the representative entity for other classes through the data, information and knowledge recreation of existing classes and relationships with the introduction of knowledge graphs.

Acknowledgments. The authors acknowledge the support of NSFC of China (No. 61363007, 61662021 and 61661019) and Hainan NSF Key project (No. 2017xxxx).

References

1. Blossfeld, H.P., Rohwer, G.: Techniques of event history modeling: new approaches to causal analysis. In: Techniques of event history modeling, pp. 236–238. Lawrence Erlbaum Associates (2002)
2. France, R.B., Kim, D.K., Ghosh, S., et al.: A UML-based pattern specification technique. IEEE Trans. Softw. Eng. **30**, 193–206 (2004)
3. Egyed, A.: Automated abstraction of class diagrams. ACM Trans. Softw. Eng. Methodol. (TOSEM) **11**, 449–491 (2002)
4. Egyed, A.: Semantic abstraction rules for class diagrams. In: Proceedings of the Fifteenth IEEE International Conference on Automated Software Engineering, ASE, pp. 301–304. IEEE Xplore (2000)
5. Fahmy, H., Holt, R.C.: Software architecture transformations. In: International Conference on IEEE Proceedings of the Software Maintenance, pp. 88–96. IEEE (2000)
6. Seemann, J.: Extending the Sugiyama algorithm for drawing UML class diagrams: Towards automatic layout of object-oriented software diagrams. In: DiBattista, G. (ed.) GD 1997. LNCS, vol. 1353, pp. 415–424. Springer, Heidelberg (1997). doi:10.1007/3-540-63938-1_86
7. Purchase, H.C., Allder, J.A., Carrington, D.: Graph layout aesthetics in UML diagrams: user preferences. J. Graph Algorithms Appl. **6**, 255–279 (2002)
8. Sugiyama, K., Tagawa, S., Toda, M.: Methods for visual understanding of hierarchical system structures. IEEE Trans. Syst. Man Cybern. **11**, 109–125 (1981)
9. Hu, H., Fang, J., Lu, Z., et al.: Rank-directed layout of UML class diagrams. In: Proceedings of of the First International Workshop on Software Mining. ACM (2012)
10. Maier, A.M., Stoerrle, H., Baltsen, N., et al.: On the impact of diagram layout: how are models actually read? In: Proceedings of the Joint Proceedings of MODELS 2014 Poster Session and the ACM Student Research Competition. ACM(2014)
11. Storrle, H.: On the impact of layout quality to understanding UML diagrams. In: Proceedings of the Visual Languages and Human-Centric Computing, pp. 135–142. IEEE (2011)
12. Ball, T., Eick, S.G.: Software visualization in the large. Computer **29**, 33–43 (1996)
13. Bassi, S., Keller, R.K.: Software visualization tools: survey and analysis. In: Proceedings of International Workshop on Program Comprehension, vol. 2, pp. 7–17 (2001)
14. Page, L., Brin, S., Motwani, R., et al.: The PageRank Citation Ranking: Bringing Order to the Web. Stanford InfoLab (1999)
15. Duan, Y., Cheung, S.C., Fu, X.: A metamodel based model transformation approach. In: Proceedings of the Acis International Conference on Software Engineering Research, Management and Applications, pp. 184–191. IEEE (2005)

Energy-Aware Composition for Service-Oriented Wireless Sensor Networks

Deng Zhao[1], Zhangbing Zhou[1,2($\boxtimes$)], Yucong Duan[3], and Patrick C.K. Hung[4]

[1] School of Information Engineering, China University of Geosciences, Beijing, China
zhangbing.zhou@gmail.com
[2] Computer Science Department, TELECOM SudParis, Évry, France
[3] College of Information Science and Technology, Hainan University, Hainan, China
[4] Faculty of Business and Information Technology, University of Ontario
Institute of Technology, Oshawa, Canada

Abstract. This article proposes a service-oriented wireless sensor networks (WSNs) framework. Sensor nodes are encapsulated and represented as WSN services, which are energy-limited, and typically spatial- and temporal-aware. Service classes chains are generated with respect to the requirement of domain applications, and the composition of WSN services is constructed through selecting appropriate WSN services as the instantiation of service classes contained in chains. This WSN services composition is reduced to a multi-objective and multi-constrained optimization problem, which can be solved through adopting particle swarm optimization (PSO) algorithm and genetic algorithm (GA).

1 Introduction

The Internet of Things (IoT) paradigm has envisioned and facilitated the interconnection and interoperation of *smart things* in a dynamic and pervasive environment [1]. Smart things typically serve as heterogenous sensor nodes and constitute wireless sensor networks (WSNs) for promoting domain applications. Due to the complexity, certain applications may require the collaboration of multiple sensor nodes. In this setting, the functional *composition* of heterogenous sensor nodes is a pressing and promising alternative, where the functionality of sensor nodes is usually encapsulated and represented in terms of a WSN service [5]. Different from traditional Web or REST services on the Internet, WSN services are usually spatial-temporal sensitive, and are mostly scarce in their energy, storage, and computational resources [7]. In this service-oriented WSNs, spatial-temporal-aware and energy-efficient techniques for the discovery and composition of WSN services are of importance.

Service discovery and composition is the long-standing research subject in the context of Web or REST services, and fruitful approaches have been proposed in recent years [3]. Generally, current approaches are promising and have inspired us when developing this technique. However, spatial and temporal-awareness and energy efficiency, which are core properties for WSN services, are not considered

© Springer International Publishing AG 2017
K. Drira et al. (Eds.): ICSOC 2016 Workshops, LNCS 10380, pp. 117–121, 2017.
https://doi.org/10.1007/978-3-319-68136-8_11

extensively, since they may *not* be relevant to traditional Web or REST services somehow. IoT resources can be encapsulated as IoT-based services, leveraging Device Profile for Web Services for instance [4], to accomplish complex tasks [5]. Generally, current approaches mainly examine the framework for the management and monitoring of IoT-resources composition, whereas the composition of IoT-based services is not explored extensively. Besides, service-oriented paradigm is adopted to promote the collaboration of sensor nodes [7] and mobile devices [2]. These approaches have explored the mobility, reliability, and spatial and temporal constraints, to the selection and composition of WSN services (or mobile devices). Usually, sensor nodes can have various functionalities, and a certain task may require the composition of heterogeneous sensor nodes. Given sensor nodes with a certain functionality, the selection of a certain sensor node should be remaining energy-aware, such that the network lifetime should be prolonged. We argue that connection-awareness and network-lifetime consideration should be important for the composition of WSN services, which has not been examined extensively at this moment, and should be explored further. To remedy this problem, this article proposes an energy-aware mechanism for promoting the composition of WSN services. Our contribution can be summarized as follows:

- A three-tier service-oriented framework is proposed, where (i) sensor nodes are encapsulated as WSN services, (ii) WSN services are categorized to service classes according to their functionalities, and (iii) service classes are composed for fulfilling the requirement of domain applications.
- Given a composition of service classes, WSN services are determined, when spatial- and temporal-constraints, and energy-efficiency, are considered. In fact, this can be reduced to the multi-objective and multi-constrained optimization problem, which can be solved through genetic or particle swarm optimization algorithms.

2   Service Classes Chaining and Recommendation

Before introducing the composing mechanism, we give a brief introduction of the concepts of WSN services. In this article sensor nodes are encapsulated and represented in terms of WSN services.

Definition 1 (WSN Service). *A WSN service sev_{sn} is a tuple (nm, dsc, op, eng, spt, tpr), where (i) nm is the name, (ii) dsc is the text description, (iii) op is an operation, (iv) eng is the remaining energy, (v) spt is the spatial constraint, and (vi) tpr is the temporal constraint, of this service.*

Generally, a sensor node may provide a single type of functionality. Therefore, a WSN service is assumed to have an operation, which is defined as follows:

Definition 2 (Operation). *An operation op is a tuple (nm, InP, OutP), where nm is the name, and InP (or OutP) is the set of input (or output) parameters, of this operation.*

Generally, a parameter can be defined by a string name, a type, and a text description. As aforementioned, service classes are abstracted from WSN services for supporting WSN services composition.

Definition 3 (Service Class). *A service class sev_{cl} for a certain WSN service sev_{sn} is a tuple (nm, dsc, op), where nm, dsc, and op are the same as that of sev_{sn}.*

Intuitively, a service class corresponds to a set of WSN services which share a certain functionality. The invocation possibility between service classes is investigated and represented in terms of a service network.

Definition 4 (Service Network). *A service network snSC is a directed graph, and represented as a tuple (SvC, Lnk, InvP), where SvC is the set of service classes, Lnk is the set of direct links that represent the invocation relationship between service classes, and InvP is the set of weights specified upon Lnk that represent the invocation possibility between service classes.*

As presented at [9], the construction of service network is mostly to calculate the invocation possibility between service classes, and to prune the links which reflects a low possibility. Specifically, the degree of similarity for two parameters is calculated through aggregating the degree of similarity for their names and text descriptions. The invocation possibility of two service classes is calculated through considering (i) the invocation possibility of their operations, and (ii) the degree of similarity for their names and text descriptions. After computing the invocation possibility for all pairs of service classes, and pruning these invocation possibility whose degree is smaller than thd_{pi}, a service network is constructed and represented as a directed graph, where the vertices correspond to service classes, and the weight specified upon directed links reflects the invocation possibility between service classes.

Leveraging the service network constructed, we propose the mechanism for the discovery and recommendation of service classes chains. We refer the reader to our previous work [9] for a detailed description about algorithms. Firstly, we determine the starting and ending service classes, and then candidate service classes chains are to be retrieved from the service network, which is performed through a graph depth-limited search algorithm with a pre-specified limitation on depth. These searched service classes chains (denoted CHN) are used for generating WSN services compositions in the following.

3   WSN Services Composition

After generating service classes chains (denote CHN) which can satisfy the requirement of domain application from the functional perspective, this section proposes to instantiate service classes chains as the composition of WSN services (denote $comp(chn)$), and to evaluate the applicability of these compositions, where the factors including spatial- and temporal-constraints, and energy-efficiency, are considered.

Generally, we propose to select the WSN services with higher spatial relevancy which provide sensory data for supporting application rq in longer time durations. The spatial relevancy (denote $spt(sev, rq)$) between a certain WSN service sev and rq can be specified by the overlap between these geographical location that are all represented by a disk. And the temporal relevancy (denote $tpr(sev, rq)$) is indicated by the overlap between the available time durations of sev and rq. On the other hand, we propose to minimize the energy consumption of the composition of WSN services $comp(chn)$. Generally, the energy consumption (denote $E(comp(chn))$) for the composition of WSN services $comp(chn)$ includes the following ingredients [8]: (i) Energy consumption for activating the instantiation of WSN services in $comp(chn)$, (ii) Energy consumption for the communication between WSN services through transmitting and receiving data packets. Besides, WSN services should be balanced for avoiding over-consumption of any single WSN service. Before instantiating a service class with a WSN service sev, sev should have enough residual energy (denoted $eng(sev_i)$) than required to be consumed (denoted $E_{cst}(sev_i)$) for implementing a certain task. A load-balancing factor (denote $lbf(comp(chn))$) of a certain WSN service composition $comp(chn)$ is specified by $eng(sev)$ and $E_{cst}(sev)$.

Given a service classes chain $chn \subset CHN$ in terms of the sequence $svC_1 \rightarrow \ldots \rightarrow svC_k$, a certain service class svC_i (where $i \in [1, k]$) may be implemented by a set of WSN services SEV_i. In this setting, discovering and selecting an appropriate WSN service from SEV_i as the instantiation of svC_i, while taking the constraints as specified above into account, is the challenge to be addressed. Intuitively, this challenge can be formulated as a multi-objective and multi-constrained optimization problem, which is formally represented as follows:

- Input Parameter Settings:
    1. $CHN = \{chn\}$: service classes chains as discovered and recommended at Sect. 2.
    2. $spt(sev, rq)$: spatial relevancy of sev with respect to application rq.
    3. $tpr(sev, rq)$: temporal relevancy of sev with respect to application rq.
    4. $E(comp(chn))$: energy consumption for a composition $comp(chn)$.
    5. $lbf(comp(chn))$: load-balancing factor of a composition $comp(chn)$.
- Output: WSN Services Composition:
    1. $comp(chn)$: the optimal WSN services composition with respect to CHN.
- Multi-Objective Functions:
    1. Minimize: $Z_{min} = \{E(comp(chn))\}$
    2. Maximize:
       $Z_{max} = \{\varphi \cdot lbf(comp(chn)) + \beta \cdot spt(comp(chn)) + \gamma \cdot tpr(comp(chn))\}$,
       where the factors φ, β, and γ are positive constant variables, and $\varphi + \beta + \gamma = 1$.
- Constraints: For each $sev_i \subset comp(chn)$ $(i \in [1, k])$, $eng(sev_i) \geq E_{cst}(sev_i)$.
- Fitness function: $fitness(comp(chn)) = w_{min} \cdot Z_{min} - w_{max} \cdot Z_{max} = w_{min} \cdot E(comp(comp(chn))) - w_{max} \cdot (\varphi \cdot lbf(comp(chn)) + \beta \cdot spt(comp(chn)) + \gamma \cdot tpr(comp(chn)))$, where w_{min} and w_{max} are objective weights representing the impact of Z_{min} and Z_{max}, respectively, and $w_{min} + w_{max} = 1$.

Generally, the fitness function measures the extent that a certain WSN services composition $comp(chn)$ can satisfy the objectives and constraints aforementioned, and an approximately optimal $comp(chn)$ is found when $fitness(comp(chn))$ is relatively small in value.

To solve this multi-objective and multi-constrained optimization problem, two evolutionary algorithms, namely particle swarm optimization and genetic algorithm [6], are adopted in this article, and readers can refer to relevant works for their procedure. Through adopting PSO and GA techniques, an approximately optimal $comp(chn)$ can be found with respect to CHN.

4   Conclusion

In this paper, a 3-tier service-oriented wireless sensor networks (WSNs) framework has been proposed, where sensor nodes are encapsulated as WSN services, and these WSN services are abstracted into service classes according to their functionalities. Consequently, the cooperation of sensor nodes is reduced to the discovery of service classes chains, which can be solved through current services composition approaches. The composition of WSN services is archived through discovering appropriate WSN services as the instantiation of each service class. This problem can be reduced to a multi-objective and multi-constrained optimization problem, which can be solved through adopting particle swarm optimization (PSO) algorithm and genetic algorithm (GA).

References

1. Botta, A., de Donato, W., Persico, V., Pescape, A.: Integration of cloud computing and internet of things: a survey. Future Gener. Comput. Syst. **56**, 684–700 (2016)
2. Deng, S., Huang, L., Hu, D., Zhao, J.L., Wu, Z.: Mobility-enabled service selection for composite services. IEEE Trans. Serv. Comput. **9**(3), 394–407 (2016)
3. Garriga, M., Mateos, C., Flores, A., Cechich, A., Zunino, A.: RESTful service composition at a glance: a survey. J. Netw. Comput. Appl. **60**, 32–53 (2016)
4. Han, S.N., Park, S., Lee, G.M., Crespi, N.: Extending the devices profile for web services standard using a REST proxy. IEEE Internet Comput. **19**(1), 10–17 (2015)
5. Ko, I.Y., Ko, H.G., Molina, A.J., Kwon, J.H.: SoIoT: toward a user-centric IoT-based service framework. ACM Trans. Internet Technol. **16**(2), 8 (2016)
6. Mohammad, A.A., Sohrab, Z., Ali, L., Ali, E., Ioannis, C.: Reservoir permeability prediction by neural networks combined with hybrid genetic algorithm and particle swarm optimization. Geophys. Prospect. **61**(3), 582–598 (2013)
7. Shah, S.Y., Szymanski, B.K., Zerfos, P., Gibson, C.: Towards relevancy aware service oriented systems in WSNs. IEEE Trans. Serv. Comput. **9**(2), 304–316 (2016)
8. Wang, T., Cheng, L., Zhang, K., Liu, J.: Energy-aware service composition algorithms for service-oriented heterogeneous wireless sensor networks. Int. J. Distrib. Sens. Netw. **10**, 217102 (2014)
9. Zhou, Z., Cheng, Z., Ning, K., Li, W., Zhang, L.J.: A sub-chain ranking and recommendation mechanism for facilitating geospatial web service composition. Int. J. Web Serv. Res. **11**(3), 52–75 (2014)

PhD Symposium

Introduction to the PhD Symposium Track

Yan Wang[1], Yuhong Yan[2], and François Charoy[3]

[1] Macquarie University, Sydney, Australia
[2] Concordia University, Montreal, Canada
[3] University of Lorraine, Nancy, France

1   Preface

This volume is the proceeding of the International PhD Symposium on Service Computing that was held in conjunction with the 14th International Conference on Service Oriented Computing (ICSOC 2016) on October 10–13, 2016 in Banff, Alberta, Canada.

The ICSOC PhD Symposium 2016 is an international forum for PhD students working in all the areas related to the service computing. Its goals are: (1) to bring together PhD students and established researchers in the field of service oriented computing, (2) to give PhD students the opportunity to present and discuss their research in a constructive and critical atmosphere, and (3) to stimulate an exchange of ideas and experiences among participants.

After a thorough review process of each submission by the program committee members, six papers out of 9 were accepted to constitute the program of the PhD symposium.

We gratefully acknowledge the support of the contributors to this PhD symposium. We express our great esteem first, to the program committee members for the time and effort they have put in reviewing papers, and second to the organizing committee of ICSOC 2016 for assisting us throughout the running of the PhD symposium.

2   Organization

PhD Symposium Chairs

Yan Wang   Macquarie University, Australia
Yuhong Yan   Concordia University, Canada
François Charoy   University of Lorraine, France

Program Committee

Hoa Khanh Dam   University of Wollongong, Australia
Marlon Dumas   University of Tartu, Estonia
Massimo Mecella   SAPIENZA Università di Roma, Italy
Stefanie Rinderle-Ma   University of Vienna, Austria
Gustavo Rossi   UNLP, Argentina
George Spanoudakis   City University London, UK
Mathias Weske   HPI/University of Potsdam, Germany
Xiwei Xu   NICTA, Australia

Searching the Web of Things:
Resolving a Real Library of Babel

Nguyen Khoi Tran[✉]

School of Computer Science, The University of Adelaide, Adelaide, SA 5005, Australia
nguyen.tran@adelaide.edu.au

Abstract. The advancement on embedded computing and low-power communication technologies allows more physical entities to participate in the Web of Things (WoT) and provide a massive range of resources, covering everything from information to interaction with the physical world. These resources are rapidly turning WoT into a real "Library of Babel" - an infinite library that holds all available information. My PhD research project focuses on making sense of this "infinite library" through developing services that provide the capability to discover and search for WoT resources. I propose to architect the WoT search engine as a Web service, which is composed from a set of interchangeable component services for maximal flexibility. I also present my research questions and three planned evaluation methods.

1 Introduction

In the Web of Things (WoT), real-world entities and services are presented as Web resources accessible through RESTful API [3,8]. This accelerating integration of physical and digital entities enables a whole new class of application and services, along with a whole range of new challenges [7].

We use the term "entity" and "resource" to denote a real-world, Web-enabled entity and the plethora of contents that it provides, respectively. Applications in WoT are built by utilizing and combining these resources. While the current progress of the field suggests that WoT is realized by providing HTML interfaces to the physical entities for interaction with human users, I believe that the future of WoT will see entities represented as Web services to facilitate their interaction with software applications and with each other. To utilize this WoT, the ability to discover and search for the relevant WoT resources are crucial. Some existing projects have addressed this problem from some specific perspectives. However, they did not consider the big picture of the problem of searching WoT nor the possibility of expanding the solution to support other perspectives.

My PhD project aims to address this problem. In this article, I describe my motivation to solve this problem and present my model of WoT search problem. I also present my proposed WoT search engine architecture and the prominent research questions that I aim to address in my project.

N.K. Tran—Supervisors: Professor Michael Sheng, The University of Adelaide, Adelaide, Australia; Dr. Lina Yao, UNSW, Sydney, Australia.

© Springer International Publishing AG 2017
K. Drira et al. (Eds.): ICSOC 2016 Workshops, LNCS 10380, pp. 127–132, 2017.
https://doi.org/10.1007/978-3-319-68136-8_12

2   Motivation

The Library of Babel, conceived in the short story of the same name by the Argentine author and librarian Jorge Luis Borges, is a universe taking the form of an infinite library containing all variations of a $1,320,000$-character string. By holding all of these variations, it has a book for every possible problem and solution in the universe. However, because the number of books in this Library is so massive that the number of digits required to write it down (approx. $10^{2000000}$) is even more than number of atoms in the observable universe (approx. 10^{80}), the knowledge of this Library is completely inaccessible to its dwellers who does not have any mechanism to organize and search the Library.

As the vision of WoT becomes reality, the Web will soon approach a "real Library of Babel" that holds information of a substantial part of the world. The capability to discover and search the WoT, provided by WoT search engines would be crucial for us - the dwellers of this infinite library. With WoT search engines, human users would be able to discover and access relevant WoT resources directly instead of having to maintain and check a list of URIs pointing to entities to find the needed resources. WoT search engines can also support WoT applications to compose themselves from WoT resources and services dynamically in real-time.

Scale and diversity are two major challenges in designing a WoT search engine. With expected 50–100 billion physical objects connected by 2020 [12], which generates orders of magnitude resources, the scale of WoT can potentially challenge the existing organization of Web search engines that revolves around a few large computer clusters managed by a few major parties. Diversity is the more challenging problem. At the Web level, the fundamental form of diversity would be the types of content that are provided as resources by physical entities. Each type of content, from sensor readings to functionalities, has different representation on the Web and requires different mechanisms to discover and search. Therefore, WoT search engines that utilize different types of contents to resolve user queries can be very different from each other. An ideal design must be able to adapt to all combinations of contents utilized in query resolution.

3   A Model for Searching WoT

To cope with the diversity of the problem, I propose a graph structure called Entity-Resource graph. Two main types of nodes in this graph are entities and resources. An entity in our model can be either a physical object or a digital entity (e.g., Website) that provides resources. A resource is a uniquely identified content, such as a stream of sensor readings or a functionality, provided on WoT by an entity. An edge in our model connects a resource to its hosting entity. Figure 1 illustrates a toy example of Entity-Resource graph its interaction with a simple WoT search engine that searches for event records of an entity having ID matching the query.

This model can be further expanded by introducing additional nodes and edges that represent humans and geo-locations. These latent relations between

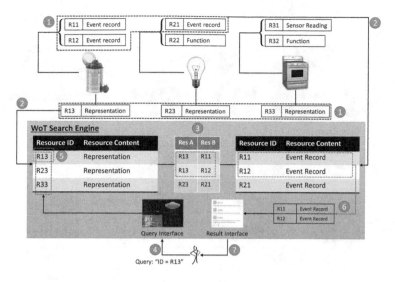

Fig. 1. An instance of Entity-Resource graph and the major activities carried by a WoT search engine in the query resolution process

human, places and things have been utilized in things recommendation [10]; thus I expect their intriguing applications in discovery and search problem.

The process carried out by WoT search engines on the Entity-Resource graph consists of two major phases:

1. Discovery: search engine utilizes the graph as a guide to detect (1) and gather available resources of the required type into a set of resource collections (2). Resources that are used to match with user queries are called Query Resources, while resources that are used for deriving search results are called Result Resources. Relations between collected resources are also recorded (3).
2. Search: search process is a traversal of the Entity-Resource graph from the query resources to the result resources. Search engine receives the query from a user (4) and matches it against the collected query resources (5). The matching resources are used to find the corresponding result resources to build a ranked list of search results (6) and return to the search user (7).

Flexibility and expandability is the key aspects of our model. By changing the starting point and ending point of search process on the Entity-Resource graph (i.e., changing type of query and result resources) and modifying the implementation accordingly, while keeping the set of activities carried out by the WoT search engine invariant, my model can describe a wide range of WoT search engines. Moreover, my graph model can be expanded with nodes representing humans and geo-locations to enable more complex form of search engines.

By modeling the identified invariant activities as loosely coupled, interchangeable Web services and organizing them in a layered architecture, I build an architecture for WoT search engines. Figure 2 provides an overview of my architecture. The bottom two layers carry out discovery activities, while the top two

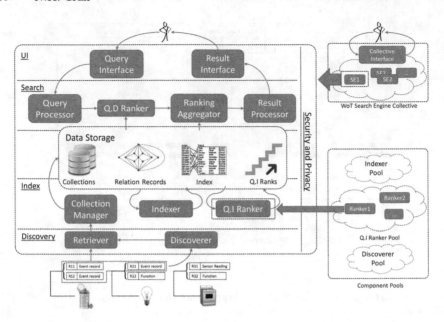

Fig. 2. Layered architecture of a WoT Search Engine and two mechanisms to address the problem of diversity and scale

layers handle search activities and the vertical layer provides security and privacy measures for the whole system. Due to the construction from loosely coupled, interchangeable Web services, my architecture allows WoT search engines to be composed from components that are designed to work with different types of resources. Moreover, the entire WoT search engine can be encapsulated as a Web service and integrated into a collective to further expand its scalability.

4   Real-Time WoT Search

My PhD project focuses on resolving queries for WoT resources using the real-time, real-world information provided by Web-enabled entities. For instance, my search engine will be able to find an available meeting room, a free parking spot using the information from WoT. Queries on real-time state or real-world entities can be resolved either by "pushing" the request to the sensors or "pulling" the sensor readings to a local device and assessing [6]. Alternatively, a proxy can be deployed to collect sensor readings periodically and resolve the query with the cached data. This approach negates the requirement for both client and sensors to know each other a priori and negates the processing stress on sensors. It also fits our WoT search engine model naturally.

The main challenge of building a real-time WoT search engine is ensuring that the cached information for query resolution is up-to-date. As the update rates of Web-enabled sensors vastly out-pace majority of Web pages, the traditional indexes utilized by Web search engines are not sufficient. The most closely related solution in the literature [6] ranks sensors by their probability of being in the required state, and then pulling each ranked sensor to validate the prediction before reporting to users. Given that the time required to contact sensors (i.e., reaching infinity) can be orders of magnitude more than the time required to resolve query locally, my main concern is eliminating or minimizing this network utilization time. My research questions are:

- Finding an optimal caching scheme that minimizes sensor pulls while ensuring that cached data is up-to-date.
- Making reliable prediction of sensor readings based on cached data to negate the need of sensor pulls for confirmation.

I will investigate these questions from two starting observations. First, the refresh rate and the rate of change of sensor readings vary between sensors. For instance, a camera sensor can capture a new image every thirtieth of a second, while a weather station might refresh every day. Moreover, majority of images from a camera sensor in a closed warehouse might be identical. Second, the state of a sensor might be derived from its nearby sensors. These observations might be used to build models to optimize the refresh rate of the search engine and predict the current readings of a sensor.

I plan three forms of evaluations in my project. First, I utilize simulation with synthetic dataset to evaluate the robustness and accuracy of my solution when working with massive datasets that are unobtainable in current public WoT data. Second, I utilize real-world data extracted from WoT data sources, such as live-maps, to evaluate the computing efficiency and response of my solution. Finally, I deploy my solution on a locally deployed test-bed to assess its operation in local-scope, where many intriguing WoT applications are deployed.

5   Related Works

Discovery and search in WoT have been mentioned as key research problems since early works on WoT [3,8]. Early efforts on this topic focus on locating a physical object by matching their embedded ID code or textual description with the user query [4,9,11]. Discovery Service concept, which denotes systems that utilize the unique identity of a physical entity to search for its logistical history [2], is also closely related to my topic. Some research groups focus on functionality, hosted by physical entities as Web services, instead of information from physical world [1,5]. Dyser search engine [6] is a rare system that utilizes the real-time state reported by WoT to search for real-world entities. This work, while targeting the same goal, is different from my project in two major points: (i) Dyser relies on the assumption that sensors reflect the periodic nature of human; and (ii) Dyser utilizes sensor pulls to validate every search result. Moreover, all of existing projects approach the problem from only a specific perspective without considering the diversity and the big picture of the problem.

6   Conclusion

Discovery and searching are crucial to utilize the "real Library of Babel" - WoT. In this paper, I present a model for WoT search engines that emphasizes on the diversity of WoT contents, as the result of the first year of my PhD study. In the rest of my PhD work, I will focus on resolving the query with the real-time, real-world information reported by WoT. This solution will lay a foundation for a plethora of novel WoT applications and services.

References

1. Christophe, B., Verdot, V., Toubiana, V.: Searching the 'Web of Things'. In: Proceedings of the Fifth IEEE International Conference on Semantic Computing (ICSC), pp. 308–315. IEEE (2011)
2. Evdokimov, S., Fabian, B., Kunz, S., Schoenemann, N.: Comparison of discovery service architectures for the internet of things. In: Proceedings of the 2010 IEEE International Conference on Sensor Networks, Ubiquitous, and Trustworthy Computing (SUTC), pp. 237–244. IEEE (2010)
3. Guinard, D., Trifa, V., Mattern, F., Wilde, E.: From the internet of things to the web of things: resource-oriented architecture and best practices. In: Uckelmann, D., Harrison, M., Michahelles, F. (eds.) Architecting the Internet of Things, pp. 97–129. Springer, Heidelberg (2011). doi:10.1007/978-3-642-19157-2_5
4. Komatsuzaki, M., Tsukada, K., Siio, I., Verronen, P., Luimula, M., Pieskä, S.: IteMinder: finding items in a room using passive RFID tags and an autonomous robot (poster). In: Proceedings of the 13th International Conference on Ubiquitous Computing, pp. 599–600. ACM (2011)
5. Mrissa, M., Médini, L., Jamont, J.P.: Semantic discovery and invocation of functionalities for the web of things. In: 2014 IEEE 23rd International WETICE Conference (WETICE), pp. 281–286. IEEE (2014)
6. Ostermaier, B., Romer, K., Mattern, F., Fahrmair, M., Kellerer, W.: A real-time search engine for the web of things. In: Internet of Things (IOT), pp. 1–8. IEEE (2010)
7. Qin, Y., Sheng, Q.Z., Falkner, N.J., Dustdar, S., Wang, H., Vasilakos, A.V.: When things matter: a survey on data-centric internet of things. J. Netw. Comput. Appl. **64**, 137–153 (2016)
8. Stirbu, V.: Towards a restful plug and play experience in the web of things. In: Proceedings of the IEEE International Conference on Semantic computing, pp. 512–517. IEEE (2008)
9. Wang, H., Tan, C.C., Li, Q.: Snoogle: a search engine for pervasive environments. IEEE Trans. Parallel Distrib. Syst. **21**(8), 1188–1202 (2010)
10. Yao, L., Sheng, Q.Z., Ngu, A.H., Li, X.: Things of interest recommendation by leveraging heterogeneous relations in the internet of things. ACM Trans. Internet Technol. (TOIT) **16**(2), 9 (2016)
11. Yap, K.K., Srinivasan, V., Motani, M.: MAX: human-centric search of the physical world. In: Proceedings of the 3rd International Conference on Embedded Networked Sensor Systems, pp. 166–179. ACM (2005)
12. Zaslavsky, A., Perera, C., Georgakopoulos, D.: Sensing as a service and big data. arXiv preprint (2013). arXiv:1301.0159

A Migration Approach for Cloud Service Composition

Jing Li[✉]

Deptartment of Computer Science and Software Engineering,
Concordia University, Montreal, Canada
jing.li.hnu@gmail.com

Abstract. Service-oriented computing offers an attractive platform for the provisioning of existing resources without investing in new infrastructure. Providers who expect to benefit from the web may bring explosive number of web services. As a result, time and space required to find a solution may be insufferable. To alleviate this problem, we propose to solve service composition problem with a database. In our previous work, we have proposed a relational database-based approach for automated service composition. We want to utilize existing resources on clouds. NoSQL databases are suitable for using as cloud data management systems. However, it is challenging to migrate relational databases to highly scalable NoSQL databases on clouds. The objective of this research project is to extend our work to cloud service composition.

Keywords: Cloud computing · Web service composition · QoS

1 Introduction

Service composition involves multiple web services in a business process now get more and more important. In general, given a user's business request and goal, the web service composition (WSC) problem is to combine different services to meet user's complex requirement. With the increasing number of web services, providers now offer candidate services with different Quality of Service (QoS) levels. QoS-aware service composition refers to composition which achieves desired functionality as well as optimizes QoS values. QoS-aware service composition can be formulated as single-objective [9, 14] as well as multiple-objective [3] optimization problem.

In our previous work, we proposed a database-based approach named FSIDB (Full Solution Indexing Using Database) to solve service composition problem [8]. In this approach, we firstly generate all possible service combinations and store them in a relational database. When a user request comes, the system composes SQL queries to search in the database and rank solutions according to their QoS values. K best solutions are returned to the user which provide backup solutions.

J. Li–Supervised by Dr. Yuhong Yan and Dr. Daniel Lemire.

© Springer International Publishing AG 2017
K. Drira et al. (Eds.): ICSOC 2016 Workshops, LNCS 10380, pp. 133–138, 2017.
https://doi.org/10.1007/978-3-319-68136-8_13

As the next step, we would like to utilize existing resources on clouds to solve the problem. Moving to clouds may also extend the scalability of the proposed system.

Nowadays, many cloud computing providers offer cloud services, e.g. Windows, Oracle, Amazon, Google. Cloud computing has emerged as a compelling paradigm where infrastructure and solutions are provided as services. Cloud computing attracts users because it provides real-time scalable resources and eases resource management. We want to solve cloud composition problem and utilize the existing resources on clouds. However, relational database is not suitable for clouds as it is designed to run on a single node in a single location. NoSQL database is suitable for using as cloud data management systems. Compared with relational database, an attractive feature of NoSQL database is: we may add records in NoSQL on the fly. Yet, we need to overcome several difficulties. First of all, the join operator is avoided from NoSQL database for high performance. However, in our FSIDB approach, we use join operator to lookup satisfying paths. One possible solution is to duplicate the same data in NoSQL database. Second, since relational database is no longer suitable to cloud environment, we need to migrate it to NoSQL database. Last but not least, we need to take care of the security problem arises from sharing resources. In this paper, we propose an approach to migrate relational database to NoSQL database. If we are able to verify the correctness and feasibility, then we can implement our approach and test the performance.

The rest of this paper is organized as follows. Section 2 describes preliminary knowledge and provides the background of our research. Based on a running example, we sketch our approach in Sect. 3. We then review related work in Sect. 4. Finally, in Sect. 5, we draw the conclusion.

2   Preliminary

A web service w is defined as a tuple with the following components:

- w_{in} is a finite set of typed input parameters of w. A web service is invoked only when all its input parameters are satisfied.
- w_{out} is a finite set of typed output parameters of w. We refer to the input and output types as *concepts*. OWL-S (Web Ontology Language for Web Services [1]) files are used to define relationships between services and concepts.
- Q is a finite set of QoS of w. The criteria for QoS are determined from users' constraints and preferences. Following [2] and [15], we use response time and throughput to measure the QoS value of a service. Response time in a data system is the interval between the arrival of the request and the beginning of delivery the response (unit: milliseconds). Throughput is the average rate of successful message delivered per time unit over a communication channel (unit: requests/min).

Service composition is the generation of a business process which fulfills business tasks that cannot be finished by individual services. A web service composition problem can be represented by a tuple with the following components:

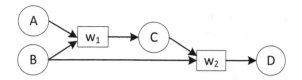

Fig. 1. A path example

- S is a finite set of services.
- C_{in} is a finite set of typed input parameters.
- C_{out} is a finite set of typed output parameters.
- Q is a finite set of quality criteria.

We say that we have a QoS-aware service composition problem if the problem should satisfy both the functional requirements and the QoS constraints. Two services can be connected if the input of a service is a subset of the output of the other service. This semantic model is consistent with many existing service composition methods, e.g., [6,10,13]

Definition 1. *A Cloud service base* $C = \{sf_k | 1 \leq k \leq m\}$ *is a set of service files and* sf_k *is a service file published by a provider.*

Definition 2. *A path is a layered graph defined as a tuple with the following components:*

$path_{\text{in}} = \{\underset{k=1}{\overset{l}{\cup}} \{w_{i.in} | w_i \in W_k\}\} - \{\underset{k=1}{\overset{l}{\cup}} \{w_{j.out} | w_j \in W_k\}\}$ *is a finite set of typed input parameters.*

$SL = \{W_k | k = 1 : l\}$ *is a set of service layers and* l *is the number of layers in the path. For each service in a layer, the input parameters are provided by either inputs of the path or the outputs of preceding layers.*

$path_{\text{out}} = \{\underset{k=1}{\overset{l}{\cup}} \{w_{i.out} | w_i \in W_k\}\}$ *is a finite set of typed output parameters.*

Q *is a finite set of quality criteria.*

Figure 1 is an example of a layered graph to represent the connection of services. We use circles to represent parameters and use rectangles to represent services. If a parameter is an input or output of a service, there is an edge between them. As mentioned in Sect. 2, we use semantic model to match services. Since the output C of service w_1 is an input of w_2, w_1 is an input service of w_2. Three paths can be found in Fig. 1 and are listed in Table 1.

Table 1. Paths in Fig. 1

ID	$path_{\text{in}}$	SL	$path_{\text{out}}$
1	A, B	$\{w_1\}$	C
2	B, C	$\{w_2\}$	D
3	A, B	$\{\{w_1\}, \{w_2\}\}$	C, D

A service composition problem is solvable if we can find a path satisfying:
$\{C_{in} \supseteq path_{in}\} \cup \{C_{out} \subseteq path_{out}\}$.

3 Proposal

An overall cloud service composition structure is illustrated in Fig. 2. "Web Service Repository" stores registered services published by service providers. It contains services' information such as name, input, output parameters and QoS values. When a user specifies his composition requirement, "Request Description" module analyzes user's requirement. After that, a path query is generated and used to query the cloud. Possible service combinations are generated and delivered to the "Composition Convertor" module, then a user readable solution is returned to the user.

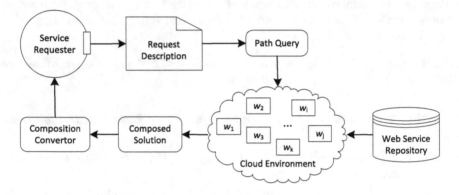

Fig. 2. Service composition in Cloud environment.

We use two tables to represent paths in Table 1 with a relational database. Path table stores the path id, inputs and outputs of the path (Table 2). The sequences of services in the paths are stated in Table 3. Our goal is to propose a method which represents paths in NoSQL database and solves cloud service composition problem.

<table>
<tr><td colspan="3">Table 2. Path</td></tr>
<tr><td>pathID</td><td>c_in</td><td>c_out</td></tr>
<tr><td>1</td><td>A, B</td><td>C</td></tr>
<tr><td>2</td><td>B, C</td><td>D</td></tr>
<tr><td>3</td><td>A, B</td><td>C, D</td></tr>
</table>

<table>
<tr><td colspan="3">Table 3. UsedService</td></tr>
<tr><td>pathID</td><td>layer</td><td>ws_name</td></tr>
<tr><td>1</td><td>1</td><td>w_1</td></tr>
<tr><td>2</td><td>1</td><td>w_2</td></tr>
<tr><td>3</td><td>1</td><td>w_1</td></tr>
<tr><td>3</td><td>2</td><td>w_2</td></tr>
</table>

We would like to migrate above two tables in a relational database to a domain D in a NoSQL database. We choose to store data in the form of key-value pairs. Each item in the database is stored as an attribute name (key) with its value. Table 4 shows how it works: a new domain "do_path" is created and the data in Tables 2 and 3 are migrated in this domain. After verifying the feasibility of this migration method, we may apply it to cloud service composition.

Table 4. Domain "do_path"

(path,2417)	(pathID,1)	(c_in,$\{A, B\}$)	(c_out,C)	(layer,1)	(ws_name,w_1)
(path,6317)	(pathID,2)	(c_in,$\{B, C\}$)	(c_out,D)	(layer,1)	(ws_name,w_2)
(path,7788)	(pathID,3)	(c_in,$\{A, B\}$)	(c_out,$\{C, D\}$)	(layer,$\{1,2\}$)	(ws_name,$\{w_1,w_2\}$)

4   Related Work

Nowadays, cloud has become a prominent platform to provide web services. Service composition approaches were first applied in cloud systems in 2009 [7,17]. After using a database to store single and composed services, a SMA algorithm is used to search matched services in the database, and a Fast-EP algorithm is used to find composition solutions [17]. Zou *et al.* studies service composition problem in multiple clouds environment [18]. Three different AI planning combination methods are presented to find composition plans. Pandey *et al.* present a high-level architectural of a Workflow Management System (WfMS) which uses cloud resources to drive workflow application [11]. Ye *et al.* utilize Bayesian Network to represent the economic model of users and model the composition problem as an Influence Diagram problem [16]. Dou *et al.,* present a privacy-aware cross-cloud service composition method [4]. In this method, they use k-means clustering algorithm to select representative history records. Besides, a tree mechanism is recruited to specify service composition context. The proposed method protects the privacy of a cloud service as well as speed up calculation of a near optimal composition solution. More researches of cloud service composition can be found in [5,12].

5   Conclusion and Future Work

The objective of this paper is to solve cloud service composition problem with NoSQL databases. Previous, we have presented an approach to solve service composition problem with a relational database. In this paper, We propose to migrate relational database to NoSQL database. If we are able to verify the correctness and feasibility, we may apply this migration method to solve cloud service composition problem. Expected benefits include decreased runtime and increased scalability. In future work, we plan to formalize and implement our proposed algorithms, and test the performance of this approach with a challenging data set.

References

1. Web ontology language for web services. http://www.w3.org/submission/owl-s/
2. Web service challenge rules (2009). http://ws-challenge.georgetown.edu/wsc09/downloads/WSC2009Rules-1.1.pdf
3. Cui, L., Kumara, S., Lee, D.: Scenario analysis of web service composition based on multi-criteria mathematical goal programming. Serv. Sci. **3**(4), 280–303 (2011)
4. Dou, W., Zhang, X., Liu, J., Chen, J.: Hiresome-ii: towards privacy-aware cross-cloud service composition for big data applications. IEEE Trans. Parallel Distrib. Syst. **26**(2), 455–466 (2015)
5. He, W., Xu, L.: A state-of-the-art survey of cloud manufacturing. Int. J. Comput. Integr. Manuf. **28**(3), 239–250 (2015)
6. Jiang, W., Zhang, C., Huang, Z., Chen, M., Hu, S., Liu, Z.: Qsynth: a tool for QoS-aware automatic service composition. In: 2010 IEEE International Conference on Web Services (ICWS), pp. 42–49, July 2010
7. Kofler, K., ul Haq, I., Schikuta, E.: A parallel branch and bound algorithm for workflow QoS optimization. In: International Conference on Parallel Processing. ICPP 2009, pp. 478–485, September 2009
8. Li, J., Yan, Y., Lemire, D.: Full solution indexing for top-k web service composition. IEEE Trans. Serv. Comput. **PP**(99), 1–13 (2016)
9. Li, J., Yan, Y., Lemire, D.: Full solution indexing using database for QOS-aware web service composition. In: 2014 IEEE 11th International Conference on Services Computing (SCC), pp. 99–106, June 2014
10. Li, J., Yan, Y., Lemire, D.: A web service composition method based on compact k2-trees. In: 2015 IEEE International Conference on Services Computing (SCC), pp. 403–410 (2015)
11. Pandey, S., Karunamoorthy, D., Buyya, R.: Workflow engine for clouds. In: Cloud Computing: Principles and Paradigms, pp. 321–344 (2011)
12. Rimal, B.P., Choi, E., Lumb, I.: A taxonomy and survey of cloud computing systems. In: INC, IMS and IDC, pp. 44–51 (2009)
13. Rodriguez-Mier, P., Mucientes, M., Lama, M.: A dynamic QoS-aware semantic web service composition algorithm. In: Liu, C., Ludwig, H., Toumani, F., Yu, Q. (eds.) ICSOC 2012. LNCS, vol. 7636, pp. 623–630. Springer, Heidelberg (2012). doi:10.1007/978-3-642-34321-6_48
14. Yan, Y., Chen, M.: Anytime QoS-aware service composition over the GraphPlan. SOCA **9**(1), 1–19 (2015). doi:10.1007/s11761-013-0134-6
15. Yan, Y., Chen, M., Yang, Y.: Anytime QoS optimization over the plangraph for web service composition. In: Proceedings of the 27th Annual ACM Symposium on Applied Computing. SAC 2012, pp. 1968–1975. ACM (2012)
16. Ye, Z., Bouguettaya, A., Zhou, X.: QoS-aware cloud service composition based on economic models. In: Liu, C., Ludwig, H., Toumani, F., Yu, Q. (eds.) ICSOC 2012. LNCS, vol. 7636, pp. 111–126. Springer, Heidelberg (2012). doi:10.1007/978-3-642-34321-6_8
17. Zeng, C., Guo, X., Ou, W., Han, D.: Cloud computing service composition and search based on semantic. In: Jaatun, M.G., Zhao, G., Rong, C. (eds.) CloudCom 2009. LNCS, vol. 5931, pp. 290–300. Springer, Heidelberg (2009). doi:10.1007/978-3-642-10665-1_26
18. Zou, G., Chen, Y., Xiang, Y., Huang, R., Xu, Y.: AI planning and combinatorial optimization for web service composition in cloud computing. In: Proceedings of the International Conference on Cloud Computing and Virtualization. CCV Conference 2010, pp. 28–35 (2010)

Towards Quality Guided Data Integration on Multi-cloud Settings

Daniel A.S. Carvalho[(⊠)]

Université Jean Moulin Lyon 3, Centre de Recherche Magellan,
IAE, Lyon, France
`daniel.carvalho@univ-lyon3.fr`

Abstract. This PhD project addresses data integration considering data quality (freshness, provenance, cost, availability) properties in a multi-cloud context. In fact, in a multi-cloud context, data is made available through a huge offer of services deployed on different clouds with heterogeneous quality of service features. By users who thank to their contracts with the clouds expressed by traditional SLA according to their rights. Consequently, data integration in this context needs to take into account these new constraints. The aim of our work is to revisit previously proposed data integration solutions in order to adapt them to the multi-cloud context. Our solution consists in defining over the clouds a layer that provides a reasoning on the best services combination that meets services and user constraints and willings, the best way to deploy the integration process. This layer should let further data integration easier thank to the definition of a new kind of SLA called *Integration SLA*. This paper gives a model-oriented vision of our proposal.

Keywords: Data integration · Query rewriting algorithm · Cloud computing · SLA

1 Introduction

Our work addresses data integration considering data quality properties (freshness, provenance, cost, availability) and service level agreements (SLA). Existing approaches - guided by heterogeneous data structures and formats, semantics and integrity constraints - have already tackled quality issues. Furthermore, this work explicitly considers infrastructure properties (reliability, computing, storage and memory capacity, and cost) imposed by the multi-cloud context and data providers quality to guide the integration process. In this new context, existing solutions are not sufficient as they need an infrastructure over the clouds that (*i*) allow services to express quality aspects; (*ii*) integration solutions to take into account the huge service offer and the multi-cloud paradigm constraints/advantages; and (*ii*) an intelligent entity to decide which services to select, where and

D.A.S. Carvalho—(Supervised by Chirine Ghedira-Guegan, Genoveva Vargas-Solar and Nadia Bennani, with inputs from Plácido A. Souza Neto).

© Springer International Publishing AG 2017
K. Drira et al. (Eds.): ICSOC 2016 Workshops, LNCS 10380, pp. 139–144, 2017.
https://doi.org/10.1007/978-3-319-68136-8_14

in which conditions further integration demands could be treated using the past integration experience. The objective is to customize data providers (services) look up and the data integration considering different data consumers requirements and expectations depending on the context in which they consume data (e.g., mobile devices with few physical capacities, critical decision making). Our work relies on two assumptions: (1) the data integration process is totally or partially externalized on different clouds that provide necessary resources under different conditions (SLA); (2) data can be retrieved from several data providers (i.e., services) with different quality properties.

Let us suppose that during Brazilian Olympic games in 2016, Lucas wants to know two days in advance the weather forecast near his location to make decisions about the events he wants to attend. According to the weather, OGApp is an application that proposes possible matches in different stadiums with available seats (sunny seats or not, in the middle or in the sides, and on the side of a specific team). Lucas has several preferences regarding privacy (i.e. he wants his personal data to be anonymous), time, schedule, budget, cost (e.g., using free data services or not). Several data provision and computing services can be composed by OGApp to integrate data that can help Lucas to make his decision. Furthermore, since Lucas often looks for data in his mobile devices he is subscribed to several clouds to externalize "costly" processes (e.g., storage of retrieved data, correlation and aggregation of data coming from different providers, data transmission on 3G). OGApp will rely on the clouds to perform the integration process for Lucas respecting his preferences and the conditions of his subscriptions in the clouds. Suppose now that later Geraldine asks for the same result as Lucas but her constraint is to obtain the results with a minimum cost. Using Lucas' previous integration plan, the OGApp could be able to answer partially her query. Consequently, the same integration plan could be replayed. Thus, the data integration process becomes a combinatorial problem where a query result is a data collection integrated by composing different data providers and data processing (cloud) services that fulfill quality constraints and SLAs specified by a data consumer. Given a user query, the integration process deals with different matching problems: (i) matching the *query* and *data provider services* - the data provider services should be able to produce a (complete or partial) result for the query; (ii) matching the *user preferences* and the *quality guarantees* provided by the data provider (iii) matching the *user preferences* and *user's type of subscriptions* - the user may have several subscriptions with different clouds that should influence the way to choose the services according to the cloud resources offered thank to user subscription; and (iv) the *data provider services* and *their type of subscriptions* - the data provider services also have subscription with the clouds, and this imposes to adapt the way the service is delivered according to the resources to which it has access.

We assume the quality conditions that the user can expect from a service are defined in service level agreements (SLA). In our context, we need to identify which SLAs measures apply to the data integration process and how they should be taken into consideration for providing a final result that fulfills data consumers requirements.

This PhD project proposes an approach for data integration guided by quality and SLAs partially or totally performed over a multi-cloud settings. The originality of our approach consists in guiding and personalizing the entire data integration process - while selecting, filtering and composing cloud services, and delivering the results - taking into account (*a*) user preferences statements; (*b*) SLAs exported by different cloud providers; and (*c*) QoS measures associated to data collections (for instance, trust, privacy, economic cost).

The reminder of this paper is organized as follows. Section 2 discusses the related works. Section 3 gives an overview of our SLA-based data integration approach. Section 4 describes the research plan, and Sect. 5 concludes the paper.

2   Related Works

Related works rely on four topics: (*i*) data integration and data quality in the database domain; (*ii*) data integration approaches in the cloud and in service-oriented contexts; (*iii*) query rewriting approaches; and (*iv*) service level agreements for cloud computing.

Data integration has been widely discussed in the database domain. [10] discussed theoretical aspects in data integration including modeling applications, query evaluation, dealing with inconsistencies and reasoning queries. Moreover, [9] reviewed several query rewriting approaches. [3] surveyed data quality aspects in data integration systems. [11] presented a data quality broker that allows to submit queries with associated quality requirements over a global schema and to provide results according to them.

[6,8] performed data integration in service-oriented contexts, particularly considering data services. However, they consider computing resources consumption versus performance for guiding the data integration process. [12] proposed an inter-cloud data integration system considering privacy requirements and the cost for protecting and processing data. [11–13] tackled quality aspects of the integration, but do not consider crucial aspects such as data consumers and data providers requirements and constraints, the associated infrastructures and the data quality itself.

As traditional databases theory, data integration on cloud and service-oriented context deals with query rewriting issues. Existing works like [1,2,4,7] have refered it as a service composition problem. Given a query, the objective is to lookup and compose data services that can contribute to produce a result. In general, these works must address performance issues, because they use algorithms that can become expensive according to the complexity of the query and on the number of available services. Although [1,4] have considered preferences and scores to produce rewritings, the multi-cloud context introduces new requirements and constraints to the integration process. Currently, the approaches are not sufficient to cover the new challenges. Thus, they should be revisited and adapted in order to make the integration efficient in this new environment.

Research contributions related to SLA in cloud computing concern (i) SLA management; (ii) inclusion of security requirements on SLAs; (iii) SLA negotiation; (iv) SLA matching; and (v) monitoring and allocation of cloud resources to detect and avoid SLA violations. We strongly believe that SLAs can be used to explicitly introduce the notion of quality in the current data integration solutions. In this sense, the use of SLAs to guide the entire data integration in a multi-cloud context seems original and promising for providing new perspectives to the data integration problem.

3   An SLA-Based Data Integration Approach: A Model Oriented Vision

To explain our solution, in this section we present a metamodel that depicts implied entities and their relationship. Then a meta-process will introduce the functionalities of the proposed solution.

According to our metamodel (Fig. 1), the *Multi-Cloud* is viewed as a set of *Cloud Infrastructures*. *Data producers* and *Data consumers* subscribe to *Cloud infrastructures*. Their subscription credentials are illustrated thanks to a *SLA* (*Consumer SLA* or *Producer SLA*) defining what the *Cloud infrastructure* offers to them through their subscription. *Data* are provided and consumed by *Data Producers* and *Data Consumers*, respectively. The *integration SLA* is a new type of SLA we introduce to reflect a multi-cloud contract between the user and the implied services according to the constraints imposed by the environment.

The data integration meta-process (see Fig. 2) implies the entities presented in the metamodel. It consists of three macro-steps. *First*, *query management* activities to process the user query and preferences; *second*, *SLA management* activities to enforce the SLA associated to the involved services, search and reuse previous *integration SLAs*, and create a new one for the current request; *third*, *query rewriting* activities [5] to search and filter *data producers*, to generate and execute the integration plan, and to compute results.

The activities defined in our meta-process bring the following challenges to our research:

1. SLA design. The issue is what are the important information that should be inserted in the integration SLA to facilitate further integration? How these information should be collected and stored during the integration to help next integrations.
2. Integration reuse. How to exploit cleverly the past integration processes?
3. Rewriting process. How to optimize it to make the execution time viable? Retrieving, integrating and delivering are tasks that requires a large amount of resources and processing time. Thus, it is necessary to study a efficient manner to make efficient the overall execution.

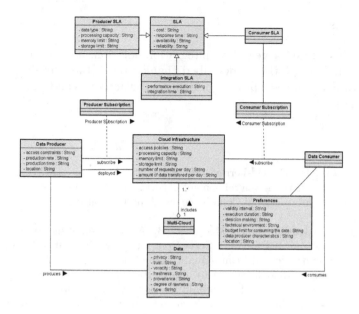

Fig. 1. Data integration metamodel

Fig. 2. Data integration meta-process

4   Research Plan

We started proposing a query rewriting algorithm called *Rhone*. It serves as proof of concept for the feasibility of our data integration process guided by cloud constraints and user preferences [5]. The first results are promising: *Rhone* reduces the rewriting number and processing time while considering user preferences and services' quality aspects extracted from SLAs to guide the service selection and rewriting. Furthermore, the integration quality is enhanced, and the integration total cost is reduced. For the time being, quality enhancement is assessed through benchmarks and use cases deployed on an experimental multi-cloud environment.

We are currently working on an SLA model for the integration process to express the constraints and the quality feature of a previous data integration. Other important research aspects are how to make efficient the rewriting process by reducing the composition search space.

5   Conclusions

This paper introduced a new data integration solution, adapted to the multi-cloud context. The solution is described thank to a metamodel describing the implied entities and a meta-process presenting the activities and the corresponding challenges.

References

1. Ba, C., Costa, U., Halfeld-Ferrari, M., Ferre, R., Musicante, M.A., Peralta, V., Robert, S.: Preference-driven refinement of service compositions. In: Proceedings of CLOSER 2014 International Conference on Cloud Computing and Services Science (2014)
2. Barhamgi, M., Benslimane, D., Medjahed, B.: A query rewriting approach for web service composition. IEEE Trans. Serv. Comput. Serv. Comput. (2010)
3. Batini, C., Scannapieco, M.: Data Quality Issues in Data Integration Systems, pp. 133–160. Springer, Heidelberg (2006). doi:10.1007/3-540-33173-5_6
4. Benouaret, K., Benslimane, D., Hadjali, A., Barhamgi, M.: FuDoCS: a web service composition system based on fuzzy dominance for preference query answering. In: 37th International Conference on Very Large Data Bases (VLDB 2011) (2011)
5. Carvalho, D.A.S., Souza Neto, P.A., Ghedira-Guegan, C., Bennani, N., Vargas-Solar, G.: *Rhone*: a quality-based query rewriting algorithm for data integration. In: Ivanović, M., Thalheim, B., Catania, B., Schewe, K.-D., Kirikova, M., Šaloun, P., Dahanayake, A., Cerquitelli, T., Baralis, E., Michiardi, P. (eds.) ADBIS 2016. CCIS, vol. 637, pp. 80–87. Springer, Cham (2016). doi:10.1007/978-3-319-44066-8_9
6. Correndo, G., Salvadores, M., Millard, I., Glaser, H., Shadbolt, N.: SPARQL query rewriting for implementing data integration over linked data. In: Proceedings of the 1st International Workshop on Data Semantics - DataSem 2010. ACM, New York (2010)
7. Costa, U.S., Ferrari, M.H., Musicante, M.A., Robert, S.: Automatic refinement of service compositions. In: Daniel, F., Dolog, P., Li, Q. (eds.) ICWE 2013. LNCS, vol. 7977, pp. 400–407. Springer, Heidelberg (2013). doi:10.1007/978-3-642-39200-9_33
8. ElSheikh, G., ElNainay, M.Y., ElShehaby, S., Abougabal, M.S.: SODIM: service oriented data integration based on mapreduce. Alexandria Eng. J. (2013)
9. Halevy, A.Y.: Answering queries using views: a survey. VLDB J. **10**(4), 270–294 (2001)
10. Lenzerini, M.: Data integration: A theoretical perspective. In: Proceedings of the Twenty-first ACM SIGMOD-SIGACT-SIGART Symposium on Principles of Database Systems. PODS 2002, pp. 233–246. ACM, New York (2002)
11. Scannapieco, M., Virgillito, A., Marchetti, C., Mecella, M., Baldoni, R.: The daquincis architecture: a platform for exchanging and improving data quality in cooperative information systems. Inf. Syst. **29**(7), 551–582 (2004)
12. Tian, Y., Song, B., Park, J., Huh, E.-N.: Inter-cloud data integration system considering privacy and cost. In: Pan, J.-S., Chen, S.-M., Nguyen, N.T. (eds.) ICCCI 2010. LNCS, vol. 6421, pp. 195–204. Springer, Heidelberg (2010). doi:10.1007/978-3-642-16693-8_22
13. Yau, S.S., Yin, Y.: A privacy preserving repository for data integration across data sharing services. IEEE T. Services Computing 1 (2008)

Revenue-Driven Service Provision for Mobile Hosts

Hongyue Wu[✉], Shuiguang Deng, and Jianwei Yin

College of Computer Science and Technology, Zhejiang University, Hangzhou, China
{hongyue_wu,dengsg,zjuyjw}@zju.edu.cn

Abstract. The development of modern technologies has greatly improved the capability of mobile devices. Along with this, mobile devices can provide their idle resources such as apps, sensors and network to others via service computing. However, mobile service hosts cannot satisfy excessive service requests due to relatively limited capabilities and resources. Therefore, how to select service requests and schedule them to an efficient utilization has become a critical problem. To deal with this problem, we propose a novel approach named RDSP4MH (revenue-drive service provision for mobile hosts) towards request selection, request scheduling and resource allocation for mobile service hosts. The experiments have demonstrated the high performance and efficiency of the algorithm.

Keywords: Mobile · Service provision · Selection · Scheduling · Revenue

1 Introduction

With the rapid development of mobile devices and wireless technologies, mobile systems have been playing an increasingly important role in our daily life. Meanwhile, the manufacturers of mobile devices have also achieved breakthroughs to extend mobile devices' capabilities in terms of memory, computational power, storage capability and embedded sensors. However, these powerful mobile devices are typically idle most of the time, which makes it realistic for mobile devices to share their surplus capabilities, resources, data, etc., as services to others to make profits. A common example of mobile service provision is that a smartphone user can create a wireless hotspot to provide his mobile network for others when he is in a meeting, on sleep or busy on other things.

Mobile service provision has nowadays emerged as a promising technology for the extension of traditional service computing. In [2], the opportunities and challenges of mobile service provision are analyzed in detail, such as it has enabled us to provide services anytime and anywhere; mobile hosts can provide services that cloud providers cannot provide, such as providing the surrounding environmental information by utilizing their sensors; mobile service provision can be delivered through free wireless networks such as Bluetooth and Near Field Communication, which are available even if the mobile network is broken-down as well as saves the cost of mobile Internet. Due to these advantages, mobile service provision can be widely applied to Internet access sharing, sensor data applications, crowd computing, etc. as illustrated in [3].

© Springer International Publishing AG 2017
K. Drira et al. (Eds.): ICSOC 2016 Workshops, LNCS 10380, pp. 145–151, 2017.
https://doi.org/10.1007/978-3-319-68136-8_15

Besides its potential benefits, mobile service provision is still facing a number of challenges. When facing excessive service requests, mobile hosts would not be able to satisfy all these requests due to intrinsically limited computing capabilities and resources. Therefore, to achieve effective service provision, a reasonable and effective strategy should have capability to (1) decide whether to accept or reject an incoming service request and (2) perform scheduling and resource allocation for the selected service requests according to required resources and their current condition.

As the computing capability and resources are limited, methods for service provision must be lightweight. Powerful cloud service providers always accept all service request and adopt heuristic algorithms or machine learning methods for request scheduling. For example, Lee et al. intended to achieve efficient resource and cost management. They proposed a heuristic algorithm based auction system to decide when and how providers should allocate their resources and to which users [4]. Albagli-Kim et al. presented a comparative study of approximation algorithms and heuristics for scheduling jobs with dwindling resource requirements [1]. However, all these researches are for powerful large-scale cloud servers. None of them address the problem from the perspective of mobile providers. In addition, most of them model service provision problem as NP-hard problems and adopt heuristic algorithms or machine learning methods, which are typically with high computational overhead. Therefore, they cannot be applied to mobile service provision.

In this paper, we address the problem of service provision for mobile hosts, and design a novel lightweight approach towards service request selection, request scheduling and resource allocation. The algorithm is of low time complexity and performed dynamically according to the current condition of mobile devices, with object to increase service provision, optimize resource utilization and eventually maximize the revenue.

The rest of the paper is organized as follows. In Sect. 2, we present basic definitions and formalize the problem. Then we describe the main operations and algorithms in detail in Sect. 3. In Sect. 4, we show the evaluation experiments and analyze the results. Finally, we conclude the paper outline our future work in Sect. 5.

2   Problem Definition

Definition 1 (Mobile Host). *A mobile host is a 2-tuple (S, A), where:*

- $S = \{s_i\}_{i=1}^{n}$, *describing the set of services that the mobile host can provide;*
- *A is a function describing the available resources the host can share. For each time point t, the available resources are denoted as a set of 2-tuples* $A(t) = \{(r_i, m_i)\}_{i=1}^{n}$, *where n is the number of types of available resources the host can provide, and r_i and m_i denotes the name and number of the i-th kind of resource, respectively.*

Mobile services can be the applications, data, etc. of service host. Service provision should not disturb the normal usage of mobile devices (e.g. phoning for mobile phones). Therefore, available resources are dynamically changing over time.

Definition 2 (Mobile Service). *A mobile service is a 4-tuple (i, h, R, QoS), where:*

- *i is the basic description of the service, including the identifier, input, output, precondition and result of the mobile service;*
- *h is the host of the mobile service;*
- *R describes the resources needed for the mobile host to execute the service, and it is denoted as a set of 2-tuples $R = \{(r_i, n_i)\}_{i=1}^{m}$, where m is the number of types of required resources, and r_i and n_i denotes the name and number of the i-th kind of resource, respectively;*
- *QoS is a set of attributes, including price, response time, reliability, availability, reputation, etc.*

Definition 3 (Revenue-Driven Service Provision). *Given a service host h, with its available resources $A(t) = \{(r_i, m_i)\}_{i=1}^{m}$, and the incoming service request sequence $q_1, q_2,...$, request selecting and scheduling is to select a set of service requests S from the sequence and schedule them to the execution sequence E to*

$$\text{Maximize} \sum_{q \in S} price_q$$
$$\text{s.t. } q^\bullet - {}^\bullet q = t_q^e, \text{ for each } q \in S \tag{1}$$

$$q^\bullet \leq t_q^d, \text{ for each } q \in S \tag{2}$$

$$\forall t, \sum_{q \in E(t) \cap S} R(r, q) \leq A(t, r), \text{ for each } r \in A(t) \tag{3}$$

Mobile service providers always provide services for some purpose (e.g. getting money, rewarding points, etc.), and they want to optimize their purpose while providing services. Specifically, we regard revenue as the purpose of mobile service provision in this paper. If mobile hosts provide services for other purpose, our method can still be applicative by simply changing the optimizing objective. In Definition 3, $price_q$ denotes the price corresponding to request q. Equation 1 implies that the arrangement of each request is in accordance with its execution time. Equation 2 illustrates that each request should be completed before the deadline in order to guarantee its response time. Moreover, the allocated resources should not exceed the available resources of the host at any time, as specified in Eq. 3.

3   RDSP4MH Approach

For each request, the host should judge (1) whether it can be completed in time, (2) whether it can be allocated with sufficient resources, and (3) whether the revenue is increased. Each request can be accepted if and only if all these three principles are satisfied. Our RDSP4MH performs request selection and scheduling based on these three principles. The algorithm is show in Algorithm 1.

For an incoming service request q_0, we should insert it to the request sequence according to its deadline first (lines 1), for the reason that if the request with later deadline is executed first, it may leads to the timeout of some requests with earlier deadline, which may decrease the revenue. The deadline of q_0 can be computed according to its arriving time and response time. Then, we should check whether q_0 can be executed before *InsertTime* (lines 2). Next, we check whether q_0 can be inserted to *InsertTime* (lines 5–6). If q_0 cannot be inserted, then the Timeout algorithm will be invoked, implying that the host cannot be able to accept all the requests and either q_0 or some requests before *InsertTime* will be rejected. If q_0 is inserted to the execution sequence, then the subsequent requests will be postponed. If a timeout occurs to any postponed request, it also needs to invoke the Timeout algorithm.

Algorithm 1. RSS4MH Algorithm

Input	The request execution sequence E, available resources R of the mobile host and the incoming service request q_0
Output	Updated request execution sequence
1	Compute the *InsertTime* of q_0 in the request sequence according to its deadline
2	**if** there is a time point t before *InsertTime* such that there is an interval following t that is long enough and with sufficient idle resources for q_0 to execute
3	insert q_0 to the execution sequence at time point t
4	**else**
5	**if** there is an interval following *InsertTime* that is long enough and with sufficient idle resources for q_0 to execute
6	insert q_0 to the execution sequence at time point *InsertTime*
7	**else**
8	**if** there is a time point t after *InsertTime* such that the time interval following t is long enough, with sufficient idle resources for q_0 to execute, and the end time does not exceed the deadline of q_0
9	insert q_0 to the execution sequence at time point t
10	**if** q_0 is not inserted to the execution sequence
11	Timeout (E, R, q_0, t)

Definition 4 (Dominance). *Given a service request q_0, an execution sequence E and a set of service requests S, q_0 dominate S if and only if*

$$\exists t_0 \text{ such that } \forall t \in (t_0, t_0 + t^e_{q_0}) \text{ and } \forall r \in R(q_0),$$
$$R(r, q_0) < A(t, r) + \sum_{q \in S \cap E(t)} R(r, q) \text{ and } price_{q_o} > \sum_{q \in S} price_q \tag{4}$$

In Definition 4, constraint 4 illustrates that there is a time interval, during which the idle resources and the resources allocated to the requests in S adds up to exceed the required resources of q_0, meanwhile, the revenue for executing q_0 is more than executing all requests in S. Therefore, if q_0 dominates S, the requests in S can be safely replaced by q_0, with the revenue increased.

The timeout process algorithm is shown in Algorithm 2. It is realized by constant searching of dominated request set with minimum price. For each time unit before the insert time point of an incoming request q_0, the algorithm tries to find the dominated request set with lowest price (lines 2–4). If no dominated request set is found, it means that q_0 should be rejected.

The time complexity of both RDSP4MH Algorithm and Timeout Algorithm is $O(lt^e n)$, where l denotes the length of the execution sequence, t^e denotes the length of the execution time of the request (the number of time unites) and n denotes the number of types of available resources. It implies that the execution time of both algorithms is in a low order of magnitude and it would not cause high overhead to mobile hosts.

Algorithm 2. Timeout Algorithm

Input	The request execution sequence E, available resources R of the mobile host, service request q_0 and insert time point *InsertTime*
Output	Updated request execution sequence
1	*MiniDominated*←q_0, *MiniPrice*←$price_{q_0}$
2	**for** $t = t_{current}$ **to** *InsertTime*
3	**if** $\forall t_0 \in (t, t+t^e_{q_0})$, there is a request set S started from t and dominated by q_0, and the total price is lower than *MiniPrice*
4	*MiniDominated*←S, *MiniPrice*←$price_S$
5	**if** there is a request or request set that is dominated by q_0
6	replace the requests in *MiniDominated* by q_0
7	move the subsequent requests accordingly

---

4   Experiments

Experiments are implemented on a HM note 1LTE mobile phone with Android 4.4.4 operating system. We set that there are 5 kinds of dynamically changing resources. Service requests are randomly generated satisfying that the price is from 1 to 5, execution time is from 1 to 5. The number of incoming requests per time unit obeys normal distribution $N(10, 5)$ and greater than 0.

To evaluate the effectiveness of RDSP4MH, we compare RDSP4MH with two classical scheduling algorithm, First Come First Serve (FCFS) and Priority Scheduling (PS). FCFS executes service requests according to their arriving time. PS perform request scheduling by selecting the request with highest price to execute first. Both FCFS and PS reject a request if there is not sufficient resources or time to execute it. We range the mean of the number of incoming requests per second from 5 to 50. The experiment is repeated 400 times and we adopt the average values. The result is shown in Fig. 1, from which we can see that our RDSP4MH approach significantly outperforms FCFS and PS, which demonstrates the high effectiveness of our approach. With the increasing of request number, the result of RDSP4MH is improved. This is because, with the increasing of request number, there are more requests for the algorithm to select.

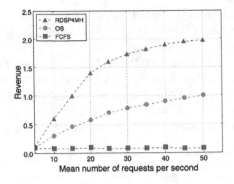

Fig. 1. Experimental result of effectiveness evaluation

To evaluate the efficiency of RDSP4MH, we range the response time of the request to examine the impact of response time on efficiency. As analyzed in Sect. 3, the efficiency can be significantly affected by the length of the execution sequence. The response time can affect the execution sequence length. In this experiment, the response time of the request obeys normal distribution $N(t, 5)$ and t is varied from 1 to 10. As shown in Fig. 2, with the increasing of mean response time, the execution time of RDSP4MH do not increase greatly, which is in accordance with the analysis in Sect. 3. In addition, the execution time of RDSP4MH is in a very low order of magnitude, which demonstrates the applicability of RDSP4MH to mobile service hosts.

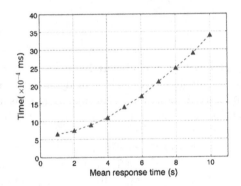

Fig. 2. Experimental result of efficiency evaluation

5   Conclusion

In this paper, we address the problem of revenue-driven service provision for mobile hosts. A novel approach named RDSP4MH is proposed to perform service request selection, request scheduling and resource allocation simultaneously, with the objective to maximize the revenue of the hosts. To evaluate the performance of the approach, we have conducted a series of experiments, which verified the high effectiveness and efficiency of RDSP4MH. In future, we will focus on RDSP4MH, trying to improve its performance.

References

1. Albagli-Kim, S., Shachnai, H., Tamir, T.: Scheduling jobs with dwindling resource requirements in clouds. In: INFOCOM, pp. 601–609. IEEE (2014)
2. Deng, S., Huang, L., Wu, H., Tan, W., Taheri, J., Zomaya, A.Y., Wu, Z.: Toward mobile service computing: opportunities and challenges. IEEE Cloud Comput. 3(4), 32–41 (2016)
3. Fernando, N., Loke, S.W., Rahayu, W.: Mobile cloud computing: a survey. Future Gener. Comput. Syst. 29(1), 84–106 (2013)
4. Lee, C., Wang, P., Niyato, D.: A real-time group auction system for efficient allocation of cloud internet applications. IEEE Trans. Serv. Comput. 8(2), 251–268 (2015)

Context-Aware Automated Workflow Composition for Interactive Data Exploration

Diego Serrano[(✉)]

University of Alberta, Alberta, Canada
serranos@ualberta.ca

Abstract. Nowadays, the Web of Data contains a myriad of structured information sources on a large number of domains. Nevertheless, most of the information is available through Web APIs that act as isolated silos of data that cannot interoperate automatically with other resources and services on the Web. My dissertation aims at synthesizing semantic web technologies over Web APIs, in order to combine the easy data integration techniques offered by semantic web, with the flexibility and availability of web services. This paper discusses the two main aspects of the envisioned thesis: (a) a description language to semantically describe functional and non-functional components of web services, and the relationships among those components, and (b) a middleware that plans composition chains, based on user's specifications, optimizing their trade-offs.

Keywords: Semantic web · Web services · Data integration · Linked data

1 Introduction

In the early 2000s, Berners-Lee *et al.* [2] envisioned a transition from an Internet of loosely interlinked text documents, designed for human consumption, to the *Semantic Web*, a thoroughly described and tightly interlinked "Web of Data", intended for automatic machine processing. The most pragmatic effort to realize the Semantic Web vision has focused on publishing interlinked datasets, in what is called the Linking Open Data (LOD) project. The project integrates multiple databases that have been translated into RDF, using a mixture of common vocabularies and terms specific to the data sources; these datasets are interconnected through the use of URIs and equivalence relations to external databases. Those datasets are typically available through SPARQL endpoints, but, in general, cross-database SPARQL queries tend to be of high complexity, since their formalization strongly depend on the ontological structure of the RDF store model and the relationships among entities, which usually has considerable variations among datasets. Therefore, the complexity and poor performance of accessing LOD datasets has limited their usage in real-time scenarios.

© Springer International Publishing AG 2017
K. Drira et al. (Eds.): ICSOC 2016 Workshops, LNCS 10380, pp. 152–157, 2017.
https://doi.org/10.1007/978-3-319-68136-8_16

Although, the LOD project has proven that, in principle, the linked-data approach is effective for integrating data from a large number of sources, nowadays, a substantial amount of Web data is exchanged through web services that expose data in formats such as JSON or XML. Those structured responses offer a common syntactic format, but they lack necessary semantics to interpret and interlink the content of the documents. In order to address this problem, the services have to include semantic annotations, as prescribed by the so-called *Semantic Web Services* (SWS).

The SWS approach attempts to describe services using domain ontologies, in order to enable automatic discovery, execution, and composition. Many SWS definitions have been proposed, such as WSMO [4], and SAWSDL [6], but few implementations of real semantic services have been produced, and the adoption of SWS in practice has fallen short. The main reason, suggested by Tosi *et al.* [8], is the focus of the research community in the definition of new ontologies and tools, disregarding real implementations of SWS, which has kept the discussion at an abstract level.

The objective of this thesis is to define a formalism that allows the creation and context-aware automatic exploration of semantically connected Web APIs, for different domains, taking into consideration functional and non-functional specifications of the resources, such as trustworthiness, authentication mechanisms and availability. Then, the middleware can specify execution plans for queries, that link and compose responses from independently deployed services, and optimize the trade-offs of data quality and performance. Additionally, this thesis will address service engineering approaches, supported by specific tools, to simplify the creation of SWS and interactive exploration of their data sets.

2   Composing and Integrating Web Services

In this section, we motivate our formalism in the context of related approaches, and we illustrate the functionalities of our middleware through an example.

2.1   Specification of Services and Their Implementation Contexts

Most of the current SWS formalizations follow a bottom-up approach, for example SAWSDL and WSMO-Lite [10]. In bottom-up approaches, Web services standards, such as WSDL, are extended by adding light-weight semantic annotations, which means that service providers need to produce the semantic and syntactic definitions. On the other hand, top-down approaches decouple the semantic description of the service from its syntactic description, on the principle that the semantics should not be influenced by implementation details. This approach was explored in classical approaches, such as WSMO, which provided a fully-fledged framework to define ontologies, goals, mediators and web services.

In our approach, we aim to combine the best of both approaches: the simplicity of the descriptions in the bottom-up approaches, to encourage its adoption, and the low coupling of top-down approaches to gain independence from the service providers, that allows us to reach a critical mass of service descriptions through crowdsourcing. In addition, one of the main guidelines in our design was to reuse and integrate existing formalisms into a simple common model, that supports publication and discovery. We introduce an RDF(S) integration ontology based on the Minimal Service Model (MSM) [5], that captures the maximum common denominator between existing conceptual models for services, enabling the representation of the semantics of services, including authentication mechanisms, provenance, quality of service metrics, and relationships among inputs and outputs.

The ontology defines a set of *Service* elements, which have a number of associated *Operation* elements. Operations, in turn, have a *Graph*, which is a collection of *Resource* triples that represent the underlying data schema of the service. The Operations also have links to input and output elements within such graph. The input elements may be defined as *required* or *optional*, and *full* or *partial*, for the cases when the input is used in partial match services, such as search functionalities. The outputs define a relation *responsePath*, that represents an XPath-like expression that is used in the lifting process, and avoids the use of other transformation technologies, such as XSLT, creating a self-contained semantic service description.

The ontology builds upon existing vocabularies. *hRESTS* [5], which is also used in MSM, is used to provide basic support for capturing grounding information necessary for Web APIs. *Web Api Authentication* [7] is used to annotate information about authentication information on top of Web API descriptions. The *Dataset Quality Vocabulary* [3] provides a lightweight vocabulary to describe functional and non-functional aspects of the service. And finally, *RDF Graph Patterns and Templates* [1] defines the terms used to describe the data schema graph patterns. The resources in the graph may contain other domain-specific ontologies and vocabularies to associate their classes and properties.

We illustrate our service modelling approach with an example based on complementary services. We consider two operations: *search actors*, and *get movie credits*. The former, searches for actors by name, and the latter, gets the list of movies where an actor, specified by his id, played a role. To keep the example concise, we only consider the graphs shown in Fig. 1 to represent the services, which were annotated using the Linked Movie Database Ontology. Traditionally, semantic descriptions consider ontological annotations on inputs and outputs to carry reference annotations between the service description and the domain ontology, for example, stating that the input of *get movie credits* is a person (or an attribute of it), and its output is a list of movies (or attributes of it). However, those annotations do not capture the specific relation between the two entities, leaving the description open to different interpretations, for instance, with other relations such as *produced* or *directed*.

In order to overcome the aforementioned limitation, we define a service operation as a 6-tuple $(E, G_s, I_{G_s}, O_{G_s}, A, Q)$ where E denotes the endpoint and other grounding parameters of the service, such as the URL and the HTTP method. G_s defines a graph representation of the service, as a finite collection of

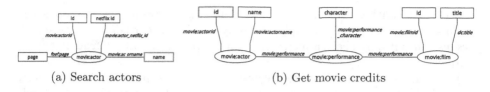

(a) Search actors   (b) Get movie credits

Fig. 1. Graph representations of the data in the example services. The green box denotes the attribute used as input. (Color figure online)

triple patterns. A triple pattern $t_s = (s, p, o)$ is a tuple composed of a subject, a predicate and an object, where $t_s \in (U \cup V) \times U \times (U \cup L \cup V)$, being U, L, and V disjoint infinite sets of URIs, literals and variables. I_{G_s} and O_{G_s} define the inputs and outputs of the service, respectively, pointing to subjects or objects in graph G_s. Finally, A denotes the authentication mechanism used by the operation, and Q defines the quality of service attributes associated to the particular operation or to the service in general.

2.2 Context-Aware Discovery and Composition

In order to query the services, we represent the queries as a conjunctive SPARQL query. More formally, a query consists of a triple (G_q, I_{G_q}, O_{G_q}), where G_q denotes a graph composed of triples, where each triple $t_q = (s, p, o)$ and $t_q \in (U \cup V) \times U \times (U \cup L \cup V)$. In turn, I_{G_q} and O_{G_q} represent the inputs and outputs, respectively. In our example, if we want to know the name of the characters that the actor *Brad Pitt* has played, we would write the following SPARQL query:

```
SELECT ?character
WHERE {
  ?person a movie:actor ;
    movie:actorname"Brad Pitt" ;
    movie:performance ?performance .
  ?performance movie:performance_character ?character
}
```

From the query, we can extract inputs and outputs. Outputs are simply the projected variables of the data query, `?character` in our example; and inputs are the bound values that appear in the triples of the query, in the `WHERE` clause, like the name `"Brad Pitt"` and the type `movie:actor` in the example. Then, the query answering problem is transformed into a subgraph isomorphism problem, in which the query graph G_q and the graph formed by all the service graphs G_S are given as input, and we must determine, first, whether G_S contains a subgraph that is isomorphic to G_q, and then extract the individual service graphs in the isomorphic graph. However, at the size of the Web, and even with a moderate load, this problem can be untractable for ad-hoc queries. In our approach, in order to discover services dynamically, we start by extracting elements from G_q that can be used as input parameters of a service request. Then, we use the input elements and authentication credentials as a filter, to consider only the services that can be invoked with the current input parameters and authentication credentials. In our example, the only service in consideration is *search persons*, since it only needs a name as an input, represented by `"Brad Pitt"` in the query.

When a query is submitted to the system, the query processor has to find a isomorphic subgraph from the set of service graphs. If such graph is not found, then it has to search a sequence of service graphs that can be composed together to fulfill the goal represented by the query. In our iterative approach, if a graph G_s can be invoked and matches partially with graph G_q, then we use the outputs of G_s as inputs of G_q in the next iteration. The algorithm stops when a sequence of service graphs $\{G_{s_1}, ..., G_{s_n}\}$ has completely covered the graph G_q, or when we reach a fixed number of iterations. In our example, the graph for *search persons* only covers the triples for the name and type of the person, leaving the performance triples uncovered. Then, in the next iteration, we can use the actor identifiers, and webpage produced as outputs from *search persons*. In this second iteration, we can use the identifier of the person to invoke the service *get movie credits*, and cover the remaining triples of the query.

The algorithm for subgraph isomorphism used in our approach, is adapted from Ullman's algorithm [9], checking recursively that the adjacent nodes and edges are equivalent. The equivalence relation considers ontological equivalence (through relations such as `owl:sameAs`), and subsumption relationships of resources and properties in the ontology.

After all the possible composition chains have been discovered, the system ranks them, according to user's preferences and non-functional properties criteria like response time, and availability. In this process, the non-functional properties values can be obtained by statistics collected during service invocations, or gathered from service descriptions.

In our system, we provide a web-based data analysis tool that empowers regular web users to explore and analyze the Linked Data produced by our integration endpoint. Currently, the system supports three different types of visualizations: (a) a tabular view, provides a familiar visualization style to read and interpret complex JSON files; (b) a force-directed graph, that provides a natural and interactive visualization, where the user can follow how the graph evolves and how clusters are formed, and (c) a JSON document, that provides support for machine-to-machine communication for third-party applications. Users can interact with the graph by expanding nodes. When the user request the expansion of the node, a SPARQL is created using the URIs and literals directly attached to the node as input graph patterns, and using the syntax SELECT *, which in our system is an abbreviation that selects all of the variables that are declared in the service definition.

3   Research Plan Overview

In the future, we plan to support semi-automatic description of services, based on a collection of sample invocation URLs provided by users. The system is able to extract input and output parameters from the example service invocations, and then, use the datatypes, names of the parameters, and popular ontologies to suggest mappings between a mediated schema and the service. In addition, we intend to provide different kinds of visualizations, depending on the nature of the data returned, such as maps, temporal charts, and different layouts for graphs and tables. In the long term, we envision a middleware that will enable system developers and end-users to transparently and efficiently access heterogeneous resources, supported through our middleware.

The evaluation strategy is divided in two phases, that involve controlled empirical studies with developers using the tools we plan to develop. First, we will demonstrate how effectively the proposed approach can be integrated into current Web APIs, including metrics of the cognitive difficulty faced by developers, and performance exhibited by the mediator system. Second, we will evaluate the exploration and visualization tools through usability assessments involving the presentation of the data, interaction with the data, the perceived cognitive offload, and the usability of the data itself.

Acknowledgement. I would like to thank my supervisor, Prof. Eleni Stroulia for her helpful suggestions. This work was supported by the KMTI NSERC Strategic project.

References

1. RDF graph patterns and templates. http://vocab.org/riro/gpt. Accessed 18 July 2016
2. Berners-Lee, T., Hendler, J., Lassila, O., et al.: The semantic web. Sci. Am. **284**(5), 28–37 (2001)
3. Debattista, J., Lange, C., Auer, S.: daQ, an ontology for dataset quality information. In: LDOW (2014)
4. Feier, C., Polleres, A., Dumitru, R., Domingue, J., Stollberg, M., Fensel, D.: Towards intelligent web services: the web service modeling ontology (WSMO) (2005)
5. Kopeckỳ, J., Gomadam, K., Vitvar, T.: hRESTS: an HTML microformat for describing Restful web services. In: IEEE/WIC/ACM International Conference on Web Intelligence (WI 2008), vol. 1, pp. 619–625. IEEE (2008)
6. Kopecky, J., Vitvar, T., Bournez, C., Farrell, J.: SAWSDL: semantic annotations for WSDL and XML schema. Internet Comput. 60–67 (2007). IEEE
7. Maleshkova, M., Pedrinaci, C., Domingue, J., Alvaro, G., Martinez, I.: Using semantics for automating the authentication of web APIs. In: Patel-Schneider, P.F., et al. (eds.) ISWC 2010. LNCS, vol. 6496, pp. 534–549. Springer, Heidelberg (2010). doi:10.1007/978-3-642-17746-0_34
8. Tosi, D., Morasca, S.: Supporting the semi-automatic semantic annotation of web services: a systematic literature review. Inf. Softw. Technol. **61**, 16–32 (2015)
9. Ullmann, J.R.: An algorithm for subgraph isomorphism. J. ACM (JACM) **23**(1), 31–42 (1976)
10. Vitvar, T., Kopeckỳ, J., Viskova, J., Fensel, D.: WSMO-lite annotations for web services. In: Bechhofer, S., Hauswirth, M., Hoffmann, J., Koubarakis, M. (eds.) ESWC 2008. LNCS, vol. 5021, pp. 674–689. Springer, Heidelberg (2008). doi:10.1007/978-3-540-68234-9_49

Towards Rules-Based Mapping Framework for RESTful Web Services

Khanh Duc Hoang Le[✉]

The School of Computer Science and Engineering,
University of New South Wales, Sydney, NSW 2052, Australia
khanhle@cse.unsw.edu.au

Abstract. Integrating web services is usually time-consuming and requires a lot of programming efforts and experiences due to documentation burden and coding style convention overhead provided by external parties. Fortunately, RESTful web services simplify the integration task compared to the traditional web service WSDL as coding convention is significantly reduced. However, the documentation burden is still evident and developers usually rely on running examples to gain better knowledge and use web service documentation efficiently. The subject of my PhD thesis is to propose a novel rules-based mapping method for mapping a desired web service to potential candidates from a predefined web service repository. In this research, the assumption is that web services are made of RESTful APIs specified in Javascript Object Notation (JSON) format. My significant thesis contributions are: (1) a hybrid model for web service similarity, (2) a rules-based mapping approach for identifying and classifying the most related and similar services against a given desired web service, and lastly (3) a concrete and detailed evaluation to show the effectiveness of the proposed approach and framework.

Keywords: Web services · RESTful APIs · Web service matching and mapping · Web service programming

1 Introduction

Services on the cloud are ubiquitous and are grown exponentially. Nowadays, the demand for integration with external platforms from existing application software is enormous, especially more and more software platforms become publicly available. On one side, software vendors wish to integrate their system with other systems. On the other side, their software platform needs to open its features to the public to increase its popularity and usage locally and globally through its dedicated APIs and web services facility. With such constant increasing of web services on the cloud in size and quantity, it becomes a challenge to developers and researchers on the field to manage and control services over time.

Supervised by Prof. Boualem Benatallah and Prof. Fethi Rabhi.

© Springer International Publishing AG 2017
K. Drira et al. (Eds.): ICSOC 2016 Workshops, LNCS 10380, pp. 158–164, 2017.
https://doi.org/10.1007/978-3-319-68136-8_17

In terms of specifying a web service, there are many common specifications used for this purpose such as Web Service Description Language (WSDL) [1] or Web Application Description Language (WADL) [1,2]. WSDL is used to describe a web service in a traditional way while WADL is used mainly for RESTful web services. In this paper, we only consider RESTful web services that are specified in JSON specification [3] which is inspired from the work of Swagger [4].

In the rest of this paper, I shall briefly discuss the related works which cover the state of the art in web service matching and mapping in Sect. 2. Section 3 discusses the proposed methodology in short. Section 4 provides a preliminary evaluation of our approach. Finally, a conclusion and sketches of future work are discussed in Sect. 5.

2   Related Works

Service mapping is a well-defined research area which is closely related to service discovery, interface matching and schema matching techniques. Service mapping is considered as a foundation for other fields such as service integration and service composition. In web service discovery, the search for a desired web service is occurred on the web service repository (usually UDDI Universal Directory Discovery and Integration). Some common search engine systems provide search capability based on keywords that result in some shortcomings. For example, when users search for web services with the keyword "zipcode", all services which are linked to "zip" or "postal code" but not "zipcode" will not be returned [5]. Fortunately, recent research in this research area has incorporated keyword search with semantics to produce better results. Usually the semantics used is based on semantic terms (i.e. synonym) of words in the online dictionary Word-Net [6]. This approach significantly improves search results, however, it leads to another shortcoming. For instance, when a user searches for search methods with "bookmark", service methods with "tag" but not "bookmark" are not returned as "bookmark" and "tag" are not synonyms according to English dictionary WordNet.

The problem of service matching is closely related to the schema matching in database field [7–9]. Schema matching refers to the process of matching two elements that are somehow semantically related and substitute each other. Schema matching is also the process of developing semantic matches between two or more schemas. The purpose of schema matching is generally either to merge two or more databases, or to enable queries on multiple, heterogeneous databases to be formulated on a single schema. Schema and Ontology matching (COMA) [10] provides a generic matching and mapping tool for schema and ontology matching. It focuses on splitting a big matching task into smaller tasks and combines matching results together. Previous matching results can be used for subsequent matching. COMA firstly attempts to provide mapping outcomes then users are required to provide feedback upon the correctness of mapping results. COMA++ [11,12] extends from its previous prototype COMA by providing more features to facilitate users with the reuse of previous mapping and user interaction. However, due to focusing on matching for inferring explicit mapping, there are some aspects of service entities are not considered such as parameter types or constraints which are not suitable for mapping in COMA. Hence, COMA mainly focuses on matching of more coarse-grain objects.

By considering a web service as a composition of service, operation and parameter entities, my approach differs from the existing approaches in the literature in the way that it focuses on the semantic relationships of parameters and operations with the introduction of different relationship operators in the rules-based mapping.

3   The Proposed Methodology

In this section, I mainly discuss the approach by introducing a hybrid model which is used to measure similarities between different service artifacts. Then different rules are discussed for triggering service mapping.

3.1   Hybrid Service Model

In order to leverage service matching, I have developed an object-oriented model for a web service. In this model, a web service object is a composition of service (S), operation (O) and parameter (P) objects. An operation object is in turn a composition of operation and parameter objects. Eventually, a parameter object is composed of different parameter attributes like name, description, datatype (i.e. String, Integer) and type (i.e. input or output). Denote Weight(name), Weight(endpoint) and Weight(desc) as the weighted values of name, endpoint and desc (description) respectively, then Weight(name) > Weight(endpoint) > Weight(desc). Similarly, denote Weight(service), Weight(operation) and Weight(parameter) are weighted values for service, operation and parameter accordingly. Following a top-down approach, the weight of each element level is increased from service level to parameter level. That means that we have Weight(service) < Weight(operation) < Weight(parameter). The generic weighting functions for comparing service elements are defined below:

$$Sim_{ser}(s_1, s_2) = \sum_{e \subset S} \delta(e) * Sim(s_1.e, s_2.e) \quad where \quad 1 = \sum_{e \subset S} \delta(e) \quad (1)$$

$$Sim_{op}(op_1, op_2) = \sum_{e \subset O} \delta(e) * Sim(op_1.e, op_2.e) \quad where \quad 1 = \sum_{e \subset O} \delta(e) \quad (2)$$

$$Sim_{par}(par_1, par_2) = \sum_{e \subset P} \delta(e) * Sim(par_1.e, par_2.e) \quad where \quad 1 = \sum_{e \subset P} \delta(e) \quad (3)$$

For example, by considering the above rules for selecting suitable variables in weight functions, we use three empirical set of values ({0.3,0.1,0.2,0.4}, {0.5,0.2,0.1,0.2},{0.5,0.3,0.2}) for variables in the generic formula.

3.2   Semantic Relationships and Rules

This subsection introduces a number of semantic relationships/operators that can be used for matching and mapping.

CONCAT Operator. When considering two strings s and t, we form a new string by concatenate string s and string t together with a delimiter (<DIM>). For example, suppose we have two strings denoted as s: abc, t: def, then CONCAT(s,t) := abc<DIM>def. For simplicity, we can choose <DIM> as a blank or a single space.

AGGRE Operator. The AGGRE of two operations Op1 and Op2 are happened by aggregation of all corresponding attributes/artifacts of Op1 and Op2. The result of an AGGRE of two operations is a newly formed operation, Op12, in which its input and output parameters are defined as a result of aggregation of input and output parameters from two operations respectively, $Op12 := AGGRE(Op1, Op2)$.

COMPO Operator. COMPO operator is used to generalise two matched operations into more generic operation. This assumes that two operations are considered to be matched as they have high matching score according to similarity metrics. The result of COMPO relationship is another operation. Like other relationships, COMPO processing happens in each corresponding attribute of two given operations. Firstly, the COMPO process starts with some string-value attributes like verb, name, description using one of different strategies like generic terms, hypernyms, synonyms, categories, dictionary lookup. For example, search := COMPO(lookup, find). Secondly, the COMPO process continues with Input and Output parameter sets in which each input(output) set from each operation are combined. Any two input(output) parameters, each from each operation, are matched, COMPO relationship can be established to form a new input(output) parameter. The composite operation has all attributes to be defined as the following formula:

$$COMPO(a, b) = \sum_{x_i \subset a, x_j \subset b}^{a,b} COMPO(a.x_i, b.x_j) \qquad (4)$$

PIPELINE Operator. A series of mapping operations can form a pipeline if and only if the output of an Operation is mapped with the input of another Operation. We call a mapping process as a mapper; a Source operation is the operation in which its inputs are not connected to any output of other operations. An Output operation is the operation in which its inputs are connected to other operations' outputs and its outputs are not connected to any other operations' inputs.

3.3   Mapping Rules

There are two main types of mapping rules namely one-one mapping and one-many mapping. One-one mapping rule focuses one single mapping between operations. The rule decides a source operation is mapped to a target operation if and only if some conditions are held. Once the mapping is established, the matched operations pair can be expressed by one of the above semantic operators in Sect. 3.2. The one-many mapping focuses on the mapping of a source operation with many operations on the target set as a result of combining possible semantic operators. The one-many mapping rules defines the mapping conditions and works on the instruction of specifying appropriate semantic operators in each mapping stage. For example, considering a source operation doABC(4, 2) and the set of target operations such as SET{doA(3, 1), doB(1, 1) and doC(1, 1)} where X(m, n) is a notation of the X operation which has m input parameters and n output parameters. When some conditions are matched, we can express the following mapping:

$$doABC(4,2) := AGGRE(PIPELINE(doA(3,1), doB(1,1)), doC(1,1)) \quad (5)$$

4   Preliminary Experiment and Results

For our mapping rules validation, at the first stage, I have collected more than 100 APIs in different categories such as Bookmarking, Maps, Payment, Social Networks and Language Translation services. For simplicity, my pre-assumption for all the APIs with the operation syntax is in the form of [VERB][OBJECT1][OBJECT2][...][OBJECTn] such as translateText, buyShare or buyNavelOrange. I have prototyped an implementation of our approach known as the Rule-based mapping system in Java with some open-source components. We have used the implementation of similarity metrics from SecondString library [13,14] for a collection atomic similarity metrics along with JSON library and Build Tools. Two similarity metrics have been used in the prototype are Jaro and Jaccard [13]. Jaccard is the metric that is suitable for comparing long texts (i.e. description) while Jaro is selected for essential metric for string matching such as name, type or path. The combination of these two metrics make an effectively harmonic outcome compared to using any single similarity metric.

I have also conducted experiments on a number of single metrics; the results confirm that using a hybrid of Jaro and Jaccard bring a dominant performance in similarity matching as shown in Fig. 1 when searching *Translate_Text* operation with unbiased syntax from the list of four operations Translate (top line), TranslateArray, Detect and GetLanguagesForTranslate.

The system has copped well with the predefined ubiquitous set of APIs for a given web service API. In our hybrid model, we have setup an offset Threshold variable (α) in order to decide if two entities are matched. By changing different parameters, we obtained different datasets of precision and recall.

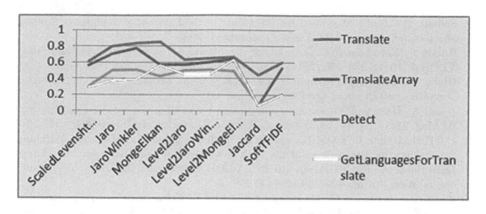

Fig. 1. Comparing similarity metrics in hybrid weighting scheme model

5   Discussion and Conclusion

Our initial evaluation has shown a great potential of using Rules-based system to address the problem of ubiquitous web service matching and mapping. We continue to collect various APIs from different domains to leverage our algorithms. At this stage, we have collected more than 100 APIs in different categories such as Book-marking, Maps, Payment, Social Networks and Language Translation services. During the wrapping of web service APIs in the JSON format, we try to maintain the originality of these web services as much as possible. Our JSON convention is much closed to Swagger specification, thus it is possible for potential API providers to register new services into our service repository automatically. Our next goal involves improving our current Rules-based system with the ability to reuse previous mapping outcomes. Although the system is designed to provide automatic mappings to the users but due to complexity and ubiquity of APIs, it is important to enable the system to interact with users for their feedbacks.

References

1. Walsh, A.E. (ed.): UDDI, SOAP, and WSDL: The Web Services Specification Reference Book. Prentice Hall Professional Technical Reference, Englewood Cliffs (2002)
2. Richardson, L., Ruby, S. (eds.): RESTful Web Services. O'Reilly Media, Sebastopol (2007)
3. JSON: Javascript object notation. http://www.json.org. Accessed 09 Jan 2016
4. Swagger: A simple, open standard for describing REST APIs with JSON (2016). https://developers.helloreverb.com/swagger. Accessed 10 Jan 2016
5. Dong, X., Halevy, A., Madhavan, J., Nemes, E., Zhang, J.: Similarity search for web services. In: Proceedings of the Thirtieth International Conference on Very Large Data Bases (VLDB 2004), vol. 30. pp. 372–383. VLDB Endowment (2004). http://dl.acm.org/citation.cfm?id=1316689.1316723

6. Fellbaum, C. (ed.): WordNet: An Electronic Lexical Database. Language, Speech, and Communication. MIT Press, Cambridge (1998)
7. Rahm, E., Bernstein, P.A.: A survey of approaches to automatic schema matching. VLDB J. **10**(4), 334–350 (2011). http://dx.doi.org/10.1007/s007780100057
8. Islam, A., Inkpen, D., Kiringa, I.: Database schema matching using corpus-based semantic similarity and word segmentation
9. Doan, A., Halevy, A.Y.: Semantic-integration research in the database community. AI Mag. **26**(1), 83–94 (2005). http://dl.acm.org/citation.cfm?id=1090488.1090497
10. Do, H.H., Rahm, E.: COMA: a system for flexible combination of schema matching approaches. In: Proceedings of the 28th International Conference on Very Large Data Bases (VLDB 2002), pp. 610–621. VLDB Endowment (2002). http://dl.acm.org/citation.cfm?id=1287369.1287422
11. Aumueller, D., Do, H.H., Massmann, S., Rahm, E.: Schema and ontology matching with COMA++. In: Proceedings of the 2005 ACM SIGMOD International Conference on Management of Data (SIGMOD 2005), New York, pp. 906–908 (2005). http://doi.acm.org/10.1145/1066157.1066283
12. Engmann, D., Massmann, S.: Instance matching with COMA++. In: BTW (2007)
13. Cohen, W.W., Ravikumar, P., Fienberg, S.E.: Second string: an opensource Java toolkit of approximate string-matching techniques (2003). http://secondstring.sourceforge.net
14. Cohen, W.W., Ravikumar, P., Fienberg, S.E.: A comparison of string distance metrics for name-matching tasks, pp. 73–78 (2003)

Demonstration

Introduction to the Demonstration Track

Jan Mendling[1], Mohamed Mohamed[2], and Zhongjie Wang[3]

[1] Vienna University of Economics and Business, Vienna, Austria
[2] IBM Research, San Jose, USA
[3] Harbin Institute of Technology, Harbin, China

1 Preface

The ICSOC 2016 Demonstration Track was held in conjunction with the 14th International Conference on Service Oriented Computing (ICSOC 2016) on October 10–13, 2016 in Banff, Alberta, Canada. This track offered an exciting and highly interactive opportunity to show research prototypes in service oriented computing (SOC) and related areas. These research prototype demos focused on developments and innovation in the areas of service engineering, operations, cloud and big data services, implementation of services as well as development and adoption of services in specific organizations, businesses and the society at large.

We received 16 submissions, of which 11 were accepted. These demos clearly showed interesting improvements and significance from recently implemented systems, and offered the ability to fruitful discussions:

- Demand-Driven SOA Simulation Platform Based on GIPSY for Context-Based Brokerage
- DeMOCAS: Domain Objects for Service-based Collective Adaptive Systems
- Anuvaad Pranaali: A RESTful API for Machine Translation
- Integration of Heterogeneous Services and Things into Choreographies
- Testing Processes with Service Invocation: Advanced Logging in CPEE
- COOL: A Model-Driven and Automated System for Guided and Verifiable Cloud Solution Design
- A Service-Based System for Sentiment Analysis and Visualization of Twitter Data in Realtime
- XDAI-A: Framework for Enabling Cross-Device Integration of Android Apps
- Desire: Deep Semantic Understanding and Retrieval for Technical Support Services
- BlueSight: Automated Discovery Service for Cloud Migration of Enterprises
- A Configurator Component for End-User Defined Mobile Data Collection Processes

We would like to thank the authors for their submissions, the program committee for their reviewing work, and the organizers of the ICSOC 2016 conference for their support which made this demo track possible.

2   Organization

Demonstration Chairs

Jan Mendling	Vienna University of Economics and Business, Austria
Mohamed Mohamed	IBM Research, USA
Zhongjie Wang	Harbin Institute of Technology, China

Program Committee

Adnene Guabtni	National Information Communications Technology Research Centre (NICTA), Australia
Armin Haller	CSIRO, Australia
Athman Bouguettaya	RMIT University, Australia
Bradley Simmons	York University, Canada
Dickson Chiu	The University of Hong Kong, Hong Kon
Djamal Benslimane	University of Lyon, France
Florian Daniel	University of Trento, Italy
Ashutosh Jadhav	IBM Research, USA
Helen Paik	University of New South Wales, Australia
Ivona Brandic	Vienna University of Technology, Austria
Jianwei Yin	Zhejiang University
Marios Fokaefs	York University, Canada
Mark Shtern	York University, Canada
MIKE SMIT	Dalhousie University, Canada
Mohammad Sadoghi	IBM Research, USA
Philipp Leitner	University of Zurich, Switzerland
Philippe Lalanda	Joseph Fourier University, France
Pierluigi Plebani	Politecnico di Milano, Italy
Raman Kazhamiakin	SOA Research Unit, Fondazione Bruno Kessler, Trento, Italy
Sonia Ben Mokhtar	LIRIS, CNRS, France
Uwe Zdun	University of Vienna, Austria
Wei Tan	IBM Research, USA
Xumin Liu	Rochester Institute of Technology
Zhiyong Feng	Tianjin University

Demand-Driven SOA Simulation Platform Based on GIPSY for Context-Based Brokerage

Touraj Laleh, Esteban Garro, Jashanjot Singh, Gurpreet Raju,
Muhammad Usman, Serguei Mokhov[✉], and Joey Paquet

Department of Computer Science and Software Engineering,
Concordia University, Montreal, Quebec, Canada
{t_laleh,mokhov,paquet}@encs.concordia.ca

Abstract. This demo complements our main research contribution to illustrate a demand-driven SOA extension of the GIPSY's multi-tier architecture as a simulation scenario testbed for scalable context aware brokerage testing and data integration.

1 Introduction

Our primary motivation is to reduce human administrator overhead required in making sure that services non-compliant with business and/or technical requirements don't get composed with during automatic service mashup and composition.

Most automatic approaches to service compositions were primarily concerned with repairing and recomposition of a composite service when its atomic services become unavailable. However, no (not many?) solutions exist that allow forcing recomposition of services when new policy requirements are introduced into the system at runtime directed by the business objectives or technical necessities and non-compliant services are still up and running and available for composition otherwise. For example, a business level requirement is introduced into a system disallowing customer data to be stored beyond service borders (e.g., Canadian banks' data on the US servers), or customers prefer their VMs to avoid multitenancy when doing VM migration. On the technical side examples include changing ciphersuite key length or cipher type change for encrypted communications and services offering lower versions of these should not be composed with. Another example where SaaS layer applications have some knowledge of run-time conditions that can hint PaaS or IaaS layers for additional resource requirements that meet the SaaS business or technical requirements (e.g., to avoid the mentioned allocation a VM beyond borders or avoiding multi-tenancy or use strong encryption).

In the current setups, system administrators would have to discover and somehow block out such non-compliant services that to avoid them being selected for automatic composition. If they are in control of those services, they would shut them down manually by turning them off or undeploying. If they are not in control, then they would have to implement network- or application-based

© Springer International Publishing AG 2017
K. Drira et al. (Eds.): ICSOC 2016 Workshops, LNCS 10380, pp. 169–173, 2017.
https://doi.org/10.1007/978-3-319-68136-8_18

firewall rules to block them. If the number of services is large, it introduces a scalability problem and time required to remedy the non-compliance issues.

Our design of the policy based broker solution allows introduction of such business or technical requirements at run-time without human administrator overhead to remove non-compliant services.

2   Evaluation

This simulation attempts to tackle three different challenges of service composition problem. First, developing an approach to generate all possible solutions for services composition problem. Second, considering constraint as an important factor in service composition and including a external constraints which has not been addressed in previous approaches. Third, designing required mechanisms to apply effects of constraints on working and future generated service composition plans. A constraint-based model using planning model is designed to express required concepts such as context and services. Unlike other constraint-based approaches [5] that only consider constraint relate to service customers and providers, we identify new sort of constraints (external constraints) that needs to considered in service composition process. Policies provide us a high-level description of what we want without dealing with how to achieve it. Thus, using policies can be a suitable mechanism to determine if the goals were achieved using existing policy refinement techniques [1]. In order to evaluate complexity of composition algorithms, many approaches have performed extensive experiments via available test sets such as [3]. However, we could not find any test set that could support the definition of constraints and effects discussed in this paper. To examine the effectiveness of the brokerage algorithm and the policy enforcement approach we designed an architecture Fig. 1 [2] for a service brokerage to implement different required components. Moreover, GIPSY [4] as a distributed multi-tier architecture for evaluation of programs in a distributed and demand-driven manner is used to generate our required data. At the time of submitting this paper our result are not statistically significant. However, our preliminary result shows significant improve in adaptability of composite services in face of different constraints specifically external constraints.

Need of a context aware system. When we consider the context of both the user and the environment, the services are updated as per the context of the environment such as the vicinity of the location and the services need to be aware of its environment. But these different services such as shopping, travelling, restaurants overlap semantically over a common parameter i.e. location. Furthermore, when we consider using different services in conjunction with each other they provide even more context-oriented results. Such as using the travel services and the civil security services in collaboration results into optimized solutions where the user will not only be able to plan his travel but also avoid places where the security might have been compromised or a state of emergency has arisen. However, in order to combine these services, in the manner of data integration, a service brokerage is forwarded. This broker works as a mediator between clients and services and also as an adaption mechanism which takes into consideration the requirements for service selection and composition.

2.1 Application Domain

The simulation testbed is a context-aware software-as-a-service (SaaS) software which aims to help clients find the most near-matching service providers based on the clients' required specifications. This framework differentiates from other service providers in that it attempts to enhance its results by providing a layer of integration among different services. This means that the context- aware service does not only consider the clients' context, but it also adds relevant parameters provided by other services. For example: "A value-added context-aware service would provide a list of shopping offers in the vicinity of the client while considering other effective factors such as the client's restrictions, transportation limitations due to disabilities, or even emergency situations in the area of the provided offers." The goal is to provide collaboration among different services, which were originally conceived independently of each other. This integration is done via a Service Broker, which will continuously monitor services and perform updates on the results of the demands stored in the DST database. This basic architecture is depicted in Fig. 1.

Client. The Client is a Demand Generator Tier which will generate Service Demands from the users using a front-end application.

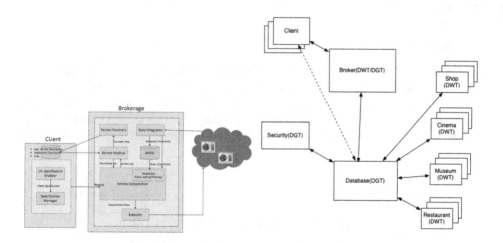

Fig. 1. The high level architecture of a brokerage simulation

These demands are sent to the broker; it will also Receive Service Responses once they have been processed and display them to the end users.

Broker. The Broker's goal is to provide the client with contextual allocation and contextual scheduling of services. It is composed by a Demand Generator Tier and a Demand Worker Tier (DWT). Further, it contains two important components: the Service-Recommender component and the Fusion-and-Monitoring component. The former is meant to perform all the logic which involves selecting and ranking the different options for a Service Demand (Service Composition). In addition, it adds different context-values that are unique to each Service Demand. The latter is in charge of Service Discovery based on the application user's location. It includes a Monitor-and-Observer and a Constrain-Generator; these allow the DWTs which are not constrained to be accessed from a database which contains all the registered DWTs (cinemas, shops, etc.).

Store/Database. The store (DST) is where all the Client and Security Service Demands are stored and retrieved by the Broker and the DWTs (once the demand has been processed). This will be implemented as a database with a table with two fields: a unique id and a value, represented as a string. Furthermore, the security services will somehow also store information about security events into the store.

Services/DWTs. The Services are either Shops, Museums, Cinemas and/or Restaurants. They will check demands of their respective type on the Store/Database and take them if the demand type matches their type, interpret the context in some way relative to the type of demand and its own constraints, and directly store it back on the Store/Database so that the Broker can retrieve it and use it accordingly. The Security Service is composed by a DGT, and it is responsible for exploring and discovering security alerts in the vicinity of the environment of the application user's location.

2.2 Scalability

Scalability testing was done using DGTSimulator with subtopic specific demands such as ShoppingDemands, RestaurantDemands and SecurityDemands etc. Since the response time (the difference of the sending timestamp and result reading timestamp) is preserved regardless of the number of items stored one the DST, this demonstrates the space-time scalability of the system for our specific demand types (Table 1).

Table 1. Response time w.r.t. increasing demands vs demand workers

Demands	1 DWT	3 DWT	6 DWT	18 DWT
10	10008.67	10008.44	10009.67	10009.07
100	10012.89	10010.15	10016.60	10009.91
1000	10013.47	10014.11	10015.14	10011.83
10000	10010.29	10013.87	10012.44	10011.17

3 Conclusion and Future Work

The extension of GIPSY to accommodate for a service-broker architecture proved challenging but successful in the sense that the introduction of such a service broker object to manage multiple different services and the filtering of their responses based on other demands and services does not have a significant impact on the demand response time while keeping the space- time scalability of the system intact. Evidently, for the type of service we are proposing, the turnaround time for a demand ultimately depends on the efficiency of the service providers to respond to that demand. However, by keeping the nature of all the service providers equal, we were then able to demonstrate that the number of incoming demands and/or the number of these standardized service providers does not have an impact on the system performance. Finally, the suitability of GIPSY as a distributed webservice provider is very promising even though further testing and extensions to other more elaborated services is needed. We are currently working to establish a test set that fully considers service constraints and other factors using GIPSY and our own data set.

References

1. Khakpour, N., Jalili, S., Talcott, C., Sirjani, M., Mousavi, M.R.: PobSAM: policy-based managing of actors in self-adaptive systems. In: Proceedings of the 6th International Workshop on Formal Aspects of Component Software (FACS 2009), vol. 263, pp. 129–143 (2010)
2. Laleh, T., Mokhov, S.A., Paquet, J., Yan, Y.: Context-aware cloud service brokerage: a solution to the problem of data integration among SaaS providers. In: Desai, B.C., Toyoma, M. (eds.) Proceedings of the Eighth International C* Conference on Computer Science & Software Engineering (C3S2E 2015), pp. 46–55, July 2015
3. ICEBE 2005 Organization Committee: Test data for web services challenge at ICEBE 2005 (2005). http://www.comp.hkbu.edu.hk/ctr/wschallenge/
4. Rabah, S., Mokhov, S.A., Paquet, J.: An interactive graph-based automation assistant: a case study to manage the GIPSY's distributed multi-tier run-time system. In: Suen, C.Y., Aghdam, A., Guo, M., Hong, J., Nadimi, E. (eds.) Proceedings of the ACM Research in Adaptive and Convergent Systems (RACS 2013), pp. 387–394. ACM, New York (2013). http://arxiv.org/abs/1212.4123
5. Wang, P., Ding, Z., Jiang, C., Zhou, M.: Constraint-aware approach to web service composition. IEEE Trans. Syst. Man Cybern. Syst. 44(6), 770–784 (2014)

DeMOCAS: Domain Objects for Service-Based Collective Adaptive Systems

Antonio Bucchiarone[✉], Martina De Sanctis, Annapaola Marconi,
and Alberto Martinelli

Fondazione Bruno Kessler, Via Sommarive, 18, Trento, Italy
{bucchiarone,msanctis,marconi,amartinelli}@fbk.eu

Abstract. DeMOCAS is a framework for the modeling and execution of service-based collective adaptive systems operating in dynamic environments. In this framework, we apply the Domain Object model and a Collective Adaptation algorithm to a case study from the mobility domain and we show its advantages in handling large-scale, decentralized and adaptive applications.

1 Introduction

Collective Adaptive Systems (CASs) are composed of distributed and heterogenous entities coming from both the real world and the back-end computer systems. Entities provide different system functionalities through their services. Services are defined as unique identifiable building blocks representing a concrete functionality in a larger, multi-service system. Implementing a functionality may involve interacting with other services through pre-defined protocols. At the same time, due to the high dynamism of the environment in which each service operates, the system must be able to re-configure its behavior at runtime in order to satisfy new users requirements and to fit new situations (i.e., unexpected and unlikely context changes). These systems ask for decentralized adaptations that can break the consistency of the whole collaboration. Thus, the adaptation must be itself collective: multiple services must adapt simultaneously to address a critical runtime condition, while preserving the collaboration and its benefits. In this paper we present **DeMOCAS**[1], a framework for the modeling and execution of service-based CASs. It includes mechanisms for services *specialization* and *adaptation* [4] and exploits the concept of *Domain Object* [3] as a way to model customizable and adaptable services. DeMOCAS is built around three main aspects: (i) *dynamic settings* (ii) *collaborative nature of systems*, and (iii) *collective adaptation*. To demonstrate DeMOCAS in action, we use a real-world scenario from the urban mobility domain[2].

---

[1] DeMOCAS is downloadable at the link: https://github.com/das-fbk/DeMOCAS.

[2] A video featuring the DeMOCAS solutions within the ALLOW Ensembles Project - http://www.allow-ensembles.eu/ can be viewed at the link: https://youtu.be/H0_LjptwZDg.

© Springer International Publishing AG 2017
K. Drira et al. (Eds.): ICSOC 2016 Workshops, LNCS 10380, pp. 174–178, 2017.
https://doi.org/10.1007/978-3-319-68136-8_19

2   Application Domain and Scenario

The scenario refers to a *Multi-modal and Collaborative Urban Mobility System* (UMS), in a smart-city context. The system's goal is that of synergistically exploit the city services (e.g., transport, smart-card, online payment services), providing real-time, and customized mobility services, for the support of the whole travel duration. Moreover, the system is able to deal with dynamic context changes affecting its execution, by allowing the application of collective adaptation techniques. The system allows users to plan and execute a journey, on the basis of a set of required information (e.g., departure and arrival time and places) and preferences (e.g., preferred transport means). It arranges the set of suitable mobility alternatives (made by one or a composition of services), among which the user can choose (e.g., the flexibus, a transportation service that manages on-demand routes defined as a network of dynamic pickup points). At execution time, *ensembles* made by different entities (e.g., the flexibus company, the route manager, the flexibus driver, the passengers) are dynamically organized. Although autonomous in their execution, the ensemble's member share common goals (e.g., being on time at the destination point). Ensembles play a fundamental role when the system needs to deal with context changes affecting its execution. The different entities can collaborate to reach the common good, in the cases in which adaptation needs arise (e.g., the flexibus route is blocked, a passenger is late to a pick-up point). If a collective adaptation is triggered, a decentralized and collective decision management strategy starts, where each entity does its best by offering its ability to handle specific problems. Furthermore, when an *intra-ensemble* adaptation (i.e., the problem is solved within the ensemble in which it arises) can not be solved, *inter-ensembles* adaptation (i.e., the problem is solved in the scope of more than one ensemble) can be performed.

3   Collective Adaptation Approach

In this Section we present the approach for modeling and execution of service-based CASs, as used in the implementation of DeMOCAS.

Application Model. DeMOCAS exploits a *design for adaptation* model, called Domain Object, defined with the purpose of modeling and executing service-based CASs. The model allows for the application of advanced techniques for dynamic adaptation (both *local* and *collective*), through specific constructs. Briefly, the system entities (e.g., system components, service providers) are modeled as domain objects (DOs from here on). Each DO implements its own behaviour (the *core process*), as well as the services (*fragments*) it provides. Both of them can be specified only partially, by defining *abstract activities* specified by their *goals*. At runtime, when a DO knows more about the context in which he is running, abstract activities are automatically refined with (one or a composition of) available fragments provided by other DOs. This also allows a DO to span its knowledge about the operational environment. Thus, the adaptive system results in a dynamic network of DOs. Moreover, over this dynamic network, *ensembles* are modeled as groups of autonomous DOs sharing common goals. For collective adaptation purposes, which are required to deal with adaptation needs spanning over the scope of a single DO, the model provides a set of *solvers* and *handlers*. While solvers model the ability of a DO to handle one or more issues, handlers are used to capture issues, during the nominal execution of a DO, and to trigger the appropriate solver.

Application Execution. DeMOCAS implements and shows the application of local and collective adaptations. The first one deals with the postponement of the concrete implementation of a service to the runtime phase (i.e., when the context is known). This kind of adaptation can be performed autonomously by a DO. The second, instead, is necessary to deal with unexpected changes in the environment and unpredictable behavior of the systems users and entities. For this kind of adaptation, a collaboration between DOs is required.

Local adaptation is performed at runtime through the refinement of abstract activities, by exploiting advanced techniques for dynamic and incremental service composition [1]. Moreover, through the refinement process, ensembles are formed. In the mobility domain, for instance, an ensemble can be made by the driver of a bus, its specific route and the passengers.

Collective adaptation comes into play to handle unpredictable changes, which usually affect different running entities. As a consequence, adaptation must be collective, for making the system resilient and avoid a halt. The collective adaptation is performed by exploiting the handlers and solvers constructs, and by associating a MAPE (Monitor, Analyze, Plan, Execute) loop [5] to each DO [2]. By monitoring the environment, handlers can both raise and–or catch issues. When an handler in a DO catches an issue, it calls the respective solver. A solver can solve the issue, or forward it outside the DO, if it is not able to provide a solution. In this case, a recursive procedure is triggered, leading to the construction of an issue resolution tree (as in Fig. 1, left side) in order to find a solution, if any. The chosen solution (the best one is selected in case of multiple solutions are available) will represent a path on the issue resolution tree. Moreover, it will be given by the union of the contributions coming for the solvers of the DOs involved in the resolution process. The best solution is eventually committed allowing the system to dynamically adapt and continue its execution. In Fig. 1 we show some panels of the *Collective Adaptation Viewer* of DeMOCAS. The *Active Issue Resolutions* table reports the issue resolution result for the issue `Intense Traffic`, triggered by a `Flexibus Driver` during its route execution, and it lists all the DOs involved in the issue resolution process. For each DO, the role, the handled issue, the issue status on its MAPE loop and the ensemble to which it belongs are given. The issue resolution tree, on the left side, relates to the `Route Manager` that owns the solver for the triggered issue. In the *Ensembles Hierarchy* panel, instead, the hierarchy of the ensembles involved in the issue resolution process, with their members, is graphically shown.

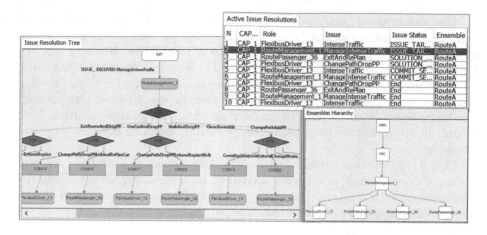

Fig. 1. Panels of the collective adaptation viewer of DeMOCAS.

4 Implementation

DeMOCAS has been implemented by using *Java* as programming language, in an *Eclipse* developing IDE. From a design point of view, we report the DeMOCAS deployment diagram, in Fig. 2. The demonstrator is composed by five modules, namely *Execution*, *Adaptation*, *AI Planning*, *Presentation* and *Model*.

The *Presentation* module implements the DeMOCAS *GUI*, together with the functionalities allowing the scenario execution to be showed in the demonstrator interface. The graphical representation of the application domain is a map, on which the user can intuitively follow the evolution of the UMS scenario. The Presentation module is constantly synchronized with the Execution module.

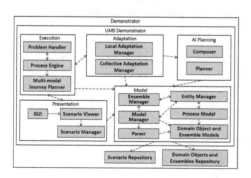

Fig. 2. DeMOCAS deployment diagram.

In the *Model* module, the *Parser* is responsible for loading the scenario files (i.e., the Domain Objects and the Ensembles) from the file system and parse it. The Process Model defines the basic building blocks for a process definition (e.g., input, output and abstract activities), while the *Model*, *Entity* and *Ensemble Managers*, are essentially devoted to handle the domain objects and ensembles life-cycles.

The *Execution* module comes into play once the scenario, modeled in terms of DOs, has been loaded and displayed. The *Process Engine* is in charge of simulating the execution of the core processes of the running DOs instances. When runtime problems occur, the *Problem Handler* creates requests for the Adaptation module.

The ***Adaptation*** module is called by the Process Engine. It tackles the refinement of abstract activities (*local* adaptations), as well as the issue resolutions (*collective* adaptations), through the *Local Adaptation Manager* and the *Collective Adaptation Manager*, respectively. The former is responsible for deriving the planning domain by driving the fragments selection and ranking (see [1]), according to the goal of the abstract activity and the specific execution context. The latter runs the collective adaptation algorithm, for the issue that has been caught, by triggering the issue resolution procedure spanning different DOs and ensembles.

The ***AI Planning*** module sustains the local adaptation of DOs, by supporting the refinement of abstract activities. It is in charge of managing the refinement procedure as an AI planning problem (*Planner*), providing the (composition of) fragments to be injected (*Composer*).

References

1. Bucchiarone, A., Marconi, A., Mezzina, C.A., Pistore, M., Raik, H.: On-the-fly adaptation of dynamic service-based systems: incrementality, reduction and reuse. In: Basu, S., Pautasso, C., Zhang, L., Fu, X. (eds.) ICSOC 2013. LNCS, vol. 8274, pp. 146–161. Springer, Heidelberg (2013). doi:10.1007/978-3-642-45005-1_11

2. Bucchiarone, A., Sanctis, M.D., Marconi, A.: Decentralized dynamic adaptation for service-based collective adaptive systems. In: Drira, K., et al. (eds.) ICSOC 2016 Workshops. LNCS, vol. 10380, pp. 5–20. Springer, Cham (2017)

3. Bucchiarone, A., De Sanctis, M., Marconi, A., Pistore, M., Traverso, P.: Design for adaptation of distributed service-based systems. In: Barros, A., Grigori, D., Narendra, N.C., Dam, H.K. (eds.) ICSOC 2015. LNCS, vol. 9435, pp. 383–393. Springer, Heidelberg (2015). doi:10.1007/978-3-662-48616-0_27

4. Bucchiarone, A., Sanctis, M.D., Marconi, A., Pistore, M., Traverso, P.: Incremental composition for adaptive by-design service based systems. In: IEEE 23rd International Conference on Web Services, ICWS 2016, pp. 236–243 (2016)

5. IBM: An architectural blueprint for autonomic computing. Technical report, IBM (2006)

Anuvaad Pranaali: A RESTful API for Machine Translation

Nehal J. Wani[✉], Sharada Prasanna Mohanty, Suresh Purini,
and Dipti Misra Sharma

International Institute of Information Technology, Hyderabad, India
{nehal.wani,spmohanty}@research.iiit.ac.in,
{suresh.purini,dipti}@iiit.ac.in

Abstract. The current web APIs are end-user centric as they mostly focus on the end results. In this paper, we break this paradigm for one class of scientific workflow problems —*machine translation,* by designing an API that caters not only to the end users but also allows researchers to find bugs in their systems by exposing the ability to programmatically manipulate the results. Moreover, it follows an easy to replicate workflow based mechanism, which is built on the concept of microservices.

Keywords: REST · API · Microservices · NLP · Framework · Docker · Workflow

1 Introduction

Machine translation (MT) systems are one of the scientific workflows which are extensively used by the researchers and industry; and they comprise of multiple components such as NER Engine, Lexical Transfer, Transliteration, etc. However, the existing systems follow a monolithic design that are not only static in nature but are difficult to debug.

We introduce a service-oriented architecture (SOA) for building scalable, distributed MT systems using composable distributed objects— *microservices* hosted in easily deployable containers. Our approach exposes components in these workflows through a simple API allowing the end users to easily construct and experiment with new systems. Our architecture builds on the approaches AnnoMarket [3], LetsMT! [5], and NLPCurator [8] by exposing microservices that not only allow access to intermediate results within a workflow, but also allow their modification. Moreover, our approach does not restrict microservices to a specific set of tools as they can be dynamically added at any point of time, during MT's life-cycle. Besides this, our proposed is not only limited to MT workflows, but can be easily adopted to any generic workflow.

In this paper, we describe our architecture and demonstrate its application to existing MT pipelines for a certain set of Language Pairs from Sampark [1][1].

---

[1] https://www.youtube.com/watch?v=XQD-155hDuA.

© Springer International Publishing AG 2017
K. Drira et al. (Eds.): ICSOC 2016 Workshops, LNCS 10380, pp. 179–183, 2017.
https://doi.org/10.1007/978-3-319-68136-8_20

2   System Design and Architecture

The existing MTs' design are inspired from monolithic architecture that use well-factored, independent modules within a single application. However, these modules are tightly coupled to a code base [7] and in most cases, are not amenable for reuse. Further, it may not be possible to build new workflows using existing modules developed by different sources due to software dependency conflicts and incompatible interfaces between them. We take a service-oriented architecture (SOA) based micro-distributed approach (*microservice* [4]) that bundles multiple independent tasks that are easy to deploy, scale and test. For example, in our system, the Urdu POS Tagger is one such microservice. We thwart the problem of monolithic approach by encapsulating the modules inside containers, which run as microservices and interact via the RESTful API. These microservices can be deployed on a cluster of inter-connected machines either in a public or a private cloud. Resource allocation and load balancing can be done at the granularity of microservices leading to a truly scalable distributed architecture.

2.1   The RESTful API

REpresentational State Transfer (REST) is an architectural style inspired by the web. This architecture provides many implementation options [6] including HTTP which uses verbs to easily state and formulate microservices as resources. We expose a simple, yet powerful API to end users where, whatever the translation task, queries are represented as HTTP POST requests of the form:

```
http://$a/$b/$c/$d/$e
$a = api-end-point
$b = src-language (ISO-639 code)
$c = tgt-language (ISO-639 code)
$d = starting-module-number
$e = ending-module-number
```

For example, to get the output up to running the *Shallow Parser* in our Hindu-Urdu pipeline, the POST request is structured as `http://$a/hin/urd/1/10`. If additional parameters are required, we pass them as additional POST parameters. Information about available language pairs in the entire system is exposed at `http://$a/langpairs`. The number of modules for a particular language pair are accessible via a simple GET request to `http://$a/$b/$c`, and the sequence of modules is available at `http://$a/$b/$c/modules`. A simple GET request to `http://$a/$b/$c/translate` should suffice, if the user wants a translation without the knowledge of submodules. All responses by the server[2] are in JSON format.

---

[2] http://api.ilmt.iiit.ac.in.

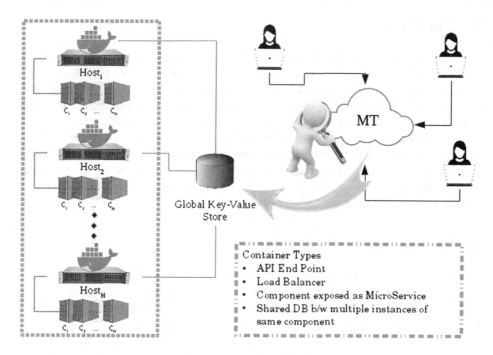

Fig. 1. An overview of the system architecture

2.2 Architecture Walkthrough

Our system architecture comprises of containers. We deploy our system using *Docker Swarm*[3] with the help of a multi-host *Overlay*[4] network. Each node in this cluster is either a microservice, or a load balancer for multiple instances of a single microservice (Fig. 1). For example, for an MT system with X well defined, isolated modules, we use at least $X + 1$ containers in the setup. The additional container hosts the public API end point. This container also holds the information about the next set of pre-defined/default modules of that scientific workflow. But the system is flexible enough to allow user to override the sequence with the route /translate/graph. All other microservices are oblivious of their position in the workflow sequence. Inside each container, the developers can write the submodules in any programming language, which are glued together and exposed as a single microservice using an HTTP server created using a REST wrapper (we use the Mojolicious Framework[5]). A generic, minimal working setup has been further explained at https://github.com/nehaljwani/ddag-sample.

---

[3] https://docs.docker.com/swarm/.

[4] https://docs.docker.com/engine/userguide/networking/dockernetworks/.

[5] http://mojolicious.org/.

3   The Client

We built a browser-based client[6] for querying exposed pipeline components. After sending the input text to the tokenizer, the JavaScript callbacks asynchronously process each sentence in parallel. The client auto-detects the input language, maintains the ordering of input sentences, and provides two key features: direct editing of target translations using JQuery IME; and direct modification of intermediate pipeline outputs and resuming the pipeline which we call ResumeMT [7]. This open source[8] client can be used for any language pair and is not necessarily limited to Indic Languages. The proposed API[9] has also been integrated with Kathaa [2][10], in a fashion where the Kathaa backend acts as a REST aggregator for all services, where, each node is processed independently.

4   Conclusion

We demonstrated an API with a browser based client as well as with a framework for creating workflows in NLP. Our approach is built on cloud-based services and an architecture that is not only easily deployable and distributed, but also resilient and composable for other NLP applications, and easier to maintain. In future, we will introduce a shared docker repository to host independent modules and a meta-language to automate the distributed setup based on a given configuration.

References

1. Sampark: Machine translation among Indian languages (2016). http://sampark.iiit. ac.in/sampark/web/index.php/content. Accessed 10 Feb 2016
2. Mohanty, S.P., Wani, N.J., Srivastava, M., Sharma, D.M.: Kathaa: a visual programming framework for NLP applications. In: Proceedings of the Demonstrations Session, NAACL HLT 2016, The 2016 Conference of the North American Chapter of the Association for Computational Linguistics: Human Language Technologies, San Diego California, USA, 12–17 June 2016, pp. 92–96. The Association for Computational Linguistics (2016)
3. Tablan, V., Bontcheva, K., Roberts, I., Cunningham, H., Dimitrov, M.: AnnoMarket: an open cloud platform for NLP. In: Proceedings of the 51st Annual Meeting of the Association for Computational Linguistics: System Demonstrations, pp. 19–24. Association for Computational Linguistics, Sofia, Bulgaria, August 2013. http:// www.aclweb.org/anthology/P13-4004
4. Thones, J.: Microservices. IEEE Software **32**(1), 116 (2015). http://dx.doi.org/ 10.1109/MS.2015.11

---

[6] http://pipeline.ilmt.iiit.ac.in.

[7] https://youtu.be/z9ugKY9UArI?t=2m40s.

[8] https://github.com/ltrc/anuvaad-pranaali.

[9] https://github.com/ltrc/ILMT-API.

[10] https://www.youtube.com/watch?v=woK5x0NmrUA.

5. Vasiļjevs, A., Skadiņš, R., Tiedemann, J.: Letsmt!: cloud-based platform for do-it-yourself machine translation. In: Proceedings of the ACL 2012 System Demonstrations, pp. 43–48. Association for Computational Linguistics, Jeju Island, Korea, July 2012. http://www.aclweb.org/anthology/P12-3008
6. Webber, J., Parastatidis, S., Robinson, I.: REST in Practice: Hypermedia and Systems Architecture, 1st edn. O'Reilly Media, Cambridge (2010). http://amazon.com/o/ASIN/0596805829/
7. Woods, D.: Enterprise Services Architecture. O'Reilly Media, Sebastopol (2003). https://books.google.co.in/books?isbn=0596005512, ISBN 10: 0596005512
8. Wu, H., Fei, Z., Dai, A., Sammons, M., Roth, D., Mayhew, S.: ILLINOIS-CLOUDNLP: text analytics services in the cloud. In: Calzolari, N., Choukri, K., Declerck, T., Loftsson, H., Maegaard, B., Mariani, J., Moreno, A., Odijk, J., Piperidis, S. (eds.) Proceedings of the Ninth International Conference on Language Resources and Evaluation (LREC 2014), pp. 14–21. European Language Resources Association (ELRA), Reykjavik, Iceland, May 2014. aCL Anthology Identifier: L14-1504

Integration of Heterogeneous Services and Things into Choreographies

Georgios Bouloukakis[(✉)], Nikolaos Georgantas, Siddhartha Dutta, and Valérie Issarny

MiMove Team, Inria, Paris, France
{georgios.bouloukakis,nikolaos.georgantas,
siddhartha.dutta,valerie.issarny}@inria.fr

Abstract. Internet-of-Things (IoT) protocols are constantly increasing in the research and industrial landscape. However, the current standardization efforts limit the incorporation of Things as first-class entities into choreographies. To tackle this interoperability barrier, we propose and demonstrate the *eVolution Service Bus* (VSB), a middleware solution targeted to enable the interaction between Things-based and business-oriented services. Particularly, we demonstrate the incorporation of a service/Thing into the following choreographies: *(i)* temperature sensors interacting with a business-oriented service, and *(ii)* business-oriented services interacting with a route planner service.

Keywords: Middleware · Service bus · Protocol interoperability · Binding Component

1 Introduction

Service Oriented Architecture (SOA) allows software entities to interact in standard ways. Choreographies [2] enable large scale integration of such entities via SOA in a peer-to-peer fashion. Interactions are realized using well known protocols such as SOAP and REST; and each service exposes its functionalities (operations, messages, etc.) by relying on XML-based standards (WSDL/WADL). The existence of standards, facilitates the development of frameworks and the wrapping of systems for interoperability. However, with the advent of paradigms such as the *Internet of Things* [4], major tech industry actors have introduced their own APIs to support the deployment of devices (Things). The resulting lack of standards limits the incorporation of Things as first-class entities into choreographies. To remedy this, heterogeneous protocols employed by Things, such as CoAP [6] supporting *client-service* interactions, MQTT [1] based on the *publish-subscribe* interaction paradigm, SemiSpace[1]. Offering a lightweight

---

V. Issarny—The work is supported by the collaborative research associate team ACHOR (inria.fr/en/associate-team/achor) and the EU-funded H2020 project CHOReVOLUTION (chorevolution.eu).

[1] http://www.semispace.org.

© Springer International Publishing AG 2017
K. Drira et al. (Eds.): ICSOC 2016 Workshops, LNCS 10380, pp. 184–188, 2017.
https://doi.org/10.1007/978-3-319-68136-8_21

shared *tuple space*, or Websockets [5] based on streaming interactions, should be made interoperable.

In this paper, we introduce and demonstrate the *eVolution Service Bus* (VSB, proposed by the CHOReVOLUTION project[2]. Its objective is to seamlessly interconnect services and Things that employ heterogeneous interaction protocols at the middleware level, e.g., SOAP and REST for Web services; CoAP, MQTT and WebSockets for Things. This is based on runtime conversions between such protocols, with respect to their primitives and data type systems, while properly mapping between their semantics. This also includes mapping between the public interfaces of services/Things, regarding their operations and data, from the viewpoint of the middleware. More specifically, middleware-level operations and data are converted, while their business semantics remains transparent to the conversion.

VSB follows the well-known Enterprise Service Bus (ESB) paradigm [3]. In this paradigm, a common intermediate bus protocol is used to facilitate interconnection between multiple heterogeneous middleware protocols: instead of implementing all possible conversions between the protocols, we only need to implement the conversion of each protocol to the common bus protocol, thus considerably reducing the development effort. This conversion is done by a component associated to the service/Thing in question and its middleware, called a *Binding Component (BC)*, as it binds the service/Thing to the service bus.

We introduce a generic architecture for VSB, which relies on the *Generic Middleware (GM)* abstraction. GM identifies and supports the basic interaction styles found in most middleware protocols: *one-way, two-way asynchronous, two-way synchronous*, and *stream* interactions. It also distinguishes between the two roles participating in an interaction, such as: *sender/receiver, client/server* and *consumer/producer*. In VSB, we define the GM API primitives, which rely on two main actions: *(i)* a `post` action for sending a piece of data; and *(ii)* a `get` action for receiving a piece of data. We then implement the primitives of every concrete middleware protocol by extending the GM API in the *Protocol Pool*.

In the following section, we present our solution for synthesizing lightweight BCs. Then, we provide details about the VSB implementation followed by the way it is to be used by developers. Finally, we demonstrate the incorporation of services/Things to choreographies.

2   System Overview

To enable the incorporation of any service/Thing into a concrete choreography, we elaborate a generic architecture for BCs. Particularly, a *Generic BC* specifies all the aforementioned interaction styles using our GM API. We determine the supported interactions and the middleware concrete protocol of each service/Thing through a generic interface description, which we call GIDL (similar to WADL/WSDL, but general enough to support a variety of protocols). To synthesize a new BC and bridge two concrete protocols (the choreography protocol

---

[2] http://www.chorevolution.eu.

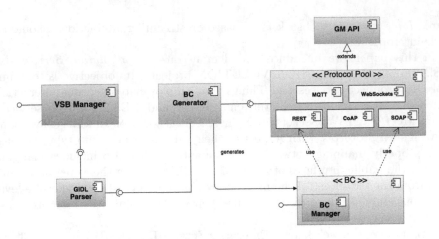

Fig. 1. VSB architecture

and the service's Thing's protocol), we use the implementations defined in the Protocol Pool.

Implementation. VSB has been implemented using Java 8 and the Maven software project management tool. A GIDL interface is in JSON format, inspired by the Swagger[3] specification. BCs are synthesized using the JCodeModel API (code generator). Regarding the *Protocol Pool*, REST has been implemented using the Restlet API, SOAP using the JAX-WS API, MQTT using the Paho project and CoAP using the Californium framework. The implementation is available as open source[4].

Use by the developer. We present the architecture of the VSB development environment in Fig. 1. VSB can be used with the following ways: *(i)* an application developer incorporates a *new service/Thing* to the choreography *(ii)* a middleware developer introduces a *new protocol*.

New service/Thing : A service/Thing is incorporated to the choreography through the following steps: *(i)* the *VSB Manager* requires the service's/Thing's *GIDL* interface and the choreography protocol (e.g., SOAP); *(ii)* if the service's/Thing's protocol (e.g., SemiSpace) is not included in the *Protocol Pool*, the VSB Manager cannot create the corresponding BC. In such case, the middleware developer must enrich the Protocol Pool with the service's/Thing's concrete protocol. *(iii)* in case the protocol is supported (e.g., CoAP), the VSB Manager requires the corresponding BC from the *BC Generator*; *(iv)* an artifact with the BC is synthesized as described above; *(v)* through this artifact, the BC can be deployed, configured, started or stopped its execution using the BC manager.

New protocol : To add a new protocol (e.g., SemiSpace) in our framework, a middleware developer should follow the steps below: *(i)* identify the protocol's

---

[3] http://swagger.io/.

[4] https://tuleap.ow2.org/plugins/git/chorevolution/evolution-service-bus.

primitives with respect to the GM API; *(ii)* implement the above primitives; *(iii)* implement the methods for the deployment (startup, shutdown, etc.) of each component role (client, server, etc.); and *(iv)* bind the protocol to the *Protocol Pool*. To facilitate middleware developers introducing new protocols, we intend to develop an eclipse plugin.

Demonstration. We consider two choreographies of services interacting using two different protocols: MQTT and SOAP. Regarding the 1st, developers desire to use a REST service to gather all the information published by temperature sensors (MQTT publishers). Sensor data should be published using the method `POST` (one-way interaction) to the resource named `sensors` through the URI: `/sensors/{id}/temperature`. We map the topic of MQTT publishers to the REST service resource and we demonstrate this communication using a synthesized BC. Concerning the 2nd choreography (SOAP protocol), developers wish to get information from a legacy *route planner* service, provided by Google. Thus, a SOAP request, `requestRoute (origin, dest)`, should be sent to the REST service which accepts requests to the URI: `/directions/{origin}/{dest}` using the `GET` method (two-way synchronous interaction). For this, we synthesize a BC that exposes a *WSDL* interface and is able to accept the requests sent. SOAP operations are mapped to the REST resources and XML data is converted to JSON for both the requests and responses. The above use cases are demonstrated in the following video: https://youtu.be/UgfM3810RS8

3   Conclusion

To allow the integration of both services and Things in choreographies, we introduce a lightweight and fully distributed ESB, which allows interconnection among smart devices and services in a peer to peer way. Different protocols can be introduced as VSB's common bus protocol with the same easiness as for integrating support for a new middleware protocol of a service/Thing; additionally, there is no need for relying on a full-fledged ESB platform. Using our approach, legacy services can be integrated into choreographies without the need for editing. VSB BCs are built and deployed as necessary; hence, no BC is needed when a service/Thing employs the same middleware protocol as the one used as the choreography protocol. We intend to extend the functionality of BCs, e.g., under certain aspects of IoT and mobile applications, to support dynamic changes in choreography scenarios.

References

1. Banks, A., Gupta, R.: MQTT version 3.1. 1. OASIS Standard (2014)
2. Barker, A., Walton, C.D., Robertson, D.: Choreographing web services. IEEE Trans. Serv. Comput. **2**, 152–166 (2009)
3. Chappell, D.A.: Enterprise Service Bus. O'Reilly Media, Sebastopol (2004)

4. Guinard, D., Karnouskos, S., Trifa, V., Dober, B., Spiess, P., Savio, D.: Interacting with the SOA-based internet of things: discovery, query, selection, and on-demand provisioning of web services. IEEE Trans. Serv. Comput. **3**, 223–235 (2010)
5. Lubbers, P., Greco, F.: HTML5 web sockets: a quantum leap in scalability for the web. SOA World Magazine (2010)
6. Shelby, Z., Hartke, K., Bormann, C.: IETF RFC 7252: The Constrained Application Protocol (CoAP). http://www.rfc-editor.org/info/rfc7252

Testing Processes with Service Invocation: Advanced Logging in CPEE

Florian Stertz[✉], Stefanie Rinderle-Ma, Tobias Hildebrandt,
and Juergen Mangler

Faculty of Computer Science, University of Vienna, Vienna, Austria
{florian.stertz,stefanie.rinderle-ma,
tobias.hildebrandt,juergen.mangler}@univie.ac.at

Abstract. Business process analysis is one of the major concerns for
companies: before processes are enacted and executed, flaws and bottle-
necks should be removed. Process simulation has been traditionally used
to simulate process paths based on stochastic information. However, the
obtained results are often not consistent with the behavior that can be
observed later during process execution as the functioning and reaction
of the orchestrated web services cannot be considered. To provide more
realistic results, a process testing environment is presented that equips
the Cloud Process Execution Engine (CPEE) with a newly developed
logging component. The contribution of the logging component is that
it incorporates simulated data from invoked services and thus allows for
the generation of more realistic log files.

1 Introduction

Simulating and testing business processes is crucial for different reasons such as
improving process performance or detecting problems with web services. Process
simulations are performed based on stochastic information and without considering the behavior of invoked services. As a consequence, the obtained results
do not reflect the behavior that can be observed later during process execution.

Instead of simulating process executions, the system described in this demo,
creates and runs process instances in a testing environment based on the Cloud
Process Execution Engine (CPEE)[1]. The CPEE – a lightweight, modular, and
service oriented process engine - has proven its maturity in many application scenarios [3]. Working with a process engine enables the testing of process instances
together with the invoked services by calling real services, which may either be
the same services used in productive execution, or demo services simulating a
specific behavior for testing purposes. On top of more realistic testing results,
the tested process instances can be directly put into "production mode" without
export/importing between execution engine and simulation environment, necessitating possibly quite some additional reworking of the simulated processes
before being able to execute them. This paper focuses on its suitability of the

---

[1] http://cpee.org.

© Springer International Publishing AG 2017
K. Drira et al. (Eds.): ICSOC 2016 Workshops, LNCS 10380, pp. 189–193, 2017.
https://doi.org/10.1007/978-3-319-68136-8_22

CPEE as a testing environment in general, and its newly extended logging capabilities in specific. In the following, the necessary steps and different options for testing process instances in the CPEE are described, starting with the import of a process model provided in BPMN notation and creating and assigning services that are to be executed. It is then shown how to spawn and execute process instances in test mode and how the generated process logs can be configured and retrieved. Application scenarios are discussed as a conclusion.

2   Process Model Creation

At first, the process model based on which the process instances to be tested will be initiated and executed has to be created. In the CPEE, a process model can be created either directly using a graph model or by importing BPMN process models created in, for example, Signavio[2].

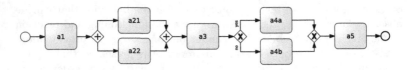

Fig. 1. Process model containing one decision and one parallel gateway (modeled in BPMN, using Signavio)

Figure 1 shows a small BPMN use case that can be imported. This model shows a parallel activity, at a21 and a22, and a decision at a4a and a4b. This use case will be employed throughout the paper.

Another option would be to compose the diagram directly in the CPEE Cockpit[3]. The result of both options can be seen in Fig. 2. Each of these activities invokes a specific web service. The CPEE can orchestrate services that are reachable over the HTTP(S) or XMPP protocols, other protocols are easy to implement. When a service is finished, the next activity is marked active.

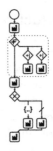

Fig. 2. CPEE process model

Our goal was to create a log file for every process instance in the CPEE to simulate a huge amount of data in a short time. These logs are created using the XES format at the moment, but any other format can be easily implemented.

---

[2] http://academic.signavio.com/.
[3] A simple frontend for the CPEE, that allows for creating and inspecting process images.

3   Implementation

Every time an activity is enacted, manipulated, or finished, the custom logging extension described in this paper[4] is called to process this information. There are many kinds of events that could be logged.

- Activity/Called. Every time a service is invoked, usually after the last activity has been finished.
- Activity/Manipulated. When a service returns some data, this data is incorporated into the process context (assigned to variables, made available as potential input for future service invocations) which triggers this notification.
- Activity/Finished. When the invocation as well as the manipulation of process context is finished, a notification is pushed.

Usually for mining a process model, we are interested to find the control flow, so we want to know when a service reports back to the CPEE and an activity is finished. For the life cycle of an event, it is also important to know when the activity started and got called. The main part of such log files are timestamps for every event. There are at least two possible options for timestamps.

Every time the process management system receives the information about an activity to be finished, the timestamp can be either (1) a timestamp provided by the service, which marks the exact time when work was finished, or (2) a timestamp generated by the process engine that includes the latency and time that is required for returning the data from a service.

Both options have their advantages when analyzing the result. Especially the first option (which is not very common) can be useful when huge quantities of data are transmitted over unreliable connections.

The developed logging service supports both options. If the services deliver a timestamp, the timestamp of the service will be used, but if no timestamp is delivered, the CPEE will create a timestamp and use this one for the log file. The minimum documentation of events are timestamps and a label of an event, but usually there is more information associated to an event. Another interesting point in logging information of the execution of a process instance are data values. For each service there is input and output. To the best of our knowledge, there is no standardized way of storing this data in the XES[5] format, but it allows to be extended in a flexible way. Thus we created two lists per event in our log file to store this additional information (see Listing 1).

Listing 1. Example of storing received data

```
1 if @log_hash.has_key?(:data_received)
2   @log_hash[:data_received].delete_if do |e|
3     if e.keys[0]=="timestamp"
4       event.add 'date', :key => "time:timestamp", :value => e.values[0]
5       time_added=true
6     else
7       false
```

---

[4] Loaded at run-time, for certain instances.
[5] http://www.xes-standard.org.

```
 8      end
 9    end
10    if @log_hash[:data_received].length > 0
11      list = event.add 'list', :key => "data_received"
12      @log_hash[:data_received].each do
13        |e| list.add 'string', :key => e.keys[0] , :value => e.values[0]
14      end
15    end
16 end
```

This allows for more than mining the process model, like decision point mining [4] for specific events. After the instance is executed and the status is finished, the log file can be retrieved directly from the CPEE[6].

Listing 2. Example of log file

```
 1 <event>
 2   <string key="concept:name" value="a22"/>
 3   <date key="time:timestamp" value="2016-07-14T12:56:36+02:00"/>
 4 </event>
 5 <event>
 6   <string key="concept:name" value="a3"/>
 7   <date key="time:timestamp" value="2016-07-15T12:56:36+02:00"/>
 8   <list key="data_received">
 9     <string key="decision" value="yes"/>
10   </list>
11 </event>
12 <event>
13   <string key="concept:name" value="a4a"/>
14   <date key="time:timestamp" value="2016-07-16T12:56:36+02:00"/>
15   <list key="data_send">
16     <string key="value" value="yes"/>
17   </list>
18 </event>
```

Listing 2 shows an example of a log file the process model described in this paper can produce. For each event the name and the timestamp is stored and for some events the used data is stored as well if available.

4   Application Scenarios

The logs retrieved from the CPEE can be utilized for different purposes such as process mining. The creation of other log types is possible, for example, change logs that are crucial for recommending changes [2] or change propagation logs that enable the prediction of change propagation behavior in distributed process settings [1]. The advantages of the CPEE combined with the new logging services are in creating a fast test environment for services, which can deployed into *real world* production environments with minimum effort. The logging service has already been used in various domains (source can be found here http://cpee. org/?t=code&c=show&CEWebS_path=server%2Fhandlerwrappers%2F).

---

[6] http://cpee.org/icsoc2016.

References

1. Fdhila, W., Rinderle-Ma, S., Indiono, C.: Memetic algorithms for mining change logs in process choreographies. In: Franch, X., Ghose, A.K., Lewis, G.A., Bhiri, S. (eds.) ICSOC 2014. LNCS, vol. 8831, pp. 47–62. Springer, Heidelberg (2014). doi:10. 1007/978-3-662-45391-9_4
2. Kaes, G., Rinderle-Ma, S.: Mining and querying process change information based on change trees. In: Barros, A., Grigori, D., Narendra, N.C., Dam, H.K. (eds.) ICSOC 2015. LNCS, vol. 9435, pp. 269–284. Springer, Heidelberg (2015). doi:10. 1007/978-3-662-48616-0_17
3. Mangler, J., Rinderle-Ma, S.: Cpee - cloud process exection engine. In: International Conference on Business Process Management. CEUR-WS.org (2014)
4. Rozinat, A., Aalst, W.M.P.: Decision mining in business processes. Beta, Research School for Operations Management and Logistics (2006)

COOL: A Model-Driven and Automated System for Guided and Verifiable Cloud Solution Design

Hamid R. Motahari Nezhad[1(✉)], Karen Yorov[2], Peifeng Yin[1], Taiga Nakamura[1],
Scott Trent[3], Gil Shurek[2], Takayuki Kushida[3], and Uma Subramanian[4]

[1] IBM Research Almaden Center, San Jose, CA, USA
{motahari,peifengy,taiga}@us.ibm.com
[2] IBM Haifa Research Lab, Haifa, Israel
{yorov,shurek}@il.ibm.com
[3] IBM Tokyo Research Lab, Tokyo, Japan
{trent,kushida}@jp.ibm.com
[4] IBM Cloud Business Unit, San Jose, USA
uma@us.ibm.com

Abstract. In this paper, we present COOL (ClOud sOlution design tooL), which is a model-driven cloud solution design tool for automatic solution generation, and solution verification. It offers a guided solutioning and customization method starting from complex client business and IT requirements, and enables verification of solution correctness by leveraging constraint satisfaction solvers.

Keywords: Cloud Solution Design · Model-Driven software engineering · Guided solution design · Cloud solution verification

1 Introduction

Over the last few years, the rate of adoption of cloud computing has accelerated significantly. In the enterprise marketplace, managed cloud services are common in which an enterprise migrates all their applications from their own data centers to cloud and expects the cloud providers to manage it for them [1]. There are different levels of managed services: managed infrastructure only (virtual machines, network, etc.), managed infrastructure, middleware, and database but not applications, and managed applications in which the service levels are defined at the application level. The first step in a cloud sales deal is capturing the client requirements including application hosting, infrastructure needs, service level requirements, the need for disaster recovery, database resiliency, backup, etc. The problem is the automated generation of correct solutions that meets client's requirements, as per the cloud provider's offering.

In this demonstration paper, we present Cloud Solution Design Tool (abbreviated as COOL), which is a model-driven and automated solution design tool for infrastructure and managed services offerings of a cloud provider. COOL makes novel contributions by supporting the end-to-end lifecycle of technical solution design, starting from client requirements to generating a deployable solution, and the associated bill of material for costing/pricing. COOL also offers a guided solutioning approach to enable solution

© Springer International Publishing AG 2017
K. Drira et al. (Eds.): ICSOC 2016 Workshops, LNCS 10380, pp. 194–198, 2017.
https://doi.org/10.1007/978-3-319-68136-8_23

architects not only to create correct solution drafts, but also to modify an existing solution configuration in compliance with the provider cloud offerings.

2   Cloud Solution Design Tool (COOL): An Overview

The conceptual architecture of the Cloud Solution Design Tool (COOL) is depicted in Fig. 1. COOL consists of 7 main components, i.e. requirement capture, client requirement analysis, automated solution generation, solution validator, solution design editor, and output generator. These components sit on top of a persistence layer containing cloud data models, solution transformation logic, and an offering description language, which makes COOL's data model extensible. The data model consists of a set of generic elements that form the model of the world, on top of which offering specific constructs are defined. The world data model includes a set of generic cloud data elements and their relationships, such as a virtual machine (VM), CPU, RAM, Storage, and network interfaces; Database, and Application. Offering-specific entities include elements for different types of VMs, database/OS types, and specific applications. For instance, for SAP Managed Services Offerings, the element of an SAP System defines a set of attributes to specify a system for an SAP Product with a specific role (production, Dev, QA– quality assurance-, etc.). An SAP system may be served by several servers/VMs. Similarly, the client requirement model is described by building on the world's model constructs. The offering model extends the data model to describe a specific provider's cloud offerings including applicable constraints, mapping and transformation rules, and solution patterns (pre-built solution offerings). The Requirement Analysis module uses formal methods to validate the client's requirements w.r.t. provider's offering including specific choice of values and types of resources/services requested. The solution generation approach in COOL employs a hybrid of model-driven and formal methods for generating correct solution drafts for given client requirements. This is done by first generating a solution skeleton using transformation rules, and then updating the solution by populating the constructs with valid values, using an approach called value propagation from constraint satisfaction domain [6], and adding any required constructs due to value assignment. At this stage, the draft solution still has attributes that may need to be further configured by the solution architect. As the architect makes changes, the Solution Validator uses a constraint solver [6], which reads the offering model, to check if the chosen values are valid with respect to the offering definition, otherwise identifies the conflicting attributes/values based on unsatisfiable core identification approach [6]. COOL's Solution Design Editor supports guided solutioning through value propagation and guiding the user to resolve identified conflicts. More detail on technical architecture and implementation of COOL can be found in [7].

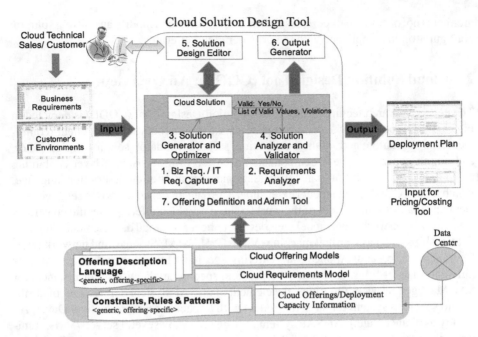

Fig. 1. The conceptual architecture of cloud solution design tool (COOL)

COOL makes novel contributions compared to the state of the art. As a cloud specification language, TOSCA [2] allows specifying application architecture and deployable application components. Similarly, CloudML [3] offers a language for representing cloud applications with a focus on managing elasticity and scalability at deployment time. OCCI [4] offers a generic metamodel and a model-driven approach for cloud application deployment. In industry, Microsoft's MAP [5] supports assessment and planning of migration of Windows-based servers to Microsoft Azure. However, all these approaches focus on the specification and deployment of cloud applications. COOL addresses the open space of cloud solution design starting from complex client's business and IT requirements, and offer a model-driven approach for solution validation and analysis, and requirement-offerings fitness in the sales lifecycle.

3   COOL Demonstration Scenario

We demonstrate the use of COOL for end-to-end cloud solution design automation. In COOL, architects can create a solution design project including one or more of supported cloud offerings. Client requirements are separated into business requirements, and IT requirements. The business requirements consist of a set of questions, some disqualifying questions to check whether the offering can address the client's need from a business point of view. COOL can take the client's IT requirements in spreadsheet format that are loaded into the tool, or directly entered through the interactive IT requirements capture UI. Next, architects are guided to requirement analysis that checks whether various combinations of requested resources and services can be supported by the chosen offering, and creates a report consists of warnings and errors. For example, in a managed application offering, there may be only specific combinations of supported OS and Databases. To resolve these issues, the architect is offered an interactive UI to either modify the requirements, or allow the tool to use default values. After all errors are resolved (and not necessarily warnings), the architects can proceed with automated solution generation. The model-driven solution generation module generates a skeleton of the solution, by mapping requirement elements to offering elements, using the mapping/transformation rules. These transformation rules are codified as parameterized JavaScript code fragments over the data domain of requirements and solution models, represented in JSON. Data domains (values) are expressed in form of tables that can be edited by non-expert users. The transformation logic lives out of the main application code, and it is updatable independently of the application. Therefore, new Cloud offerings can be added to the tool, or existing ones modified, without impacting COOL's application code.

After the model-driven transformation step, the generated solution object is passed to a constraint satisfaction solver, which understands the offering model and associated solutioning constraints (these are automatically generated from the offering models). In this process, it progressively populates the attributes with allowable values based on other chosen values (the same as in the example of specific allowed combinations of OS and database types). Value propagation logic may add new elements to the solution object based on attribute values, as well, for example additional CPUs, RAM, Storage or VMs to meet progressively updated solution. Once a solution draft is generated, if some attributes are note automatically populated, COOL marks the solution as incomplete, and points architects to make applicable selections. If the architect's updates lead to an incorrect solution, COOL flags the solution as incorrect and identifies conflicting solution elements and values. Once the solution is valid and complete, the COOL allows generation of deployable solution specification, according to the offering logic, and also outputs detailed billing feature codes for a downstream solution costing/pricing tool. In the demonstration, we will also show accelerated solutioning options through predefined requirement and solution templates, based on best practices.

References

1. Linthicum, D.: The case for managed service providers in your cloud strategy (2016). http://www.infoworld.com/article/2923441/cloud-computing/the-case-for-managed-service-providers-in-your-cloud-strategy.html
2. Binz, T., Breitenbucher, U., Kopp, O., Leymann, F.: TOSCA: portable automated deployment and management of cloud applications. In: Bouguettaya, A., Sheng, Q., Daniel, F. (eds.) Advanced Web Services, pp. 527–549. Springer, New York (2014)
3. Ferry, N., Rossini, A., Chauvel, F., Morin, B., Solberg, A.: Towards model-driven provisioning, deployment, monitoring, and adaptation of multi-cloud systems. In: IEEE CLOUD 2013, pp. 887–894. IEEE Press (2013)
4. Merle, P., Barais, O., Parpaillon, J., Plouzeau, N., Tata, S.: A precise metamodel for open cloud computing interface. In: IEEE CLOUD 2015, pp. 852–859. IEEE Press (2015)
5. Microsoft Assessment and Planning (MAP) (2016). https://technet.microsoft.com/en-us/solutionaccelerators/gg581074.aspx

6. Boni, O., Fournier, F., Mashkif, N., Naveh, Y., Sela, A., Shani, U., Lando, Z., Modai, A.: Applying Constraint programming to incorporate engineering methodologies into the design process of complex systems. In: 24th Conference on Innovative Applications of Artificial Intelligence. Toronto, Ontario, Canada (2012)
7. Trent, S., et al.: Resolutions to technical challenges regarding the distributed development and deployment of a node.js web application for cloud solution design. In: Software Engineering Symposium, Tokyo, Japan (2016)

A Service-Based System for Sentiment Analysis and Visualization of Twitter Data in Realtime

Yehia Taher[1(✉)], Rafiqul Haque[2], Mohammed AlShaer[3,5],
Willem Jan v.d. Heuvel[4], Karine Zeitouni[1], Renata Araujo[4],
Mohand-Saïd Hacid[3], and Mohamed Dbouk[5,6]

[1] DAVID, Université de Versailles Saint-Quentin-en-Yvelines, Versailles, France
{Yehia.taher,Karine.Zeitouni}@uvsq.fr
[2] Cognitus, Paris, France
rafiqul.haque@cognitus.fr
[3] LIRIS, Université Claude Bernard 1, Villeurbanne, France
{m.alshaer,mohand-said.hacid}@univ-lyon1.fr
[4] ERISS, Tilburg University, Tilburg, The Netherlands
[5] Universidade Federal do Rio de Janeiro, Rio de Janeiro, Brazil
renata.araujor@uniriotec.br
[6] Lebanese University, Beirut, Lebanon
mdbouk@ul.edu.lb

Abstract. The existing solutions for sentiment analysis suffer from serious shortcomings to effectively deal with Twitter data as they can merely exploit hashtags. In this demo, we present SANA: a reusable, service-based architecture for dealing with streaming data, analysing this data on the fly taking into account more comprehensive semantics of Tweets, and dynamically monitoring and visualising trends in sentiments through dashboarding and query facilities.

Keywords: Sentiment analysis · Realtime analysis · Big data · Twitter

1 Motivation and Challenges

Recently, organizations have commenced to rely heavily on external data - specially Twitter data - to perform sentiment analysis in order to get a better grasp on how their enterprise, products, services and processes are perceived by customers at real-time. In particular, a vast volume of the Twitter data exhibit emotions of consumers. A realtime analysis with Twitter data results in timely decisions and interventions from the organization, such as adapting their offer to the consumer expectations. However, realtime analysis on Twitter data is enormously challenging. The most critical challenges are two-fold: (i) unlike the classic relational data, Twitter data are *unstructured*, whilst (ii) the *velocity* (speed) of data is extremely high and unpredictable. For instance, on average, more than 6000 tweets are tweeted every second. Several sentiment analytics are proposed in literature *e.g.*, [1–4]. Unfortunately however, to the best of our

© Springer International Publishing AG 2017
K. Drira et al. (Eds.): ICSOC 2016 Workshops, LNCS 10380, pp. 199–202, 2017.
https://doi.org/10.1007/978-3-319-68136-8_24

knowledge, these solutions merely exploit hashtags which contain a small fragment of a tweet. In our view, this is clearly not sufficient for performing complete analysis because it lacks the ability to realize the contexts of tweets. In addition, these solutions are built-on traditional architectural paradigm. Therefore, in this paper, we propose SANA, a service-based solution for realtime sentiment analysis with the Twitter data, which takes into account the context and the content of the tweets.

2   System Overview

The multi-layered architecture of SANA consists of various components, which are briefly described in the following.

Data Collection and Ingestion Layer: This layer contains two components: a data collector and a data ingestor. The data collector is a client which binds one or many data source APIs that enable an access to remote repositories with an authentication check through their public keys. Once the connection is established, the data collector starts fetching data streams (*i.e.*, tweets) in realtime. The data ingestor consists of two interfaces. The first interface taps data into SANA *data lake* which is a distributed Hadoop cluster, reside in the storage layer. The other interface opens a channel to push tweets directly to the data processing components.

Data Processing Layer: The components contained in this layer perform several tasks. The two main tasks are carried out in this layer include *data analysis* and *visualization*. *Data distribution* and *query execution* are two additional tasks performed in this layer. The analysis starts with filtering incoming Twitter data. SANA's data filter eliminates unnecessary strings from tweets and keeps the core text required for analysis. Also, it allocates an *unique identifier* to each tweet. Then, the text classifier extracts and classifies positive and negative sentiments from the texts. We used the multinomial naïve-bayes classifier (a machine learning technique for supervised learning) along with Chi Square (χ^2) feature selection. The multinomial naïve-bayes classifier is used to train our model with labeled training datasets that are classified as positive or negative sentiment. The Chi Square (χ^2) function tests whether the occurrence of a specific string and the occurrence of a specific class is independent. The NER tagger extracts the contexts of classified texts. It labels the sequence of context related strings (*e.g.*, person, location, and organization) in a tweet. After the classification is done, the data distributor sends the results to local disk, the data lake (Hadoop cluster), and the graph storage. Queries to find the comprehensive detail of the results are submitted through SANA's query interface.

Data Storage Layer: Two different types of storage is integrated in SANA: *data lake* and *graph storage* where the results are stored. The data lake is a cluster of nodes where data blocks are distributed. SANA adopts data lake to deal with massive-scale data. The graph based storage of SANA assists to building knowledge graph of classified texts and their contexts.

Presentation Layer: SANA provides a graphical user interface (GUI) which consists of a *control panel* and a textbox for *data visualization*. The control panel provides three services. The *data collection service* calls and loads the data collector. The *backend services* call processing servers, the graph database server, the coordination server which maintains configuration information, and provides the distributed synchronization service. The *query execution* service calls and loads the query processor. Lastly, the visualization interface loads the data visualizer and visualizes pie chart that shows the percentage of positive and negative sentiment.

3   Demonstration

SANA is offered as a desktop-based solution and a software as a service (SaaS) on the cloud. Therefore, it provides two different user interfaces: *desktop based* and *web based*. In this paper, we describe the former. In the first step, an user starts all the servers by clicking a button called *running background services* provided in the user interface (We assume that these servers are installed and configured in user's machine). This starts data acquisition server, processing servers, Haddop cluster, and graph storage server. In the next step, the user starts SANA sentiment analytics application. Upon clicking on *start application* button a window pops up, the user then selects the application jar file provided by SANA. Once the file is imported, the SANA realtime application starts and the tasks are performed automatically from this point until visualization. SANA's data collector establishes a connection with the Twitter data center using an authentication API and starts fetching data (the user can view the data collection step on the screen); then it ingests the raw data into SANA's topology which is essentially the processing logic. Figure 1A shows the topology.

The topology contains: Tweet filter, Tweet classifier, and Tweet NER which perform three tasks, filtering data, sentiment classification, and context extraction. Then, in the next step three tasks are carried out in parallel. First, the consumer sentiments are visualized in a pie chart which shows the percentages of positive and negative views on a concept/product or service which in our demonstration is a *land*. Figure 1B presents the results produced in every less than a second. The users will observe that sentiment analysis results are updated constantly, as classification is carried out in realtime over the incoming tweets. Second, SANA's data distributor stores the results in data lake (Hadoop cluster), and the graph storage server. Also the results are stored in local disk. Third, the knowledge graph – consisting of extracted sentiments and their contexts – are visualized by our graph storage. Figure 1C shows the knowledge graph.

Finally, an user might be interested to perform correlated queries to extract more knowledge from the tweets. The user clicks *Analysis* button, a textbox appears on the screen. Then the user types queries such as, "match (n) --> 2 with n, count (*) as rel-cnt where rel_cnt > 2 return n. Id n. text Limit 15". This

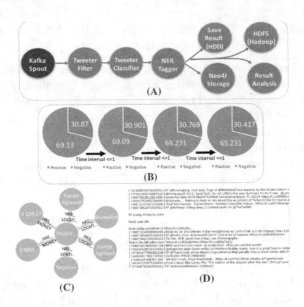

Fig. 1. (A) The SANA Topology **(B)** The percentage positive and negative sentiment **(C)** The Knowledge graph **(D)** The Knowledge Graph

demonstration query in our demo returned 15 tweets. Each of these tweet contants more than two relations among the nodes that represent context and sentiment. Figure 1D shows the textual representation of the results of the query. We provided a video of this demonstration in here: http://cognitus-research.webs.com which gives more detail.

References

1. Agarwal, A., Xie, B., Vovsha, I., Rambow, O., Passonneau, R.: Sentiment analysis of twitter data. In: Proceedings of the Workshop on Languages in Social Media, pp. 30–38. Association for Computational Linguistics, June 2011
2. Chong, W.Y., Selvaretnam, B., Soon, L.K.: Natural language processing for sentiment analysis: an exploratory analysis on tweets. In: 2014 4th International Conference on Artificial Intelligence with Applications in Engineering and Technology (ICAIET), pp. 212–217, Kota Kinabalu (2014)
3. Nasukawa, T., Yi, J.: Sentiment analysis: capturing favorability using natural language processing. In: Proceedings of the 2nd International Conference on Knowledge Capture, pp. 70–77. ACM, October 2003
4. Neethum M.S., Rajasree, R.: Sentiment analysis in twitter using machine learning techniques. In: 2013 Fourth International Conference on Computing, Communications and Networking Technologies (ICCCNT), pp. 1–5, Tiruchengode (2013)

XDAI-A: Framework for Enabling Cross-Device Integration of Android Apps

Dennis Wolters[1(✉)], Jonas Kirchhoff[1], Christian Gerth[2], and Gregor Engels[1]

[1] Department of Computer Science, Paderborn University, Paderborn, Germany
{dennis.wolters,engels}@uni-paderborn.de, jonaskir@mail.uni-paderborn.de
[2] Faculty of Business Management and Social Sciences,
Osnabrück University of Applied Sciences, Osnabrück, Germany
c.gerth@hs-osnabrueck.de

Abstract. A lot of people are managing multiple computing devices suited for different purposes, like private and work devices. Integrating applications running on different devices is often a problem, because the services provided by those applications are not meant to be integrated. In this demonstration, we present our XDAI-A framework which enables cross-device integration of services provided by Android apps. The framework uses adapters to convert Android-internal service interfaces of existing apps into external services with a platform-independent interface that can be accessed from applications on other devices and even other platforms. Our ready-to-use framework does not require to alter existing Android apps, since the adapters are installed separately. For the convenient specification of adapters, our framework comes with a domain-specific language (DSL). Additionally, we provide an infrastructure to find and integrate devices and their applications' services.

Keywords: Cross-Device · Integration · Android · Services

1 Introduction

In our everyday life, we use several different types of computing devices, like desktop computers, smartphones, or tablets. Since those device types have different strengths and weaknesses, we use them for different tasks or in different situations. As a result, our favorite applications and our data are distributed across multiple devices [2]. Integrating the applications running on different devices is often a cumbersome task performed manually by the user. This is due to the fact that most apps only offer a user interface and not a service interface that can be accessed by other applications. As a consequence, users use workarounds to simplify the cross-device integration, e.g., by using tools like Dropbox, to realize some form of data level integration. In contrast, our framework supports integration on a higher level. Instead of working with the data produced by another app, we want to directly integrate the service creating the data. This, however, requires the existence of consumable service interfaces.

© Springer International Publishing AG 2017
K. Drira et al. (Eds.): ICSOC 2016 Workshops, LNCS 10380, pp. 203–206, 2017.
https://doi.org/10.1007/978-3-319-68136-8_25

The Android platform encourages developers to create apps that offer services which can be integrated by other apps on the same device. For instance, a phonebook app on an Android smartphone can integrate the service to take a picture offered by the camera app. Yet, these services can only be accessed when both apps run on the same device, since Android-specific communication means are used and data is exchanged using local plattform-specific data stores. However, based on this interaction, the framework to be demonstrated is able to provide the integration of services offered by Android apps even across devices.

2   System Overview

In this section, we give an overview of our framework enabling **Cross-D**evice **A**pplication **I**ntegration of **A**ndroid apps (XDAI-A). For this purpose, we relate the different buildings blocks of our approach as visualized in Fig. 1 to the steps performed during the cross-device integration at runtime (see Fig. 2).

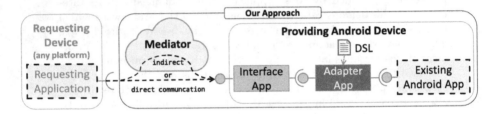

Fig. 1. Overview of our implementation [3]

Infrastructure on the Providing Device: In order to provide services for applications running on other devices, we install two types of apps on the providing Android device: The first is an adapter app that communicates with the existing Android app and is responsible for the adaptation of requests and responses. Secondly, an interface app is responsible for providing the external service interface and receives the request and transmits the responses back to the requestor. External service requests received by an interface app are translated into an intermediate format and delegated to the adapter app. The adapter app interprets adaptation rules defined using a DSL to translate the request (details in [3]). The rules define the local data stores in which data contained in the request shall be stored, e.g., databases or file system, and which local services need to be invoked. Furthermore, these rules define how responses of the local services are translated back into the intermediate format. Within this translation, the data referenced by the local response is embedded into the response for the requestor, since references on device-internal data stores cannot be resolved by external requestors. The interface app again translates the intermediate response to the desired external response format, like JSON, and sends it to the requestor.

The decoupling of interface and adapter apps allows to support different kinds of external interfaces, e.g., a RESTful interface and an XML-RPC interface.

Currently, our framework includes an interface app which provides the services of Android apps over a RESTful interface. Moreover, by realizing the adapter as a separate app, our approach can be used without having to change existing Android apps. We have defined adaptation rules for several common Android apps and by providing a DSL, we simplified the specification on further adapters compared to programmatically defining adapters.

Mediator: The mediator is a central entity, implemented as a node.js webserver, that can be compared to a service registry. The interface apps of providing devices register their provided services at the mediator. For this, the mediator has a RESTful API, which also provides different ways for the requestor to select a device which shall provide a service: (i) The mediator can be queried for a list of devices capable of providing a service. This list can be shown on the requesting device in order to select the providing devices. (ii) The mediator can broadcast requests to all devices capable of providing the requested service and the user can claim the request on one of those devices. (iii) A QR or PIN code can be created by the mediator, which is shown on the requesting device and scanned/entered on the providing device to indirectly bind the service. With respect to privacy, options (i) and (ii) are limited to devices of the same owner but option (iii) can be used to in situation where both the providing and requesting device have different owners, e.g., integrate an app running on a private smartphone into an application running on a public internet terminal. The requestor and the provider can communicate directly with each other or indirectly via the mediator. The latter has the advantage that the mediator can translate between different communication protocols or can buffer requests/responses.

Changes to the Requesting Application: External services created using our framework need to be integrated into a requesting application. If a requesting application already has an import interface, the interface of an external service can be directly defined in a way that it can be used by the requesting application. Alternatively, mismatches between the external service's interface and the import interface can be resolved by using approaches to build adapters on the requestor's side, i.e., Iyer et al. [1] developed such an approach for the Android platform. If the requesting application has no import interface, it has to be adapted by the application's developer. For web applications, we provide a JavaScript library that can be used to integrate services running on Android devices.

System in Use: Figure 2 shows an example of an application running on a tablet that uses our framework to integrate the camera app on a smartphone. The upper part of the figure shows what is happening in the background and the lower part shows what is visible to the user. The application on the tablet retrieves a list of devices able to provide the service to take a picture from the mediator. The user selects a device and the request is sent via the mediator to this device. There, the request is received by the interface app and translated into the intermediate format. Thereafter, the corresponding adaptation rules are applied by the adapter app. As a result of this adaptation, the camera app is opened and the user can take a picture. Subsequently, the adapter app receives the response and adapts it for the requestor. The interface app delegates the adapted response back to

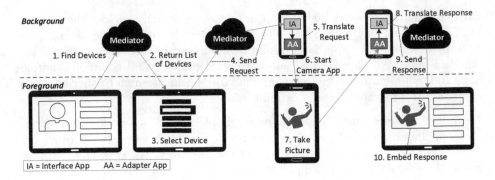

Fig. 2. Example usage of the XDAI-A framework

the requestor, which can further process it, e.g., by embedding the picture. Steps 1–3 look differently if options (ii) or (iii) are used to determine the providing device. Moreover, instead of sending the request/response via the mediator, it might be directly sent to the corresponding device.

3   Demonstration

The demonstration is twofold: In the first part, we demonstrate the user benefits by showing a demo web application that integrates services of different existing Android apps across devices using the XDAI-A framework[1]. In addition to the example illustrated in Fig. 2, the demo application integrates various other services, e.g., sharing text and images using a messenger app, selecting an existing picture using the file explorer, adding events to the calendar, and retrieving contact information from the phonebook. The demonstration shows that the adaptation of requests and responses is only noticeable in form of a delay if files have to be up-/downloaded. The different techniques to determine the providing device are demonstrated and we discuss the implications of those techniques with respect to privacy. The second part of our demonstration focuses on the internals of our approach: We explain the specification of adaptation rules using our DSL, provide various specifications for the demonstrated integrations, and discuss how multiple services can be aggregated into a single external service.

References

1. Iyer, A., Roopa, T.: Extending android application programming framework for seamless cloud integration. In: MS 2012, pp. 96–104. IEEE (2012)
2. Santosa, S., Wigdor, D.: A field study of multi-device workflows in distributed workspaces. In: UbiComp 2013, pp. 63–72. ACM (2013)
3. Wolters, D., Kirchhoff, J., Gerth, C., Engels, G.: Cross-device integration of android apps. In: Sheng, Q.Z., Stroulia, E., Tata, S., Bhiri, S. (eds.) ICSOC 2016. LNCS, vol. 9936, pp. 171–185. Springer, Cham (2016). doi:10.1007/978-3-319-46295-0_11

---

[1] A demo video can be found at http://xdai.dwolt.de/.

Desire: Deep Semantic Understanding and Retrieval for Technical Support Services

Abhirut Gupta[✉], Arjun Akula, Gargi Dasgupta, Pooja Aggarwal, and Prateeti Mohapatra

IBM Research, Bangalore 560045, India
{abhirutgupta,arakula2,gaargidasgupta,
aggarwal.pooja,pratemoh}@in.ibm.com

Abstract. Technical support services involve enterprises providing after-sales support to users of technology products. The current support structure is labor intensive with practitioners manually consulting support documentation to troubleshoot users' problems. We propose a cognitive technical support system as one that: (a) can understand technical problems expressed by users, (b) can automatically provide relevant resolution information and (c) can learn and improve its understanding and resolution over time. A typical technical problem description contains a combination of symptoms experienced by the user, explanation of attempts already made to resolve the problem, and sometimes, a clear expression of the requirement to solve the problem. Handling such intricate descriptions is outside the scope of current retrieval based systems and requires a deep understanding of the problem, combined with reasoning over a knowledge graph.

Keywords: Knowledge graph · Semantics · Technical support

1 Introduction

Currently, the operating model in technical support services is human-intensive where skilled experts are hired to support users with their queries. The science of support services is aimed at providing high quality support at lower cost by: (a) driving performance optimization from data analytics and (b) reducing manual effort by building cognitive interfaces where machines and human work together. In this paper, we focus on the latter goal of reducing manual effort by building a cognitive technical support system. This support system can interact with users of a technology, understand intricate problem definitions and respond with an accurate answer.

Large IT service providers, having realized the transformation brought in by cognitive technology, are experimenting with cognitive service agents like Amelia [4] and Watson [1] for IT problem resolution. Building blocks of such cognitive technology include components that can automatically parse text (or speech) to reliably perform problem determination, root cause analysis and automated

© Springer International Publishing AG 2017
K. Drira et al. (Eds.): ICSOC 2016 Workshops, LNCS 10380, pp. 207–210, 2017.
https://doi.org/10.1007/978-3-319-68136-8_26

resolution in the domain. There are two non-trivial challenges in building the next generation of cognitive systems: (1) Automatic understanding of problems expressed in natural language and (2) Using that understanding to retrieve correct responses from an Information Retrieval system.

In recent times, a number of classifiers using deep learning techniques have been built for question answering systems [2]. When there are commonly repeating questions, these classifiers perform well. However, the sheer combinations of products, versions and platforms make technical support questions follow a long-tailed distribution [3]. Hence, it is unlikely that two questions will be similar. In this domain, it is thus imperative to semantically understand each question and use the semantics for retrieval. To this effect, knowledge graphs representing entities and relations have become very popular [6, 7]. We present Desire(Deep Semantic Understanding and Retrieval for Technical Support Services), a cognitive system for technical support that builds a domain specific knowledge graph and uses deep parsed text fragments for traversing it.

2   Desire Architecture

Figure 1 presents an overview of the Desire system architecture and its main components:

- **Offline Component** Which comprises of - (i) Knowledge Graph Builder that extracts common entities and relations for building a Knowledge Graph (KG), and (ii) Deep Question Understanding that builds a model for recognizing symptom, intent and attempt from user queries expressed in natural language.
- **Online Component** Which comprises of - (i) Query Parser that consults the understanding model to parse out intent, symptom and attempt from the user generated query (ii) Query Builder: Uses the intent, symptom and attempt for semantic traversal of the KG.

We describe these components in detail in the following subsections

2.1   Deep Question Understanding

On analyzing several thousands of problem descriptions, it was observed that troubleshooting queries in technical support often have three distinct parts - Symptom (description of the problem), Attempt (actions that the user has already tried to resolve the problem), and Intent (an explicit request for a certain service) Fig. 2 has an example of all three parts extracted from a user question. Note that some or all of these parts might be present in a given question. Formally, we can formulate the problem of identifying these parts from a problem as follows. Given a problem description as a sequence of words - $T = [t_1, t_2, .., t_n]$, we identify three non-overlapping, possibly empty, subsequences $T_{symp}, T_{att}, T_{int}$ which denote the symptom, attempt and intent respectively.

We use Statistical Information and Relation Extraction (SIRE) [5] for detection of symptom, intent and attempt mentions. The mention detection currently is based on maximum entropy models. It requires a dataset of (hundreds of) manually annotated problem descriptions.

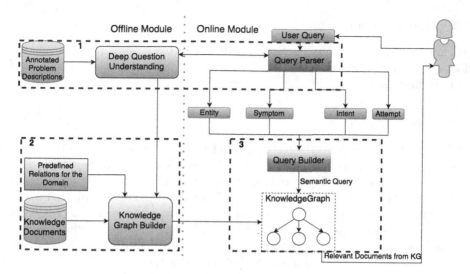

Fig. 1. System architecture with the offline and runtime modules

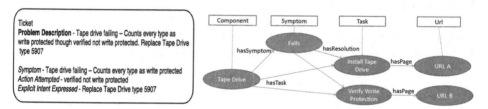

Fig. 2. A sample ticket regarding a failing tape drive

Fig. 3. A section of the Knowledge Graph applicable to the problem.

2.2 Knowledge Graph

A Knowledge Graph is essentially a Knowledge Base that is organized as Entities and the Relations that connect them. Figure 3 shows the KG section that is applicable to the example in Fig. 2. The relations *hasSymptom, hasTask, hasSymptom* and *hasPage* are used to connect entities of the type *Component, Symptom, Task* and *Url*, and are predefined. Instances of these relations are, however, extracted from both the knowledge source documents and by mining frequent patterns in annotated problem descriptions.

Finding the correct resolution documents for a query reduces to a constrained traversal problem in the knowledge graph over the entities and relations. While these queries can be formulated as simple traversals on a KG, they are very difficult for traditional text retrieval systems.

2.3 Query Parser

At runtime, the natural language query that comes to Desire is parsed using the deep question understanding model. The parser extracts out the intent, symptom and attempt from the query.

2.4 Query Builder

The Query Builder utilizes the Relationship Extractor model learnt in the offline module, and translates the parts extracted into a semantic query on the KG. For e.g. the question in Fig. 2 translates to a traversal in the KG as follows - look for all documents for the "Tape Drive" entity and "Fails" symptom where the resolution mentions "replace tape drive" and does not mention "set write protection". Since it is not necessary that all three of intent, symptom and attempt be present in all questions, the module prioritizes different parts of the question in the presence and absence of other parts.

3 Demonstration

We will demo our real-live cognitive technical support system, the Desire system. We have also included a video of our demo in the submission.

References

1. Ante, S.: Ibm set to expand watsons reach. Wall Street J. (2014)
2. Bengio, Y.: Learning deep architectures for AI. Found. Trends Mach. Learn. **2**(1), 1–127 (2009)
3. Buckley, J.J.: Long tailed distributions. In: Buckley, J.J. (ed.) Fuzzy Probabilities and Fuzzy Sets for Web Planning, pp. 147–159. Springer, Heidelberg (2004). doi:10. 1007/978-3-540-36426-9_16
4. Flinders, K.: Meet amelia new artificial intelligence platform interacts like a human. http://www.ipsoft.com/
5. Kambhatla, N., Qian, L., Roukos, S., Sun, Z.: Statistical information and relation extraction (sire). http://researcher.watson.ibm.com/researcher/view_group. php?id=2223
6. Mitchell, T.: Never-ending learning. Technical report, DTIC Document (2010)
7. Pelikánová, Z.: Google knowledge graph (2014)

BlueSight: Automated Discovery Service for Cloud Migration of Enterprises

Dannver Wu[1]([⊠]), Jinho Hwang[2], Maja Vukovic[2], and Nikos Anerousis[2]

[1] University of California, Berkeley, CA, USA
dannver@berkeley.edu
[2] IBM T.J. Watson Research Center, New York, USA
{jinho,maja,nikos}@us.ibm.com

Abstract. Migrating legacy enterprise infrastructures to the cloud is highly desirable due to greater versatility, lower management costs, as well as improved scalability. However, the large scale of these systems makes transforming the current architecture a long and difficult process that involves weeks or even months of manual collection and analysis of data. BlueSight serves to expedite and simplify this process by collecting the data through an agentless process and analyzing the collected data to determine which and how applications should migrate.

Keywords: Cloud computing · Migration analytics · Workload discovery

1 Introduction

The benefits of cloud platforms, which include reduced management costs and greater versatility, create a need to migrate existing applications running on older systems. However, this migration process typically involves a lengthy and costly process that requires human-to-human interactions and user input. In this process, engineers must decide which applications to migrate and if the application should be directly moved as a single entity or be broken down and refactored into independent micro-services.

On the large scale of enterprise systems, ranging from hundreds to thousands of servers, it is difficult to understand and analyze the legacy applications to construct a plan for migration. Currently, an experienced team of migration engineers is required to decide the best method of migration for each application. Different applications require different changes to move to a cloud platform (e.g. re-hosted, re-factored, etc.).

In this paper we describe an automated discovery service for the migration and transformation of enterprise systems to the cloud. Discovering the architecture is particulary challenging due to the complexity of the application dependencies. The service automatically collects the necessary data and generates a detailed report to be used by migration engineers to determine a plan for the transformation process. In this report, we provide detailed information about

© Springer International Publishing AG 2017
K. Drira et al. (Eds.): ICSOC 2016 Workshops, LNCS 10380, pp. 211–215, 2017.
https://doi.org/10.1007/978-3-319-68136-8_27

the infrastructure, as well as classify the applications based on their suitability for transformation to the cloud, and propose a migration pattern for the application. Additionally, a clear visual interface provides users the ability to clearly understand their infrastructure by filtering, clustering, ranking, and viewing the dependency and geographical information.

2   System Overview

BlueSight consists of two main steps, collection and analysis, in order to create a comprehensive system report for migration teams. Applications have many significant dependencies on a multitude of underlying components, such as the OS, various system and security configurations, etc. The collection process is executed as an agentless method, either automatically through remote access or manually uploaded by the user, providing detailed data about the complex dependencies within the architecture, as well as various server metrics. Once this data is collected, the entire system is displayed through a clear visual graph with filtering, ranking, and clustering functionalities to allow the user to understand and prioritize specific applications for migration.

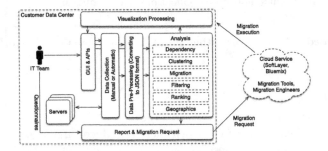

Fig. 1. BlueSight architecture.

Figure 1 illustrates the BlueSight architecture and workflows throughout the migration analytics process. The IT team in the customer data center can use BlueSight through a GUI or through APIs. When the IT team registers migration candidate servers and triggers "Data Collection", BlueSight accesses the servers automatically through ssh (linux) or samba (Windows) connections and collects information [6,7]. Then, the raw data is parsed and converted into the JSON format. The analysis engine takes over the data and runs through the different analytics: dependency, clustering, migration, filtering, ranking, and geographics [1,3–5]. The visualization processing engine generates graph data for the GUI interface. When the IT team decides to migrate any applications or servers, BlueSight will trigger the migration and generate a report of specific information about the applications or servers will be sent to cloud migration engineers who will make a migration plan [8]. Migration orchestration tools, such as the IBM cloud migration orchestrator, can also be integrated into the process [2].

3   Functions/Features

3.1   Collection

BlueSight takes an agentless discovery approach, using automated scripts to collect data from the servers [1]. Since enterprise customers are very sensitive to security, it is extremely hard to obtain machine credentials without compromising privacy. Thus, BlueSight is deployed into the customer's data center and isolated from the outside (even from IBM). The collection process can be executed automatically through remote access, or alternatively the user can run the scripts themselves and upload the resulting archived files to BlueSight. This process collects data about system properties, CPU/memory/disk/network usages, network statistics, as well as specific dependencies, services, processes, and applications of each server.

3.2   Analysis

Once the data is collected, the user is presented with a visualization of all of the servers, OS, middlewares, instances, applications, and databases in the system. There are several ways to get more detailed information. Users can view a summary of the entire infrastructure enumerating the unique applications, total discovered applications, servers, as well as overall averages of system metrics and a list of the unique applications. Additionally, clicking any node in the visual graph will display specific information about the server, including the applications/middlewares that are being run on that server and the hardware resources and usage statistics.

Users are also provided functionalities to manipulate the graph. In the top right corner are options to show or hide components based on type. Filters allow users to display servers that fit user-defined thresholds of CPU usage, disk usage, network usage, etc. A search-box and an application list on the side allow users to search for and display specific applications along with the connected components (e.g. OS, server).

Being able to group servers by a variety of metrics helps users to determine the significance of migrating each application. BlueSight conducts a migration analysis of the architecture, classifying servers into different migration patterns, suggesting whether each could be retained in the current state, retired, re-hosted, re-platformed, re-factored, or re-architectured. Each pattern is a good indication of where the servers migrate into. BlueSight also allows users to cluster the servers in the graph through a variety of statistical algorithms and view each group of servers visually.

4   Case Study

In our case study we will demonstrate the service using the data of an anonymous customer that consists of 121 servers running 631 instances of 37 unique

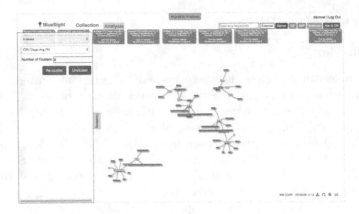

Fig. 2. Clustering in BlueSight.

applications. The collection script collects data and analyzes the application dependencies. In the GUI view, as seen in Fig. 2, the user is presented with the entire architecture as a graph with the various components as nodes, and the relationships and dependencies represented as edges. There are options to filter the graph by types of nodes. On the left, there are menus to further filter the graph through various system metrics, rank the applications using these same metrics, as well as generate clusters. Figure 2 is the result of clustering the graph by average CPU usage using k-means, to form 9 groups. The clustered nodes are displayed on the top as larger gray nodes, and each one can be expanded to show the contents. Clicking the cluster node shows additional details concerning the contents of the selected cluster.

One of the most exciting parts of this interface is in the menu on the top of the screen, which shows the results of the automatic migration analysis. This shows the user which migration pattern each application fits, which allows the customer to quickly and easily decide which applications to focus on first during the transformation. A more in-depth video of the service is available at http://bit.ly/BlueSightDemo.

5   Conclusion

In this paper, we described an automated discovery service for the migration of enterprise systems to cloud platforms. BlueSight solves the issue of being able to understand large enterprise infrastructures and assists both the user and migration teams in deciding what applications to transform, as well as how to do the transformation.

References

1. Hwang, J.: Computing resource transformation, consolidation and decomposition in hybrid clouds. In: 2015 11th International Conference on Network and Service Management (CNSM), pp. 144–152, November 2015

2. Hwang, J., Huang, Y.W., Vukovic, M., Anerousis, N.: Enterprise-scale cloud migration orchestrator. In: 2015 IFIP/IEEE International Symposium on Integrated Network Management (IM), pp. 1002–1007, May 2015
3. Hwang, J., Liu, G., Zeng, S., Wu, F.Y., Wood, T.: Topology discovery and service classification for distributed-aware clouds. In: 2014 IEEE International Conference on Cloud Engineering (IC2E), pp. 385–390, March 2014
4. Hwang, J., Huang, Y.W., Vukovic, M., Jermyn, J.: Cloud transformation analytics services: a case study of cloud fitness validation for server migration. In: Proceedings of the 2015 IEEE International Conference on Services Computing, SCC 2015, pp. 387–394. (2015). http://dx.doi.org/10.1109/SCC.2015.60
5. Hwang, J., Vukovic, M., Anerousis, N.: FitScale: scalability of legacy applications through migration to cloud. In: Sheng, Q.Z., Stroulia, E., Tata, S., Bhiri, S. (eds.) ICSOC 2016. LNCS, vol. 9936, pp. 123–139. Springer, Cham (2016). doi:10.1007/978-3-319-46295-0_8
6. Jermyn, J., Hwang, J., Bai, K., Vukovic, M., Anerousis, N., Stolfo, S.: Improving readiness for enterprise migration to the cloud. In: Proceedings of the Middleware Industry Track, Industry papers, NY, USA, pp. 5:1–5:7 (2014). http://doi.acm.org/10.1145/2676727.2676732
7. Nidd, M., Bai, K., Hwang, J., Vukovic, M., Tacci, M.: Automated business application discovery. In: 2015 IFIP/IEEE International Symposium on Integrated Network Management (IM), pp. 794–797, May 2015
8. Vukovic, M., Hwang, J.: Cloud migration using automated planning. In: NOMS 2016–2016 IEEE/IFIP Network Operations and Management Symposium, pp. 96–103, April 2016

A Configurator Component for End-User Defined Mobile Data Collection Processes

Johannes Schobel$^{(\boxtimes)}$, Rüdiger Pryss, Marc Schickler, and Manfred Reichert

Institute of Databases and Information Systems, Ulm University, Ulm, Germany
{johannes.schobel,ruediger.pryss,marc.schickler,
manfred.reichert}@uni-ulm.de

Abstract. The widespread dissemination of smart mobile devices offers promising perspectives for collecting huge amounts of data. When realizing mobile data collection applications (e.g., to support clinical trials), challenging issues arise. For example, many real-world projects require support for heterogeneous mobile operating systems. Usually, existing data collection approaches are based on specifically tailored mobile applications. As a drawback, changes of a data collection procedure require costly code adaptations. To remedy this drawback, we implemented a model-driven approach that enables end-users to realize mobile data collection applications themselves. This paper demonstrates the developed configurator component, which enables domain experts to implement digital questionnaires. Altogether, the configurator component allows for the fast development of questionnaires and hence for collecting data in large-scale scenarios using smart mobile devices.

1 Introduction

In many application scenarios (e.g., clinical trials), data collection is still based on paper-based questionnaires (so-called *instruments*), which reveal many drawbacks (e.g., huge efforts for digitizing and analyzing the data collected). Using smart mobile devices with specifically tailored services offers promising perspectives in this context. The development of respective mobile services, however, is both time-consuming and costly. Furthermore, the mobile support of mobile data collection scenarios often requires profound domain-specific knowledge. Hence, a generic and flexible approach to speed up the development of mobile data collection applications is demanded by domain experts [3]. In the QuestionSys project, we developed an advanced framework for supporting the lifecycle of mobile data collection scenarios. On one hand, IT experts are relieved from costly manual tasks (e.g., deploying mobile applications to devices). On the other, domain experts (e.g., medical doctors) are empowered to create sophisticated data collection instruments following a process-centric approach for their design and enactment. This paper demonstrates the configurator component that enables domain experts to create sophisticated instruments for large-scale data collection scenarios.

The paper is organized as follows: Sect. 2 presents selected services of the framework. Section 3 discusses related work and Sect. 4 summarizes the paper.

© Springer International Publishing AG 2017
K. Drira et al. (Eds.): ICSOC 2016 Workshops, LNCS 10380, pp. 216–219, 2017.
https://doi.org/10.1007/978-3-319-68136-8_28

2   The QuestionSys Framework

This section introduces the QuestionSys framework (cf. Fig. 1) and its underlying mobile data collection lifecycle: The *Design & Modeling* phase allows domain experts to create an instrument by applying a graphical questionnaire definition tool. The resulting specification is then transformed into an executable process model based on a well-defined mapping. The *Deployment* phase then handles the installation on smart mobile devices. During the *Execution* phase, multiple instances of the instrument may be started. In order to allow for a robust but still flexible enactment, a mobile process engine is used. During the *Analysis* phase collected data may be evaluated in real-time in order to provide immediate feedback if needed. Finally, the *Versioning* phase deals with release management of the created instruments and collected data respectively. This paper focuses on the configurator component. However, more details regarding the other components of the QuestionSys architecture and the mobile data collection lifecycle are provided in [4].

Figure 2 (a) shows the *element creation* view of the QuestionSys configurator (cf. Fig. 1, ①). First, the domain expert (i.e., end-user) chooses the respective questionnaire from the left. Then, elements of different types (e.g., *Headlines* or *Questions*) may be selected. In the rightmost part, the content of an element may be edited. In particular, the configurator allows versioning and handling multiple languages. To enable an immediate feedback when editing elements, an *interactive preview* is provided. The feature further allows simulating different devices and switching between languages. The most important function allows combining elements to *pages* using a drag & drop approach.

Figure 2 (b) illustrates the modeling perspective. Domain experts may use the created pages and drag them to the model depicted in the center view. Furthermore, the modeling component allows creating sophisticated navigation operations to guide interviewers through the process of data collection. Note that the modeling editor follows a *correctness-by-construction* approach; e.g., it is not possible to create a *non-executable* model. Finally, the questionnaire model is mapped to an executable process model (cf. Fig. 1, ②).

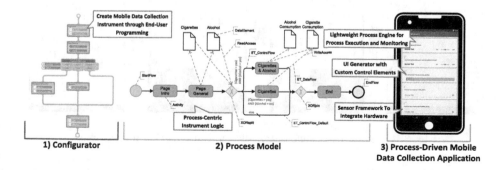

1) Configurator   2) Process Model   3) Process-Driven Mobile
                                                   Data Collection Application

Fig. 1. QuestionSys approach

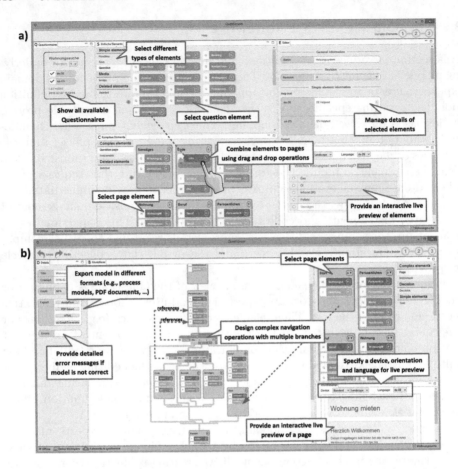

Fig. 2. QuestionSys configurator: (a) Combining elements to pages; (b) Modeling a data collection instrument

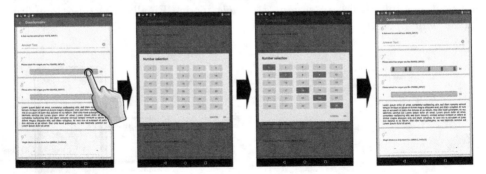

Fig. 3. QuestionSys mobile data collection application impressions

The configurator component and its model-driven approach allows domain experts to visually define executable instruments. In turn, it contributes to reduce costs and increase productivity regarding mobile application development.

To validate the approach, a mobile application (cf. Fig. 1, ③) supporting scientists during data collection was realized and applied in large-scale trials. More details regarding the mobile process engine, capable of executing data collection instruments, are discussed in [5]. Figure 3 presents impressions of the developed mobile data collection application.

3   Related Work

There exist various approaches supporting non-programmers in creating software. Their feasibility and applicability were proven in several studies. [2] provides a tool assisting administrators in their daily routines, allowing them to visually model scripts. In turn, [1] presents a graphical notation for implementing block-structured programs. Evaluations showed that subjects prefer this approach compared to text-based programming. Due to their limitations, however, these approaches cannot be applied for more complex data collection scenarios.

4   Summary and Outlook

The paper presented two components of the QuestionSys framework. In particular, we demonstrated the configurator component enabling domain experts to create instrument themselves. In addition, the mobile application was discussed. Currently, we are conducting a study evaluating the usability of the configurator component. Information regarding the process of creating elements and combining them to instruments are of particular interest in this context.

References

1. Begel, A., Klopfer, E.: Starlogo TNG: an introduction to game development. J. E-Learn. **48**, 5–15 (2007)
2. Kandogan, E., Haber, E., Barrett, R., Cypher, A., Maglio, P., Zhao, H.: A1: end-user programming for web-based system administration. In: Proceedings 18th ACM Symposium on User Interface Software and Technology. ACM (2005)
3. Schobel, J., Pryss, R., Schickler, M., Reichert, M.: Towards flexible mobile data collection in healthcare. In: 29th International Symposium on Computer-Based Medical Systems. IEEE Computer Society Press (2016)
4. Schobel, J., Pryss, R., Schickler, M., Ruf-Leuschner, M., Elbert, T., Reichert, M.: End-user programming of mobile services: empowering domain experts to implement mobile data collection applications. In: 5th International Conference on Mobile Services. IEEE Computer Society Press (2016)
5. Schobel, J., Pryss, R., Wipp, W., Schickler, M., Reichert, M.: A mobile service engine enabling complex data collection applications. In: Sheng, Q.Z., Stroulia, E., Tata, S., Bhiri, S. (eds.) ICSOC 2016. LNCS, vol. 9936, pp. 626–633. Springer, Cham (2016). doi:10.1007/978-3-319-46295-0_42

Author Index

Printed in the United States
By Bookmasters

Printed in the United States
By Bookmasters